About Island Press

Island Press is the only nonprofit organization in the United States whose principal purpose is the publication of books on environmental issues and natural resource management. We provide solutions-oriented information to professionals, public officials, business and community leaders, and concerned citizens who are shaping responses to environmental problems.

In 2003, Island Press celebrates its nineteenth anniversary as the leading provider of timely and practical books that take a multidisciplinary approach to critical environmental concerns. Our growing list of titles reflects our commitment to bringing the best of an expanding body of literature to the environmental community throughout North America and the world.

Support for Island Press is provided by The Nathan Cummings Foundation, Geraldine R. Dodge Foundation, Doris Duke Charitable Foundation, Educational Foundation of America, The Charles Engelhard Foundation, The Ford Foundation, The George Gund Foundation, The Vira I. Heinz Endowment, The William and Flora Hewlett Foundation, Henry Luce Foundation, The John D. and Catherine T. MacArthur Foundation, The Andrew W. Mellon Foundation, The Moriah Fund, The Curtis and Edith Munson Foundation, National Fish and Wildlife Foundation, The New-Land Foundation, Oak Foundation, The Overbrook Foundation, The David and Lucile Packard Foundation, The Pew Charitable Trusts, The Rockefeller Foundation, The Winslow Foundation, and other generous donors.

The opinions expressed in this book are those of the author and do not necessarily reflect the views of these foundations.

The
Coming
Democracy

The
COMING
DEMOCRACY

NEW RULES FOR
RUNNING A NEW WORLD

Ann Florini

ISLAND PRESS

Washington • Covelo • London

ISLAND PRESS is a trademark of The Center for Resource Economics.

Library of Congress Cataloging-in-Publication Data

Florini, Ann.
The coming democracy : new rules for running a new world /
Ann Florini.
p. cm.
Includes bibliographical references and index.
ISBN 1-55963-289-5 (alk. paper)
1. Civil society. 2. Democracy. 3. Globalization. I. Title.
JC337 .F56 2003
306.2—dc21
2002153428

British Cataloguing-in-Publication Data available.

Book design by Brighid Willson

Printed on recycled, acid-free paper ✪

Manufactured in the United States of America

09 08 07 06 05 04 03   8 7 6 5 4 3 2 1

To Monica and Pamela

CONTENTS

PREFACE

This book began as a relatively short monograph on a relatively narrow subject—rethinking the meaning of international security after the end of the cold war. The Rockefeller Brothers Fund (RBF), like many other grant-giving organizations active in the international arena, was reconsidering how best to channel its grants, and it wanted to contribute to the broader debate then raging over how best to define security in the chaotic international environment of the 1990s. The contours of that debate included calls for expansion of security to include all major threats to human well-being, from armed conflict to disease to environmental degradation. As research director of the RBF project on redefining security, I spent several months drafting a monograph that dealt broadly with such big questions.

At the end of the year, I took the draft monograph to the RBF's president, Colin Campbell; vice president, Russell Phillips; and special assistant to the president, Priscilla Lewis—and asked them not to publish it. I had come to the conclusion that there was a better way to define the issue with which we were all grappling. I believed we were concerned not so much with how broadly to define global security as with how well the world could deal with all the threats that could be loosely grouped under that heading. The monograph was insisting on evolving into a broader book, one that focused on the processes by which global decision making occurs—the book you have in your hands.

Having worked closely with these three extraordinary people over the past year, I was delighted but not surprised by their enthusiastic response to my request to indulge in a larger intellectual odyssey. For the next three years, the RBF generously funded my work at the Carnegie Endowment for

International Peace both directly on the book and in support of other projects related to transparency and transnational civil society. For that support, and for their forbearance when the book took an additional two years to finish, I offer heartfelt thanks to the RBF's board and staff. I owe far more than the usual debt to a funder. In the early stages, people at the RBF served as sounding boards, editors, and unfailing sources of encouragement and good ideas.

I also want to thank the Carnegie Endowment for International Peace, particularly its president, Jessica Mathews, and its vice president for studies, Thomas Carothers, for providing the ideal intellectual environment for the writing of this book. Several of my Carnegie colleagues were kind enough to review all or parts of the manuscript at various stages: Tom Carothers, Robert Cavey, and Virginia Haufler before she returned to the University of Maryland. Special thanks to P. J. Simmons for intellectual and moral support far beyond the call of collegiality. Others to whom I owe a debt of gratitude for comments include Todd Baldwin, John Boli, Martha Finnemore, Allen Hammond, Tim Kessler, Priscilla Lewis, Russell Phillips, Peter Riggs, Strobe Talbott, and Lynn Whittaker. Several research assistants helped with various stages of the book: Wendi Adelson, Cara Carter, Yahya Dehqanzada, Andrew Eggers, Robert Johnson, Wynne Rumpeltin, and Jordan Tama. Four authors on whose work I drew were kind enough to allow me to read their works in manuscript form: David Brin, Allen Hammond, Margaret Keck, and Kathryn Sikkink.

My family deserves thanks on several grounds. My sister, Karen Florini, and my husband, Sunil Sharma, not only delivered the usual moral support but also provided helpful substantive input, including detailed comments drawing on their substantial relevant expertise. My mother, Barbara Florini, gently but persistently reminded me as the years dragged on that the book would be useful only if I actually got it finished.

Above all, thanks to my daughters. They did not help, of course—instead, they actively interfered, clearly believing that paying attention to them was a better use of Mommy's time than scribbling on paper. They were often right. But in a larger sense, the book exists because of them. They will live in a world that could flourish or fall apart, depending on how well the current generation resolves the conundrums of global governance. This book is my effort to contribute toward that resolution, and it is dedicated to them.

The
Coming
Democracy

⟨1⟩

A Time of Transformation?

They were unlikely sparks for a revolution. The bibles that rolled off the newly invented printing press of German goldsmith Johannes Gutenberg in the 1450s were massive, painstakingly crafted works of art, meant to catch the eye of the church leaders and secular rulers who could afford the two-volume tomes.[1] Gutenberg, a chronically indebted businessman with an eye for beauty, may have created masterpieces, but he was primarily out to make a living. If he thought about any broader effects of his invention, he probably assumed that it would help unify Christendom by replacing the many error-filled local variants of hand-copied religious documents with single, authoritative, Church-approved versions. Gutenberg could not have foreseen the Protestant Reformation, the Enlightenment, the emergence of the nation-state as the dominant political form, the spread of mass literacy, or the rise of representative democracy. Yet all were made possible by the printing press.[2]

The Reformation was the most immediate beneficiary. Martin Luther's ninety-five theses railing against the corruption of the Catholic Church—which were mailed in a letter in 1517 to the archbishop of Mainz, not, as legend has it, nailed to the door of the Wittenberg castle church—quickly leaked. By the end of 1517, they were all over Germany, translated into German.[3] And over the next seven years, Luther's works amassed a total print run of perhaps 300,000 copies—one-third of all the books published in Germany during that time. Previous reform-minded tracts may have been written, but none received so wide an audience as Luther's.

Over time, Gutenberg's invention also changed the geography of language. Authors trying to reach broad audiences had to deal with a bewildering variety of dialects, creating standardized languages that sidelined Latin and provincial vernaculars alike.[4] It is hard to imagine the rise of the nation-state and, eventually, the rise of nineteenth-century nationalism in the absence of such ease of communication within national borders.

Most important of all, print changed the way in which knowledge could be accumulated. Printers could improve works from edition to edition, relying on large networks of readers to point out errors and provide new data on any subject, from mapping to botany. Print also, of course, made it possible to reproduce errors far more widely, but on the whole, error correction outweighed error duplication. Scottish philosopher and historian David Hume wrote to his publisher, "The Power which Printing gives us of continually improving and correcting our Works in successive Editions appears to me the chief advantage of that art."[5]

Part of the knowledge that was accumulated was political. Now everyone could know what laws existed, what agreements rulers had made with the ruled. Censorship became problematic. The Catholic Church tried to cope with the explosion of unwelcome books by regularly issuing the *Index librorum prohibitorum* (Index of prohibited books), which provided invaluable free publicity for the listed authors and, as historian Elizabeth Eisenstein notes, "may have spurred sales."[6] Over time, the explosion of knowledge opened the door to vastly greater individual freedom and to forms of governance that required the ongoing involvement of literate, attentive, and informed populations.

These consequences were not inevitable. Movable type presses were available in China as early as the eleventh century, but they were little used and had essentially no influence.[7] The European invention of the printing press transformed Europe because Europe was ready to be transformed. The Renaissance was already under way, and Europe was in the painful process of recovering from the devastation of the bubonic plague. The growing demand for books and other written materials was outstripping the capacity of scribes to make their copies. Public disgust with the corruption rife in the Catholic Church provided fertile ground for Luther's theses. Thus, the advent of print holds powerful lessons for us today.

We are now, potentially, at a similar turning point. Information technology may once again be poised to transform politics and identity. If the print revolution made possible the nation-state system and eventually national democracy, where might the digital revolution lead us? Can it help us create new, and possibly better, ways of running the world?

As was true in the early days of print, we live in an extraordinarily fluid time, when choices made today will have massive consequences for tomorrow. To see this, imagine living in a wonderful world a few decades from now. The gut-wrenching poverty that left half the world eking out a bare existence at the turn of the millennium has become little more than a distant memory as ever freer and more equitable global markets have ushered in a new era of prosperity for almost everyone. Population has grown far more slowly than predicted, with birthrates dropping dramatically in a "demographic transition" that reflects the world's improved standards of living (the richer people become, the fewer children they have). The population growth that has occurred has created larger markets and bigger labor forces for the growing economies. New environmentally sustainable technologies, from "green" cars to organic farming, are so widely adopted that Mother Nature smiles benignly on her 8 billion or so human children. This extraordinary progress in the human condition has become possible thanks to the information revolution and the related spread of education. People around the world have become capable of demanding, and getting, effective and competent governments, which are closely monitored by a global array of citizens' groups looking out for the public interest.

Now imagine a different scenario for that not-too-distant future. Economic globalization has forced all societies to subordinate concerns about equity and social justice to productivity and competitiveness. With the private sector ever more powerful and the wealthy ever more isolated from the rest of society, governments find themselves unable to compel those with money to help pay for such basic social needs as defense and police functions, economic infrastructure, environmental protection, or a social safety net. Organized crime runs rampant through porous borders. The technologies of the information revolution have spread, but inequitably, leaving the poor well aware that others are living far better than they but unable to participate in the information-based global economy. Growing and aging populations that are increasingly organized into self-interested activist groups put heavy demands on governments to provide services. Environmental degradation compounds those demands by undermining the ability of the poorest to fashion a living for themselves as supplies of water, firewood, and arable land diminish. The failure of either market or government to meet the demands of both the truly desperate and the merely relatively deprived masses is provoking growing frustration and thus violence. And everyone is suffering the consequences of climate change and ecosystem collapse as weather runs wild, fisheries are devastated, and much of humanity ends up poisoned by the by-products of industrial activities.

There are plenty of people who say we are already well on our way toward one or the other of these outcomes. Panglossian pundits foretell a "long boom" of ever-increasing prosperity: Peter Schwartz, Peter Leyden, and Joel Hyatt, in their book of that name, lay out a vision of a future made glorious by rapid economic growth, technological innovation, and the power of net-working.[8] Others, like the well-traveled writer Robert Kaplan, foresee a world at best divided between the privileged few and the miserable many, headed for conflict and possibly wholesale collapse.[9]

These are not the only views of our likely future, of course. A number of pundits prefer to promulgate paradigms that look more like the recent past, with the world defined primarily by antagonisms between countries. The United States is always one of the antagonists, given the preponderance of U.S. power, and its enemy is posited to be China or a unified transnational Islam (replacing earlier renditions that put Japan or a revitalized Russia in that role).[10] Most well known in the wake of the September 11 attacks on New York and Washington, D.C., is Samuel Huntington's imaginative vari-ant on the Great Enemies idea, contending that whole civilizations, rather than mere countries, will clash.[11]

All these views reflect a palpable hunger for a single theme that will bring coherence to the confusing cacophony that has prevailed since the cold war ended. The hunger is understandable: we need some means of attributing meaning to the myriad events and trends we observe, some basis for decision making. But such simplifications of reality appear to describe inevitabilities rather than possible futures. And some of their arguments have a dangerous propensity to generate self-fulfilling prophecies. If claims about new enemies are taken seriously, peoples who need not become enemies may start treating each other as such. That is clearly what the terrorists behind the September 11 attacks hoped to bring about with their ill-founded claims about hostil-ity between Islam and the West. If assumptions of inevitable prosperity are accepted, the real threats to that outcome will be ignored until too late. And if fears about possible catastrophes are accepted as descriptions of an unavoidable future, that future will come.

Reality is not as simple, and human destiny is not as fixed. Major stresses are inevitable, given the sheer size of the growing human population and the need to adjust to technological changes. But within those constraints, humanity has enormous freedom. People decide which problems matter most and how, or whether, to try to solve them. Cultures and civilizations need not clash if people decide to work out their differences in nonviolent ways. Climate change need not continue. Humanity can wait and see whether ecological catastrophe will strike, or we can reduce the emission of greenhouse gases. We can wait until the bombs go off, or we can act to constrain the proliferation of conventional weapons and weapons of mass destruction. We can confront the problem of growing income disparities, or we can wait and see whether such divisions really will rip societies apart, as many social scientists predict.

The difference between the rosy and gloomy scenarios boils down to a single word: governance. Governance is something more than the familiar processes of governments. *Governance* refers to all the ways in which groups of people collectively make choices. Just as operating systems set the parameters within which computers function, governance systems set the parameters within which societies function. At the global level, however, the operating software is still in the beta-test stage of an early version—not able to do much, and with plenty of bugs still in the code.

Governments are obviously a big part of global governance—they agree on treaties, constitute international organizations that set international standards, and enact and enforce national laws to implement internationally agreed-on rules. But corporations are also taking an increasingly large part in global governance by lobbying governments, regulating themselves through industry associations, and establishing codes of conduct for their own behavior. And a vast and growing array of nonprofit groups is beginning to participate in global governance, whether by demanding changes from the streets or by sitting down with representatives of governments and corporations to write the rules.

This current system for running the world is based on rules that were set in the middle of the twentieth century, in the wake of World War II. It is based on assumptions that a handful of great powers will make most of the decisions, with other national governments involved as needed and with intergovernmental efforts at times coordinated through treaties or international organizations such as the United Nations. It was designed for a time when war between countries seemed the greatest threat to international well-being, when national economies engaged in trade but otherwise operated quite separately, and when environmental concerns were scarcely a blip on the radar screen.

The world of the early twenty-first century is obviously quite different. In late 2002, the "war" against terrorism was uppermost in many minds. But humanity faces many threats. True believers in doomsday scenarios have many potential catastrophes to pick from. The cold war may be over, but the world still hosts thousands of nuclear weapons. Dozens of countries (and, increasingly, subnational groups) have or could get chemical weapons, biological weapons, or both, as well as missiles to deliver them. The international treaties and safeguards in place to prevent such proliferation have serious flaws. Although we are unlikely to experience another war like World War II, in part because the United States is so militarily dominant that no conceivable enemy could hope to win a conventional war against it, millions are still dying and suffering from the cumulative murder and maiming made possible by the global trade in small arms. Such violence is particularly hard to control when it comes, as it increasingly does, from rebel groups and criminal organizations (often now one and the same) rather than national governments. The international community, in the form of the United Nations and national leaders, is increasingly recognizing a moral obligation to stop the slaughter of innocents, but those national leaders generally accomplish little beyond hand-wringing and buck-passing until thousands have already died.[12] Much of the violence is fueled by the escalating profits of drug traffickers and other smugglers, whose goods are easily disguised in the surging flows of legitimately traded goods and whose profits are readily laundered through the vast global financial system. Other large-scale threats to human well-being include everything from economic instability to environmental degradation, as later chapters will show.

So far, although people are becoming more aware of the global nature of humanity's most urgent problems and opportunities, the responses, with some notable exceptions, add up to unimaginative muddling through. The thousands of international conferences, treaties, and declarations of pious intent have (again, with some notable exceptions) done more to salve the conscience than to save the world.

To see the gap between rhetoric and reality, consider an example: the globalization of disease.

Watching a child die of illness or infection used to be a common parental experience. It still is common in the poorer half of the world, where infectious and parasitic diseases remain a leading cause of death.[13] But for the rich, literate, and lucky, the prospect became a remote horror in the last half of the twentieth century, thanks in large part to the miracle of antibiotic drugs. Now, however, the germs are fighting back, and all too often they are winning. That is due to the remarkable stupidity with which humanity has been squandering its pharmaceutical treasure.

Bacteria are not defenseless against antibiotics. Any given infection may contain some bacterial cells that are slightly resistant. If not enough of the drug is taken to overwhelm the slightly resistant bacteria, those will survive—and reproduce, passing on their resistance to their heirs. Thus, over time, use of antibiotics promotes the existence of resistant bacteria.[14]

That may be inevitable, but the stupidity comes in the multiple ways we are drastically, if inadvertently, speeding up the rise of resistance. All over the world, antibiotics have been prescribed lavishly, often for diseases against which they are entirely ineffective, such as viral illnesses. When they are used against bacterial diseases, where they can work quite well, people often stop taking them as soon as they feel better but before all the bacteria have been wiped out. The very poor often cannot afford to take a full course of pills over several days, leaving the most antibiotic-resistant bacteria lurking in their bodies. Even worse, we have been giving vast quantities of the stuff to healthy cattle, pigs, and chickens, to make them grow slightly faster and to compensate for the unsanitary conditions in which they are raised, and we have been spraying antibiotics on fruit trees to control or prevent infections. So we are eating a steady low-level diet of antibiotics.

All this is leading to the resurgence of diseases that once seemed well under control, even in rich countries with well-developed public health systems. New York City is contending with the emergence of strains of tuberculosis resistant to known treatments. Some strains of a bacterium called *Staphylococcus aureus,* which frequently causes postsurgical infections, are becoming resistant to the antibiotic vancomycin, until recently the drug of choice; other strains are already resistant to everything else.[15]

At the same time that diseases thought to be under control have come back to haunt us, new ones are popping up. As global population increases, humans are encroaching on new environments. That encroachment provides opportunities for microbes to jump from animal hosts to new human ones.

This may be how acquired immunodeficiency syndrome (AIDS) arose. And AIDS, as is well known, is becoming the most serious health threat in recorded history. It has already killed in excess of 20 million people—more than all the soldiers who died in the twentieth century's vast wars and as many as the total death toll from Europe's Black Death in the fourteenth century. AIDS is a peculiarly vicious epidemic, robbing societies of adults in the prime of life. Africa has been worst hit, with as many as one-third of all adults infected in such unfortunate countries as Botswana.[16] But it is hardly just an African problem. Already, more than 10 million people outside Africa have been infected.[17] China alone could have that many cases by 2010.[18]

The third element in the global disease picture comes from the same technological advances that have me sitting 37,000 feet over the Atlantic Ocean as I write this. Unless humanity decides to put a stop to international airplane travel and global shipping, the rise of new and resurgent infectious diseases will be a global problem. Whenever previously isolated human populations begin to interact, disease spreads as viruses and bacteria find new hosts who have not developed immunity to them. Multiple such epidemics struck in ancient Rome. Europe's Black Death of the fourteenth century, probably carried back from Asia by traders, killed nearly 40 percent of the population. The indigenous peoples of the Americas endured devastating waves of disease after European contact. Such outbreaks are the fully predictable consequence of growing contacts among people. Although such epidemics are nothing new, modern transportation technologies intensify the danger of the spread of virulent infectious disease. Because people move so quickly, even fast-acting diseases can spread before killing off their initial victims. Already today, millions travel for business or pleasure, and even in a time when many people are cutting back on travel plans, the number of short-term visits to other countries is growing much faster than total population levels. Tourism now accounts for some 10 percent of the world's annual economic growth, with people taking 6 billion such trips per year. By 2020, experts predict, 1.6 billion people, from what will then be a total population of about 7.8 billion, will travel internationally as tourists.[19]

Put all this together—the lessened effectiveness of antibiotics; the emergence of previously unknown diseases for which treatments are scarce, expensive, or simply unavailable; and modern transportation—and we have a chilling reality. Everyone, literally everyone, is vulnerable to the threat posed by new and resurgent diseases.

So what great global initiative has been launched to save us all from the scourge of pestilence? Several are indeed under way. But efforts seem alarmingly feeble compared with the scale of the problem.

For starters, the World Health Organization (WHO), a United Nations agency, has undertaken several initiatives, often in partnership with private businesses and nongovernmental organizations, from the Roll Back Malaria campaign to the Global Alliance for Vaccines and Immunization. And WHO is not alone. The Bill & Melinda Gates Foundation is pouring tens of millions of dollars into vaccination programs and other health initiatives. At the urging of the United Nations' secretary-general, Kofi Annan, a global fund has been established to address such big killers as AIDS, malaria, and tuberculosis. A group of scientists in the United States has established an electronic mail network called the Program to Monitor Emerging Diseases (ProMED) to facilitate reporting on disease outbreaks, with more than 10,000 participants in 120 countries as of 1999. Some big pharmaceutical corporations are giving some of their products to people too poor to afford them. And the shameful neglect of public health systems around the world is, at least, being noticed now that such systems are seen as the first line of defense against bioterrorism.

But such efforts provide a sparse defense against the bacterial arsenal. Tuberculosis, for example, kills 2 million people per year, and that number is rising, not falling.[20] No serious efforts are under way to stop the vast misuse of antibiotics. And this is nothing compared with what could happen if some demented soul decided to give the bacteria a helping hand in the form of biological weapons more potent and easily distributed than anthrax.

Why is there such an enormous gap between the scale of the problem and the resources being devoted to it? One reason is that, as in most things in life, it is the poor who suffer first, and they lack the resources and power to do much about the problem. Rich countries have been notable tightwads when it comes to providing assistance to poor ones to support their public health systems. There might be a certain poetic justice in the prospect that epidemics that break out in poor countries may come to plague the miserly rich. But presumably most of us would prefer good health and long life, especially for our children, over poetic justice.

The broader problem is that it is not clear *who* should do what. Organizations such as WHO could do more, but only if the governments that control and constitute them provide the necessary resources and marching orders. And it is not clear that a centralized bureaucracy like that of WHO, or of any intergovernmental organization, is the ideal mechanism for dealing with highly decentralized problems such as antibiotic resistance or diseases carried by travelers.

The globalization of disease is just one of the knotty transnational problems whose causes lie and whose effects are felt in more than one country. Because the problems are transnational, their resolution lies beyond the authority of any single national government. Environmental degradation and microbes alike blithely ignore political boundaries—air molecules and fish go where they choose.

Because political authority is held by national governments, there is an increasing disjunction between the (transnational) problems to be solved and the (mostly national) systems and procedures available to solve them. And to the extent that transnational and multinational systems are emerging to address transnational issues, these systems are not directly accountable to the people whose lives they affect. No constituency elects international organizations, multinational corporations, or nongovernmental activists.

Moreover, those new systems are often organized as though the issues on the global agenda could be resolved separately. Reality refuses to stay neatly confined in orderly bureaucratic and analytic boxes. Instead, the problems interact with and exacerbate one another. Trade and environment, for example, are becoming tightly linked, but when the two conflict, the people who decide which takes priority understand only one. Among the protestors at the ministerial conference of the World Trade Organization (WTO) in Seattle, Washington, in November 1999 were environmentalists outraged by the organization's tendency to judge trade–environment disputes solely on the basis of trade laws. The governments that write the rules the WTO enforces fear that allowing environmental standards to influence trade policies could lead to ever more barriers to trade and provide a handy smoke screen behind which protectionists could hide. Environmentalists argue that "our trading system must find ways to operate within environmental limits."[21] Such attempts to solve complexly interacting problems across dramatically different issue areas cause confusion for overburdened states and for the international organizations they create.[22] These outdated rules for running the world seem likely to fall short.

But what are the alternatives? One obvious possibility would be a world government wherein the United Nations and other international institutions are built up to the point that they take on the whole range of functions currently served by modern national governments. This is a truly bad idea. The prospect of world government is as undesirable as it is unrealistic. If the world has learned only one thing from the bloody history of the twentieth century, it is that highly centralized, top-down systems of governance are economic and political nightmares. Although such governments are able to mobilize populations, both the means and the ends are horrendous, making them ultimately unsustainable even on their own terms. A single world government would very likely be worse than anything yet seen. No centralized government on such a scale could be responsive to the highly diverse needs and desires of billions of people. And even if it were desirable, world government is politically impossible. Neither governments nor their citizens will allow any strong centralized supranational authority to collect taxes and regulate behavior across the board in the foreseeable future. No plausible kernel exists around which a world government with coercive powers might develop, paranoid delusions about the United Nations' black helicopters notwithstanding.

A second proposition calls for reducing the need for global governance by returning to the good old days of impermeable national borders. Some, though certainly not all, of the anti-globalization protestors, not to mention various xenophobic anti-immigrant political movements in rich countries and at least some terrorist networks, have exactly such an approach in mind. But that would be throwing the baby out with the bathwater. As later chapters will argue, economic integration (if handled better than it is currently being handled) could dramatically and sustainably improve the lives of vast numbers of people around the globe. And even after throwing out both baby and bathwater, stepping back from globalization would still leave us stuck in a bathtub contaminated with the dirty scum of global environmental degradation.

A third option, much favored in some circles, would have us rely on the "invisible hand" of the market. The invisible hand is indeed a powerful force—but only under certain conditions.[23] Not everything that is desirable has a market, that is, people able and willing to pay. Even when a group of people share a desire for a good or service, such as a well-educated populace or protection from attack, individual members of the group may not find it rational to pay for that good or service, no matter how much they each want it. To clean up a lake, each local homeowner must stop dumping untreated sewage into the lake, but those who do not stop still benefit from the actions of those who do. To provide for the national defense, citizens must pay taxes, but those who cheat on their taxes do not go undefended. This, in social science jargon, is the collective action problem: when there is no way to exclude people from enjoying a good or service, people are tempted to free ride, that is, to enjoy the benefit while letting someone else pay the cost.[24] This is not mere selfishness. It is often futile to pay up unless enough others will join in. If only a single homeowner treats his sewage, the lake will not become noticeably cleaner. As one leading scholar put it, "a man who tried to hold back a flood with a pail would probably be considered more of a crank than a saint, even by those he was trying to help."[25] Because of the collective action problem, many things that people collectively want are underprovided—the market fails.

In short, world government will not work, a retreat to national borders is impossible, and market forces cannot deal with most collective action problems. Where each of these proposals fails is in its lack of means for carrying out the five basic steps needed to deal with problems of the collective good. The steps are as follows:

1. There must be agreement that the problem is indeed a collective, not an individual, matter.
2. Those concerned must negotiate about how to solve the problem and how to divide the cost.
3. If the group (whether local, regional, national, or global) manages to reach an agreement, it must implement this agreement.
4. The group has to check to make sure everyone is complying with the agreement.
5. Often, the group must have some means for punishing free riding, to deter those who might be tempted to shirk.

At the transnational level, mechanisms for all five steps are poorly developed and often ineffective. Setting the agenda of what constitutes collective problems is always hard, even at the national level. But it is even harder in the global arena. There may be broad agreement on the desirability of peace, prosperity, community, and (increasingly) individual liberty, but translating those ideals into concrete agenda items requiring action on someone's part is no easy matter.[26] Global problems rarely inspire a sense of crisis, even though their long-term effects may be devastating. Unlike the clear-cut tasks of fighting a war, the world faces a series of gradual erosions of the good (e.g., environmental degradation) and accumulation of the bad (resurgent disease). By the time it becomes readily apparent to all that a significant problem has arisen, solving it may be extremely expensive, especially given the degree to which vested interests will by then have entrenched themselves in implacable opposition to change. And at the global level, no system exists for forcing a ranking of issues or an allocation of resources. Priorities reflect a hodgepodge of the interests of the most powerful states (or their most powerful constituents), the whims of the media spotlight, and blind chance. Citizens can lobby governments to act as their interlocutors, but many governments lack the capacity—and sometimes the motivation—to serve as effective representatives of their citizens' interests in the wide range of transnational issues. And there is often a big problem in deciding whose agenda a problem should be on (the United Nations? the Group of Seven great powers? the TransAtlantic Business Dialogue?). Of course, who it is that benefits from a decision typically depends on who makes it.

Even if the agenda-setting problem is solved, the other steps of global collective action present formidable obstacles. Negotiation too often takes place in cumbersome intergovernmental forums that are unable to keep pace with fast-changing problems and that often fail to represent the interests of large numbers of people. Implementation too often depends on explicit case-by-case reciprocity, which can easily break down, rather than general patterns of diffuse reciprocity that keep cooperation going beyond the inevitable snags.[27] The still-resilient norm of national sovereignty can wreak havoc with efforts at monitoring as governments resist letting outsiders in to check on them. Enforcement across borders remains seriously problematic because the available tools, from diplomatic persuasion to economic sanctions to military force, are blunt, ineffective, or both.

Effective global governance requires ways to carry out the five steps despite all these obstacles. There have been occasions on which the world could rely on a single country to bear the whole cost and let everybody else free ride, although in the realm of international politics such apparent altruism usually has some self-interested explanation lurking beneath it. The United States often played this role in the decades just after World War II as part of its campaign to contain the Soviet Union, serving as a "benevolent hegemon" for allies and potential allies in the anti-Soviet camp. In this role, the United States showered Europe with aid under the Marshall Plan, brought about the reintegration of Germany and Japan, led in creating international financial institutions such as the International Monetary Fund to stabilize the international economy, led the charge in lowering the barriers to trade, and often opened its own markets to the exports of countries that did not fully reciprocate as a means of fostering economic rebuilding or development.[28]

There is still something of a tendency to look to the United States to solve the world's problems. But relying on the benevolence of hegemons is a risky strategy. Governments, answerable only to domestic electorates, face few incentives to act for the benefit of someone else's constituency. The United States, the obvious candidate for the role as the world's dominant economic and military power, shows few signs of willingness to bear the burden of others' free riding now that it is no longer trying to stave off the threat of Communism. And for many global issues, there is not much even the extraordinarily powerful United States could accomplish by itself. It cannot unilaterally preserve the global environment or stop the global trade in drugs and small arms. Most of the time, global problems will have to be solved globally, not unilaterally.

Another way of providing for the collective good is tried and true: coercion, *making* people contribute to the common good. As chapter 4 will show, national governments can do this. Governments, at least when they are functioning well, can make people pay taxes to support collective goods such as police forces and armies, which in turn make it possible for governments to enforce compliance with laws and regulations (including the ones about paying taxes). But even at the national level, governance that relies primarily on coercion does not work very well. Countries such as North Korea and Iraq are poor for a reason. And coercive power is even less likely to work at the global level. In the absence of black helicopters, the one plausible enforcer of a world order is the one remaining superpower, the United States. Given its reluctance to sign on to international agreements aimed at solving global problems or to come up with its own solutions to such global problems as climate change, the United States seems no more likely to serve as a coercive hegemon than it is to bear the burden of the world's free riding.

In short, providing for the collective good at the global level will require something more imaginative than the extension or replication of national government power at the global level or a return to the sharply defined borders of the past. Hints are already emerging as to what that something might be. New systems of global decision making are emerging that go beyond cooperation between states to a much messier agglomeration of ad hoc mechanisms for solving the many and varied transnational problems. No one is planning this system. It is evolving, with many disparate actors who are largely unaware of the roles of other sectors and their relationships to other issues. The private sector and the amorphous third sector of nongovernmental organizations that are grouped under the heading of "civil society" are becoming key figures in transnational governance, filling some of the gaps that governments are leaving open. Increasingly, as later chapters will show, agreements are being worked out and implemented directly between the private sector and activist groups on issues ranging from environmental protection to labor standards. And nongovernmental organizations are increasingly taking on the role of monitoring compliance with international accords.

But these groups lack the democratic systems of accountability that have so painfully evolved in the past few centuries. No one elected Amnesty International to serve as the human rights conscience of the world, no one elected Greenpeace to set and enforce environmental standards for multinational corporations, and no one elected the corporations themselves. Of course, until recently no one had elected most national governments, either. But since there is now a clear global consensus on the desirability of democratic rules of governance, in principle if not always in practice, surely we do not want to create unaccountable forms of transnational governance just as we are finally getting some momentum in the spread of democracy at the level of national government.

This is where hard thinking is needed about what constitutes "democracy" in the context of global governance. It is important not to confuse the form with the function. Democracy requires two things: a system for providing people with a voice in the making of decisions that affect them and a mechanism for holding representatives accountable to those whom they represent. At the national level, opportunities for voice are provided by such mechanisms as civil society and political parties. Accountability is provided by elections. But national elections give no say to people outside a country who are nonetheless affected by that country's national decisions. At a meeting in Buenos Aires just before the November 2000 U.S. elections, a senior

Argentine diplomat told me in all seriousness that he would rather have a vote in the U.S. elections than in Argentina because Argentine citizens are at least as affected by what the United States does as by what their own government does. Unfortunately, it is hard to dream up mechanisms that would enable people to vote anywhere in the world where decisions are made that affect them.

The world badly needs to devise institutions and frameworks that can make it possible for people affected by decisions to have a voice in those decisions and to hold the decision makers accountable. The tools are now available to do at a global level what the printing press helped do for national governance—to decentralize the flow of information, enabling democracy to emerge. The speed and scale at which decision making must now take place has outstripped the capacity of purely electoral systems of democracy to cope. If democracy is to survive globalization, it must attend to the free flow of information.

The following chapters explore how to do all this. Chapter 2 introduces the most important concept for global democracy in the twenty-first century: transparency. If voice and accountability are to exist across borders, decision makers must explain their actions and decisions to the broader public whose destiny is thereby affected, and they must allow that public greater say in those decisions. Such transparency will not automatically ensure that good and just decisions are always made, but it is the most effective error correction system humanity has yet devised.[29] It can, must, and increasingly does apply not only to people already explicitly responsible for governance—leaders of national governments and intergovernmental organizations such as the World Trade Organization—but also to corporations and even the civil society groups accustomed to seeing themselves as the watchdogs monitoring everybody else. Changes in both technology and behavioral norms are making such transparency-based governance increasingly feasible.

Chapter 3 examines one reason why collectivities other than nation-states can participate in transparency-based governance—the slow but significant changes in the way people identify themselves. After all, people are more apt to work on behalf of a group goal if they identify themselves as part of that group. People can now identify themselves as members of all sorts of groups, and many types of groups now have the capacity to form cross-border networks that enable them to participate in making (or disrupting) global rules. Although most of what we hear about groups these days is pretty nasty—

ethnic or religious or nationalist groups that define themselves in opposition to some hated "other"—there are grounds for hope that humanity can grow up enough to get beyond these divisive definitions of group identity.

The following three chapters address the knotty questions of who can and should do what in global governance; chapters 4, 5, and 6, respectively, investigate the appropriate roles of national governments (and the intergovernmental organizations they create), private enterprise, and civil society in making and implementing the new rules of global governance.

The next two chapters apply all the foregoing to some of the most pressing issues facing the world. Chapter 7 delves into what most people think of when they think of globalization: economic integration. Partly thanks to new communications and information technologies and partly as a result of deliberate government and corporate decisions, barriers to the flow of goods, services, and money have fallen dramatically. But this facet of globalization is a political as much as a technological process, one desperately in need of revitalized rules and fairer ways of making those rules. Although living standards have risen for many, some of those lifted out of poverty by the forces of economic integration have been plunged right back into it by the various economic crises of recent years. Moreover, more than a billion people have been left out of this globalized system all along, scrabbling for a living in a world that is placing less and less value on their unskilled labor, and their share of the world's population is growing. The massive protests now surrounding virtually every economics-related meeting of international organizations and governments reflect a broad sense that there is something fundamentally unfair at work in the global economy.

Chapter 8 looks at why we need new forms of global governance if we are to take sustainability seriously. Partly because there are so many of us and partly because a significant fraction of us live lives of unprecedented and astonishing wastefulness, there is no part of the planet that remains unaffected by humanity's presence. The effects are generally not good. Although some environmental spillovers are purely local, an increasing number, from climate change to the catastrophic extinction of species, are matters of global concern. And because environmental degradation results directly from economic activity, as economic policy making goes global, considerations of what were once local environmental issues should—but do not—follow suit.

Chapter 9 pulls all the strands of the book together in a scenario that projects how the world might evolve a better system of global governance.

This book is based on a view of the future that is fundamentally, if nervously, optimistic. The nervousness sets in because the book does call for significant change in the way we think about political and social organization. Such a change in thinking and in doing needs to occur—and is already beginning to occur—not just among politicians and corporate executives but also among ordinary citizens, who are collectively far more able to contribute to solving transnational problems than either they or the elites generally recognize. The optimism comes from the belief that humanity can in fact figure out ethically acceptable ways of governing itself at the global level. Along with the urgent threats to human well-being explored in the coming pages are examples of innovative solutions that might prove to be more effective mechanisms for governance than those currently in use.

Those innovative solutions often do not look much like the electoral, representative systems that are the usual focus of works on governance. Indeed, there is not much discussion in this book of the formal structures of political decision making. Instead, the focus is on what can be truly new when technology and politics combine to open up the information floodgates, in a time of transformation potentially as great as was the period following Gutenberg's invention more than half a millennium ago.

2

The Global Spotlight

About 10:30 on some cloudless morning, step outside and look straight up. You may be posing for a picture taken from 400 miles above. That is not altogether new, given that the United States and Russia have been operating spy satellites since the 1960s. But those were secret. Now, satellite images of extraordinary detail and clarity are showing up regularly under newspaper headlines and on the evening news, showing everything from secret military installations to people's backyards. This started in September 1999, when Space Imaging, Inc., a private company based in the United States, launched a satellite called *Ikonos,* which can detect objects on Earth as small as one meter across from 400 miles up. Spy satellites are even better, reportedly able to detect objects only a few centimeters in size, but *Ikonos* imagery is available for sale to anyone able and willing to pay.

We all know that information is power, and once high-resolution imagery became available, it did not take long for people to see the political potential.[1] As soon as Space Imaging started selling *Ikonos* imagery, in January 2000, John Pike of the Federation of American Scientists started buying.[2] Pike, an intense man with a maniacal laugh, is a public policy advocate, not a trained imagery analyst. He bought and publicized the imagery to force open debates on subjects that have long been the province of people with security clearances. For the next several months, Pike bought imagery of a whole series of sensitive military installations around the world, posted them on his organization's World Wide Web site, and added his (often very controversial) interpretations of what the imagery showed. In January, it was North Korea's main missile test site—Pike concluded that the infrastructure was too primitive to constitute a serious threat, an assessment sharply at odds with the official U.S. government view. In March, it was Pakistan's nuclear and missile facilities—Pike concluded that things were *more* threatening than had previously been publicly revealed. In April, it was a U.S. site known as both Area 51 and Groom Dry Lake Air Force Base, a Nevada aircraft test site so secret that the air force only recently admitted it existed.

When Pike started doing this, much muttering was heard in the halls of U.S. intelligence agencies, complaints that Pike lacked the expertise needed to assess the imagery and its implications. The mutterers had a point—satellite imagery is notoriously difficult to interpret.[3] But Pike was not trying to change U.S. policy on those specific issues with just a few satellite images. He had a bigger point to make: in a democratic society, such matters should, and now can, be the subject of informed public debate. If he wanted to stir up debate, he succeeded. In all these cases, both the imagery and Pike's analyses appeared in major newspapers and on television news broadcasts.

Pike is not alone. A whole slew of nongovernmental organizations (NGOs) now use publicly available satellite imagery and other information to challenge long-standing government monopolies on the analysis of national security issues. Analysts with a U.S. environmental group, the Natural Resources Defense Council (NRDC), spent three years using *Ikonos* imagery and a wealth of other data to determine how many nuclear warheads the United States actually needs to cover likely military targets in Russia and elsewhere. That exercise publicly duplicated a big chunk of what the U.S. Strategic Command had done secretly for decades to come up with the Single Integrated Operational Plan, better known as the SIOP (pronounced *seye*-op). That puts the NRDC, and anyone else using its data, in a position to challenge military assessments of what the United States actually needs and, therefore, what the country can afford to negotiate away in arms control negotiations. Others have used satellite imagery to monitor the volatile South China Sea, where multiple claims over which country has possession of which islands regularly spark fears of conflict,[4] and to see whether NGOs can use the imagery to help contain the spread of nuclear weapons.[5]

Ikonos was just the beginning. The U.S. Department of Commerce has granted licenses to more than a dozen private satellite companies, two of which are now selling high-resolution imagery. ImageSat International, licensed in Israel (originally called, for some reason, West Indian Space and now headquartered on Cyprus), put a high-resolution satellite in orbit in December 2000. Several other countries, including Russia, Canada, India, and France, already sell impressively detailed satellite imagery, and those planning to join the bandwagon include Japan, China, and Brazil.

All these eyes in the sky are beginning to reveal a great deal of information previously unavailable to the public. It is not as portrayed in the movies—commercial satellites cannot pick out individual people. At best, their imagery can sometimes show shadows. One image, posted on Pike's Web site, shows what appear to be shadows of individuals on a road in Afghanistan. Space Imaging also has a scene of Egypt near the Great Sphinx at Giza that shows a bunch of tiny black dots near what appear to be buses. I was told that those dots are the shadows of people, presumably members of tour groups. But I could not tell whether this is true—the dots are barely the size of the period at the end of this sentence. You need not bother to smile when you step outside for your celestial photo op.

What the satellites *can* reveal, however, is a wealth of data good enough to enable observers to distinguish between tanks and trucks, see the path of destruction in the wake of a tornado, determine how far floodwaters or fires have extended, or detect likely sites of mass graves. Thus, the longer-term effects of *Ikonos* and its ilk are potentially far greater than embarrassment of governments or complication of arms control debates. These and other new ways of gathering information provide comprehensive data available to all on everything from the status of the environment to the location of refugees. They provide a potential basis for shared understanding of what is happening in the world—a critical and much-neglected first step in global-scale governance.

And such imagery is just one piece of the "information revolution," the whole range of technologies that have transformed the way people gather and analyze data and communicate information.

Panopticon Plus

More than a century ago, English jurist and philosopher Jeremy Bentham proposed a new approach to prison design to keep inmates under control. He suggested building a prison in the shape of a tower, with a central area from which the guards could watch the prisoners in their cells. Each cell would have a transparent wall facing the central area, but the walls between cells would be opaque. Most important, the central observation deck would be shuttered so that guards could see out but prisoners could not see in—and thus could not know from moment to moment whether they were under observation. Bentham called his design, intended to make prisons more humane, the Panopticon.[6]

The metaphor has proved irresistible to a host of social theorists. Michel Foucault seized on the Panopticon as a symbol of the nature of modern society, in which people are controlled by being isolated from one another and being made to believe they are being watched.[7] But it is the technologies of the information revolution that have rendered the Panopticon a plausible metaphor for daily life. Privacy advocates have raised the specter of a relentless swarm of Little Brothers watching us all from behind those central shutters, putting every detail of our shopping trips and medical records in huge databases for who knows what nefarious purposes.[8] And video cameras are everywhere, noting whether we are speeding or shoplifting or merely walking down the street. But there is a different way of designing the Panopticon.

Author David Brin calls it a tale of two cities.[9] Imagine the following scenario taking place a decade or so from now. In City A, there is a stunning difference from most of today's large metropolises. There is no street crime. That is because tiny cameras peer down from every lamppost, rooftop, and street sign, feeding their imagery right into Police Central. That also means that any "private" meeting among citizens may well be monitored, and they have no way of knowing whether they are under scrutiny. Panopticon Plus indeed. City B has the cameras, too, and enjoys the same safe streets. But here, "each and every citizen of this metropolis can use his or her wristwatch television to call up images from any camera in town," including the ones *inside* police headquarters.[10]

Brin is making an "if you can't fight it, join it" argument about the intrusiveness of modern information-gathering technology, asserting that loss of privacy is technologically inevitable. He may well be wrong—legal and social restrictions could go a long way toward reducing the pressure on personal privacy. But the fundamental principle may well be right.

The cameras are already starting to point both ways, with examples extending well beyond the famous case of the videotaped beating of Rodney King by police. In 1995, a California-based group called Communities for a

Better Environment (CBE) got fed up with waiting for corporations and government authorities to do something about major releases of toxic substances from oil industry facilities. The CBE was motivated particularly by a major disaster at the Unocal refinery in Rodeo in August–September 1994, when over the course of sixteen days, an accidental release of 125 tons of particularly nasty pollutants sickened 1,500 people. The organization and local citizens decided to form a community air pollution patrol. They got themselves an optical sensor, a device that emits a beam of light (in this case, infrared light) and measures the concentration of various gases in the beam. That device makes it possible for this nonprofit organization to determine for itself what concentrations of various toxic chemicals are emerging from which facilities.[11]

Such data collection technologies represent only one of the revolutionary information technologies that matter for governance. Surveillance systems such as cameras and optical sensors are not in themselves sources of information. They are sources of data, raw facts that lack meaning without context. The data have to be turned into useful information—facts placed within a context. That is where the extraordinarily fast evolution of the number-crunching and data management capacity of computers comes into play. Geographic information systems (GIS), for example, can now insert data from satellite imagery into databases containing other information, such as a city's property tax assessment records. Using that, city officials—or neighbors—could see who is putting a big new addition on a house without a permit. Computing power and memory capacity show no signs of slowing their relentless advance. Moore's law—that computing power doubles about every eighteen months—seems likely to hold as true in coming years as it has since the 1970s.[12]

But what really gives the information revolution the potential to be more than a set of mere technical advances is the ease and power of communication. Advances in telecommunications keep connecting more people and allowing them to share more information. This has been an escalating evolution, from telegraph to telephone to television to fax machines to, most recently, the Internet and the World Wide Web. Just in the 1990s, the number of Internet hosts went from a bare handful to nearly 20 million. Some twenty companies are planning, or already launching, constellations of satellites that will permit wireless "roaming" telephone connections anywhere on the planet—we will be able to take our phones with us and use them to call anyone (or be called by anyone) on Earth who has access to a phone. Some will transmit data and even video, not just voices.

The pace of technological innovation will keep escalating. In a few years, technologies that currently seem breathtaking will appear hopelessly archaic. Access to the Internet should be vastly speedier. Search engines are already able to find useful information, not just enormous piles of data. And the technology will be ubiquitous and increasingly invisible. We will find it incorporated into not only our computers and telephones but also our refrigerators and, say, our preschool daughter's bracelet—with a global positioning device connected to the Internet so that when she wanders off in the mall, we can log on via cellular telephone and find her.

That is, we will enjoy these benefits if we live in a rich country. The gee-whiz factor in all this needs to be tempered with recognition of the continuing reality of the global digital divide. Although vast quantities of data are newly available, most of the world is excluded from the cornucopia. Billions of people lack access not only to the Internet and the Web but also to newspapers, television, and books.[13] Although almost all countries now have at least one Internet service provider (ISP) somewhere within their borders, most people outside the rich countries still have no real access. Few can afford a personal computer. Even where computers are available, the charges for logging on are often, ironically, higher in poor countries than in rich ones and require a vastly higher percentage of income. In Cameroon, for example, Internet access costs about $3 per hour, in a country where the average income for civil servants is $200 per month and the general population gets by on just $610 per year.[14] The high charges in part reflect deliberate government policy to gain revenues from what often are still government telephone monopolies, monopolies that may provide as much as one-fifth of total government revenues.[15]

Awareness of the digital divide has led to an increasing number of initiatives aimed at expanding access to information and communications technologies. For example, a series of big conferences have brought together government officials and telecommunications professionals by the thousands to discuss ways of developing Africa's notoriously poor communications infrastructure.[16] Such groups as World Links, Schools Online, and World Computer Exchange are working to get computers into schools and villages around the world.[17]

But charity is probably too weak a reed on which to base the wiring of the world. Commerce is a more likely candidate. Even though poor people are by definition not the most lucrative market, there is money to be made. In some cases, entrepreneurs from poor countries who have been educated in the West are returning home to set up communications networks. Marwan Juma, the son of a Jordanian diplomat, was educated in the United States and now runs Jordan's largest ISP, the National Equipment and Technical Services Company (NETS). With 4,500 accounts at the end of 1999, NETS is minuscule by the standards of rich countries—but it represents several thousand people who previously had no access at all.[18]

Big companies show signs of interest in reaching beyond traditional markets. In March 2000, Hughes Electronics Corporation reached an agreement with a private company in India to supply and deploy 50,000 community access terminals for satellite-based Internet service in more than 1,000 cities there. The intended customers are people who lack not only home computers but also home telephone service. Located in accessible sites such as coffeehouses and restaurants, the kiosks will provide Internet access for a per-use charge, as phone booths do for telephone service.[19]

The bridging of the digital divide need not involve Western companies or entrepreneurs educated in the West, or even personal computers. Bangladesh is getting connected by cellular telephone. The renowned Grameen Bank, famous for its innovative strategy of providing microcredit—very small loans—to destitute villagers to enable them to start or expand businesses, has branched out into the communications business. Grameen Telecom follows the same basic model as Grameen Bank. It provides a small loan to a villager to enable her (almost always a woman) to buy a cell phone. It also buys airtime and resells it at cost to its loan recipients. In this country with only one phone for every 333 inhabitants, many people have never before made a call.[20] Phone access can quite directly improve people's lives. One villager who formerly spent five hours on a bus every two weeks to order supplies for his brick factory now simply calls his suppliers. Farmers can find out what prices their crops are commanding and thus eliminate the middlemen who routinely exploit them.[21]

In short, although the rich countries are clearly far ahead of the poor in benefiting from information and communications technology, it is not talking refrigerators that is politically consequential. Even if the digital divide persists, those who lack the latest gadgets will have much more access and better communications capability than ever before. The digital divide is a symptom of the fundamental inequality that prevails in the world, but it is not so grave as to eviscerate the potential for new approaches to global governance. Even a persisting digital divide would see an enormous number of formerly marginalized people able to monitor the activities of governments and corporations, to express their views, and to participate in a bigger range of groups than ever before.

Governments Fight Back

Then there is the question of whether governments can or should try to constrain access to information, technology, or both.

Governments do have some legitimate motives for imposing controls on the content of information flowing through digital systems, just as content is regulated in older informational systems, from the printing press to radio and television. On the Internet, anything that can appear in the form of words, pictures, or sounds can be found: images of Mars, the *New York Times,* conspiracy theories, pornography, wild rumors, and outright lies. No one currently plays the role of gatekeeper to sort through the mishmash. Garbage circulates unrestricted. Privacy is threatened by massive databases on consumer spending, medical records, and the like.[22]

At the same time, the growing dependence of many economies on information technology has created new vulnerabilities.[23] Hackers can tap into computers connected through the Internet, and they have succeeded in diverting funds from banks, damaging medical records, and gaining access to national security systems. So far, hackers have been primarily mischief-makers, but computer networks are vulnerable to the actions of terrorists and organized crime syndicates as well as deliberate attack in acts of war. And information technology promises to facilitate money laundering and other financial crimes through potentially untraceable electronic transfers of money.[24]

For all these reasons, governments may legitimately want to shackle the flow of information. But the truly ominous part of the information revolution, from the perspective of governments, is the *political* consequences it may have. Even well-intentioned and competent government officials are likely to have qualms about the uses, or misuses, to which political opponents may put information. And any government that performs less than perfectly may find informed citizens asking awkward questions and even banding together to take independent action.

What can governments do to hang on to power? One tempting solution is to make sure they can at least know what is being done in cyberspace by restricting people's ability to encrypt their communications. Encryption formulas can be just complex enough to provide protection from the casual hacker, or they can potentially be strong enough to frustrate even the code-breakers extraordinaire at the U.S. National Security Agency. Since the early 1990s, governments and industry in developed countries, particularly the United States, have fought over just how secret secrets should be on the Internet. Electronic commerce requires the availability of systems that can protect such financially sensitive data as credit card numbers. Global companies need effective encryption to protect proprietary information contained in their internal communications. Human rights organizations do not want the governments they are monitoring to have access to their files and communications. On the other side, governments do not want criminals—or, sometimes, political opponents—to carry on communications and financial transactions that governments cannot monitor.

The U.S. government, concerned about such things as the increasing use of global telecommunications on the part of organized crime syndicates, initially imposed export controls on encryption codes; an American would be committing a felony if a laptop computer taken overseas had a moderately good encryption system. But early in 2000, the government essentially gave up, allowing exportation of virtually any commercially available encryption program to any country (except for the handful on the U.S. Department of State's terrorist list).[25] It turned out to be unworkable for the United States to conduct a unilateral export control policy on a technology that is globally available.

Another tactic is to shut down the flow of information when it seems especially alarming. Even well-established democratic governments are reacting with fear to the transparency imposed by the new technologies. The U.S. government could have stopped Space Imaging from selling any or all of the images John Pike published. Under a (possibly unconstitutional) policy known as shutter control, the government has given itself the right to order satellite operators licensed in the United States to turn off the cameras anytime the secretary of commerce (on advice from the secretary of state, the secretary of defense, or both) decides that "national security or international

obligations and/or foreign policies may be compromised."[26] The government clearly has the right to protect national security, but the protection
extended to undefined foreign policy concerns goes far beyond the usual
U.S. understanding of the appropriate role of government in controlling
access to information. Although this policy has not yet been invoked, the
government seems to have found an equally effective, more politically palat-
able alternative. During the fall 2001 war in Afghanistan, the government
signed an exclusive contract with Space Imaging (at that time the only private satellite operator in the country) for *all* imagery of the region, even in
areas where no military operations were being carried out. At a cost of less
than $2 million per month, the government's "checkbook shutter control,"
as it was dubbed, neatly circumvented the First Amendment challenges that
might have arisen had the government invoked the regulatory kind of
shutter control.

The U.S. government is not alone in its fears of this new form of
transparency. India's central government was sufficiently alarmed by the
possibility of Indian citizens gaining access to high-resolution imagery of
their country that it instituted a policy requiring all purchases of foreign-
supplied imagery to be made through a central agency. And both of these
countries are democracies that have been selling good-quality satellite
imagery around the world for years.

Autocracies are likely to be even more wary, and they have more options
for shutting down information flows. In countries that already have effective
political surveillance systems in place, governments can limit the number of
ISPs to what they can monitor, or they can ensure that Internet service is
provided only by companies closely tied to the government. They can
require citizens to have an identification number to get an Internet account
and then hold account holders responsible for all Internet use from that
account. They can make the use of encryption subject to criminal penalties.
In places where people are accustomed to censoring themselves, such measures could chill, if not freeze, the flow of politically sensitive information.

These things are happening. According to a report by the NGO
Reporters sans frontières (Reporters without Borders), forty-five countries
restrict Internet access, often by requiring all subscribers to use a single ISP.
Some (Iraq, North Korea, Libya) allow virtually no Internet access.[27] It is
pretty easy to dismiss those refuseniks as a few scattered, pathetically poor
countries whose governments just do not understand what they are up

against. The more interesting cases are those in which governments try to reap the economic benefits of information technology without allowing it to disturb their tight political control.

Singapore's government, for example, has encouraged an especially rapid growth in Internet access as a way of becoming a hub for regional economic and financial transactions. Singapore's rate of civilian Internet use—between 5 and 10 percent of the population—rivals that of the United States. Access to and use of the Internet, however, can be monitored, given that Internet services and telephone lines are controlled by government-owned or government-linked companies. Moreover, the stiff legal penalties faced by violators of Singapore's laws against political dissent or distribution of objectionable material further discourage efforts to use the Internet to conduct free-ranging discussions.[28] Political and religious organizations are required to register with the government, and the nation's three ISPs are required to block access to some 100 sites.

At the other end of just about every scale—total population, level of economic development, penetration of information technology—is China, which, like Singapore, is trying both to open the information floodgates and to control the resulting floodwaters. In January 2000, the Chinese government issued rules requiring government approval for all content posted on the World Wide Web. Another law adopted about the same time forbade the use of foreign encryption software and required all users of encryption software to register with the government.[29] In October 2000, new rules forbade "the teachings of evil cults" (presumably meaning Falun Gong), required Internet companies to maintain records of all information posted on their Web sites for sixty days, and stipulated that news on domestic Web sites could come only from official sources.[30]

Singapore and China are not isolated examples. Russia requires ISPs to install surveillance equipment. Burma (Myanmar) closely monitors electronic mail.[31] In Vietnam, rigorous monitoring of ISPs and close regulation of content have given the government a significant degree of control over Internet use.[32]

Will all this work? Can governments succeed in channeling the floodwaters? In the short run, some can, although they are not finding it easy. Singapore's restrictions work well at chilling open political discussion on the Internet, largely because people believe they are being monitored.[33] China's bewildering array of overlapping regulations, encouragement of

self-censorship via threats to shut down or fine troublemaking Internet content providers, and outright physical intimidation has proven reasonably
effective, particularly at a time when citizens seem reasonably satisfied with
economic conditions.[34]

But over the longer term, all these governments are most likely fighting
a losing battle. Unilateral shutter control policies make little sense now that
imagery is becoming readily available from other suppliers. It is easy for
small groups to set up new Web sites quickly, leaving governments scrambling to keep up. With an estimated 9 million to 17 million Internet users
in China in 2000, the administrative burden of monitoring all those connections would be daunting, even for the most sophisticated police state. Even
Singapore, a rich country with a well-paid and very effective bureaucracy, is
beginning to question its ability to control all possible forums. The Singapore Broadcasting Authority states that it does not monitor users' Web site
access or e-mail or check on chat groups. Prime Minister Goh Chok Tong
recently acknowledged, "We've got to live with the Internet and I have just
got to move."[35]

Moreover, once connections are made, they are hard to break, even for
governments that would dearly love to do so. That helps explain why the
August 1991 coup attempt in the Soviet Union was foiled. The coup leaders did what coup leaders are supposed to do—they seized control of the
press and broadcasting agencies. But they forgot about the telephone
lines.[36] That allowed a range of communications to flourish both within the
country and with outsiders. Thanks to the availability of phones, both U.S.
president George H. W. Bush and British prime minister John Major were
able to call Boris Yeltsin and voice support for his opposition.[37] Accounts of
Yeltsin's defiance of the coup leaders were also faxed, e-mailed, and tele-
phoned across Russia.[38]

A few years later, the Internet had spread widely enough to figure in the
failure of a different government crackdown. In late 1996, Yugoslav president Slobodan Milosevic tried to shut down what remained of his country's
independent media when large anti-government demonstrations were staged
in protest of his annulment of municipal elections. The Internet made it possible for his opponents to outwit him. The independent radio station B92
shifted to digital broadcasting in both Serbo-Croatian and English over
audio Internet links. The head of the radio's Internet service, Drazen Pantic,
noted: "The irony is that the Government meant to silence us, but instead

forced us to build a whole new technology to stay alive. The drive to close us down has given us a tool to vastly expand our audience."[39]

The *Boston Globe* reported similar Internet involvement in the 1998 overthrow of Indonesia's longtime president Suharto.[40] In a country of more than 17,000 islands, where the government controlled television and radio stations, dissidents used e-mail and chat rooms to share information with one another, received updates on foreign news coverage from contacts overseas, and flooded news groups with stories of presidential corruption. Analysts argue over how much difference all this made—at the least, as one said, the Internet "fast-forwarded things."[41]

The inability of governments to cut such links has powerful political implications. Clearly, authoritarians are in for an increasingly difficult time. Governments may retain the power to impose controls, but only at the cost of shutting their countries off from the rest of the world. Even where they manage to cling to power, their more daring citizens will be able to use phones, fax machines, and e-mail to let the rest of the world know what is going on behind increasingly porous walls.

A different challenge to unconstrained access to information comes from the increasing worldwide control of the Internet by large corporations. Since corporations have so much money to spend on technological development, they may have the power to shape the new technology to their own ends. Rather than decentralizing and democratizing production and employment, the technology may instead aid the exploitation of labor by isolating workers and by facilitating technological monitoring of employees.[42] And it could conceivably enable the corporations that control a few dominant portals to select which voices are widely heard.

This is not impossible, but it is implausible that corporate control of information will be more restrictive in the Internet age than it was in the days of only a few television channels (in most countries, government-run) and one- or two-newspaper towns. The new technologies are more likely to diffuse information widely and to allow a multitude of voices to be heard than were the older media. This poses a threat to any organization that is vulnerable to public sanction. Like governments, corporations are being forced to respond to information outside their control that seeks to influence their practices and policies.

Nonetheless, neither governments nor corporations will lose control completely. Anything that can be seen by satellite may be known—but many things cannot be seen by satellite. Government, corporate, and other networks may be zapping huge quantities of information via the Internet, but much will be encrypted, and the ongoing race between encrypters and codebreakers may at any given moment favor the encrypters. Furthermore, there is a basic asymmetry that technology alone cannot overcome. People inside an organization—government, corporation, crime ring, whatever—always know more about the organization's activities and plans than those outside. Overcoming that asymmetry requires something more than technology. It requires a normative standard. And here, there has been only one plausible proposal to date: an idea called transparency.

Transparency

Advocates of well-established norms such as corporate privacy and national sovereignty want to hide information from prying eyes, whereas promoters of transparency tout it as the solution to everything from international financial crises to arms races and street crime.[43] Transparency means deliberately revealing one's actions so that outsiders can scrutinize them. This element of volition makes the growing acceptance of transparency much more than a resigned surrender to the technologically facilitated intrusiveness of the information age. It is a choice, a potential standard for the way powerful institutions ought to behave.

It is an open question whether such a standard will take root and function effectively. This will be the great political experiment of the information age. But historical cases can give us an early read as to the likelihood of success.

The norm of transparency has spread widely in a field where it seems most unlikely: military security. The world's major military powers, and many of the minor ones, have enmeshed themselves in a web of agreements to disclose an astonishing level of detail about their military capabilities and practices. By the end of the cold war, members of both the North Atlantic Treaty Organization (NATO) and the Warsaw Pact took for granted the need to open their territories to highly intrusive inspections by the other side. In a series of arms control treaties negotiated in the 1980s, the two sides agreed to allow each other to inspect missile facilities, to host each other's monitoring personnel for years at a stretch, to allow each other's airplanes to overfly their territory to check for any untoward goings-on, to exchange information about military budgets, and to permit random inspections on short notice.

In the 1990s, that acceptance of transparency spread to much of the rest of the world. By the end of the decade, 170 countries had signed on to a treaty banning chemical weapons. This treaty imposes an impressive number of disclosure requirements, not only on governments but also on the chemical industry. This is necessary because the same chemicals that revolutionized agriculture and medicine during the twentieth century can be used to make chemical weapons. Because these substances are so widespread and so thoroughly integrated into the fabric of the international economy, with a few exceptions they cannot simply be banned. Instead, the verification net must be cast both wide and deep, covering an enormous range of chemicals and imposing stringent requirements to ensure that the chemicals are properly used. These verification requirements include routine and very-short-notice surprise inspections of a vast array of often privately owned chemical facilities. By the end of the 1990s, the Organization for the Prohibition of Chemical Weapons, established by the terms of the Chemical Weapons Convention to carry out implementation, had carried out more than 500 such inspections in some thirty countries.

Given the newness of the idea that giving potential adversaries such detailed information is a good thing, rather than an act of treason, it is not surprising that compliance with all these requirements for disclosure is mixed. Some countries have yet to file even the mandatory initial declarations of which facilities in their territories produce or use certain chemicals. Yet others display a surprising degree of openness. In 1996, the U.S. Department of Defense not only disclosed information required by the treaty but also declassified a multitude of details about the U.S. chemical weapons stockpile.[44] Great Britain makes all its declarations publicly available.[45] In July 1997, India, after years of denying that it had any weapons of mass destruction, openly declared its possession of stocks of chemical weapons, even though Pakistan had not yet ratified the treaty and even though India's chemical weapons program had not been publicly revealed.

Transparency has emerged in other issue areas as well. In politics, "freedom of information" laws, which require government bureaucracies to provide information to citizens, are becoming something of a fad. In the 1990s, some thirty countries adopted laws, regulations, or constitutional provisions to increase the flow of government information, and many others are debating whether to do so.[46] Many of the laws have serious flaws or are not fully implemented, but it is remarkable that so many countries have them at all.

In the economic and environmental arenas, as later chapters will show, the trend toward greater transparency has gone even further. Rather than merely facilitating mechanisms of governance such as intergovernmental arms control agreements or cleaner national government, economic and environmental transparency measures have been conceived as direct mechanisms of governance in and of themselves. And there have been successes in this regard. The public release of information about which corporations are polluting has helped push many to cut wasteful emissions. Availability of information about the state of national economies or individual companies is increasingly required for those countries or companies to attract foreign investment. Corporations that refuse to disclose detailed information about their labor practices find that secrecy leads to a presumption of guilt in the court of public opinion.

The pace of change is remarkable. In the mid-twentieth century, few countries routinely released information about their economies. Indeed, many treated such information as state secrets. Now, scores of countries post the details on international Web sites. Then, the argument that countries should routinely open their most sensitive military facilities and plans to outside scrutiny would have seemed laughable. Now, it is standard practice for most major military powers. Then, only Sweden and Finland had laws requiring government officials to provide information to citizens on demand. Now, some forty countries do, and the number is growing rapidly.

Transparency is becoming the norm. Coupled with information technology, it creates an explosive combination, one that could change the nature of governance as drastically as the print revolution did half a millennium ago. Where information technology, globalization, and democratization converge, we may be seeing the emergence of a dynamic new alternative to the coercive power of states: regulation by revelation.

Governments generally solve problems by telling people what to do. Polluters, for example, are told to reduce pollution. Since pollution can be hard to measure directly, regulators sometimes require that companies use specific manufacturing technologies known to be less polluting than those the companies would otherwise use, rather than leaving it up to the company to figure out how to meet specific targets for reducing emissions. At the international level, many efforts to regulate behavior consist of a few major powers telling everyone else what to do. The United States in particular plays this role, from nonproliferation to trade to human rights, imposing economic sanctions at an unprecedented rate on countries that fail to comply with standards of behavior set somewhere in the U.S. government.

Regulation by revelation is a very different approach to governance. No government need tell corporations, or other governments, exactly what they must do or cannot do. Instead, governments and corporations are required simply to own up publicly to whatever it is they *are* doing in the expectation that such a requirement will cause them to alter undesirable behavior. That public admission often brings about big changes in behavior.

Will Transparency Endure?

Much of this book's argument for new approaches to global governance depends on continued growth in availability of information. Earlier sections explored whether governments might prove able to reimpose centralized controls over information technology, concluding that it is unlikely. That leaves the question of whether the trend toward greater transparency—voluntary disclosure—will last. What is driving the trend toward transparency?

Obviously, as already suggested, technology itself is part of the answer. It is a matter of simple economics. If information becomes cheaper and easier to supply, supply goes up. But technology merely enables transparency. There is much more to the story.

The spread of democratic norms is fostering the belief that powerful entities, such as states and corporations, should account for their behavior. A fundamental tenet of democracy is, after all, consent of the governed, and consent is meaningless unless it is informed. The essence of democracy, indeed, is not elections. Elections are merely a means to an end, and that end is accountability. Globalization itself is spreading the demand for transparency. Now the consent must come from ever wider groups. As globalization shrinks the world, governments and corporations find themselves under intense pressure to divulge secrets about activities ranging from military security to environmental emissions. And thanks to the rise of civil society around the world, more and more groups are demanding a say in what used to be other people's business. None of these trends is likely to dissipate anytime soon.

But information flows are not the same as transparency. Even if voluntary disclosures escalate, they might not affect governance. One concern is the "fire hose effect": the possibility that so much information will pour out that capturing and using it becomes impossible. Already, most people with the education and leisure to read this book are glutted with information. It is conceivable that the amount and diversity of information being transmitted will overwhelm everyone.[47]

But, as David Brin points out, such data smog is not inevitable:

> There is a good chance that the problem would be solved by the development of new software agents, sophisticated autonomous servant programs designed to cull and search through the morass, adroitly sifting the information byways with our needs foremost in mind, clearing away dross and eventually restoring clarity to cyberspace, the way the air of Los Angeles is gradually becoming breathable once again.[48]

Our forebears adapted to the glut of information made possible by the print revolution by developing systems of checks by editors and publishers, attributing greater credence to some publications than to others on the basis of their reputations for credibility and accuracy. For transparency to work, we will have to create systems for winnowing through the chaff.

Resistance to Transparency

Governments and corporations are not uniformly persuaded by the idea that they should open themselves to scrutiny. Transparency's popularity is inversely proportional to its distance. Everyone thinks it is a good idea to subject the behavior of others to intense public scrutiny. Few wish to be subjected to it themselves. To governments or corporations that are just doing what they have always done, the expectation that they should now report on their activities to outsiders can seem like an affront or an inconvenience, if not an outright threat. Government bureaucrats struggle to keep up with the endless reporting requirements of international environmental, human rights, and financial institutions. Corporations find themselves besieged by demands for information about their environmental and labor practices, not only from governments but also increasingly from NGOs, which may be based in distant parts of the world. International organizations such as the World Bank and the International Monetary Fund face growing pressure to open up their decision-making processes to public review. All find the bright light of scrutiny at best uncomfortable, at worst paralyzing. Many states, corporations, and organizations have instead retreated behind more traditional norms of privacy or sovereignty, insisting that although calls for transparency are all well and good, *they* should not be required to hew to its demands.

The forces of resistance got a big boost on September 11, 2001. Transparency's traditional proponent, the United States, began backpedaling furiously. Most notable has been the newly popular practice of "scrubbing" Web sites—removing information that someone believes might aid terrorists in planning attacks. Ironically, the Project on Government Secrecy of the Federation of American Scientists, one of the leading NGO proponents of government transparency, removed information from its own Web site—primarily concerning the location of secure intelligence facilities—on the grounds that such information was not publicly available elsewhere.[49] Other scrubs raised more serious concerns about the appropriate balance between protecting legitimate secrets and ensuring that citizens have the information necessary to protect themselves.

The U.S. Environmental Protection Agency (EPA), for example, removed a database with information about chemicals used at 15,000 industrial sites in the United States.[50] The database was the result of a congressional requirement established after the disastrous 1984 chemical leak at the Union Carbide plant in Bhopal, India, that companies submit information about the potential for toxic waste spills so that local emergency services and residents could make appropriate plans to deal with worst-case scenarios.[51] But after September 11, the EPA apparently decided that the danger of giving terrorists ready access to such information outweighed citizens' right to know whether their children's day care centers are located next to potentially dangerous chemical sites.

Other government agencies, including many at the state level, pursued a similar course of action. The U.S. Nuclear Regulatory Commission temporarily closed down its Web site altogether; when the site reopened, it contained only "select content." The Internal Revenue Service prohibited unescorted public access to the reading rooms the United States Congress required it to establish, ostensibly out of concern for employee safety. The state of Pennsylvania removed some environmental information from its Web site, and the state of Florida blocked public access to information about crop dusters.[52]

This backlash may not make much difference. It is confined almost entirely to the United States. And it is proving difficult even in the United

States to impose retroactive controls on information that used to be public. As a news article about the scrubs pointed out a couple of months after the attacks, "on the World Wide Web, almost nothing truly dies."[53] Search engines keep their indexes up to date by using small computer programs called "bots" to monitor the Web, and the nonprofit Internet Archive's bots have enabled that archive to store perhaps 10 billion Web pages. Steven Aftergood, head of the Federation of American Scientists' project on government secrecy, belatedly discovered that his well-intentioned scrub of his organization's Web site provided little protection from the misuse of information—bots had copied the relevant photographs to other sites.

The Dark Side

Part of the reason the administration of President George W. Bush and those of other governments are able to put the clamps on such information is that transparency is not always good. If people do not agree on what constitutes good or bad behavior by a government or corporation, revealing that behavior may just spark conflicts over competing views of the public good. Some institutional secrets are legitimately worth protecting—there is no inherent right for one corporation to know its rival's trade secrets, and military disclosure can allow adversaries to find weaknesses and locate targets. Misinterpretation, accidental or deliberate, can transform disclosure from an opportunity for public accountability to an exercise in scapegoating.

Even where transparency would in principle be good, it may not work. Nobel Prize–winning economist Amartya Sen has pointed out that transparency prevents famines—there are no famines in countries with a reasonably free press.[54] But it does not seem to do much good in combating chronic malnutrition, which exists even in the richest and most open countries, including the United States.

From Knowing to Doing

Even if all disincentives to transparency are overcome, this new governance tool will not by itself lead to the rosy scenario of chapter 1. Transparency by itself will accomplish nothing at all. People have to interpret and act on the information revealed. As it happens, that is getting easier.

Information and communications technologies are making it ever easier for new groups to form and maintain bonds, even across boundaries, and to act as collective entities. This change is altering the nature of social organizations in a transformation as fundamental as the emergence of hierarchical governments or competitive markets.[55] Dispersed groups can readily share information and coordinate their efforts. These networks can be ephemeral and yet effective as parts of different organizations come together as needed in cyberspace. And these cross-border networks, whether ephemeral or long-lasting, are the channels through which data might be transformed into global collective action.

Such networked coalitions are not just a product of the computer revolution. Western societies have been organizing effective ephemeral coalitions in substantial numbers since the 1960s. Lacking a large permanent base of grassroots activists, these movements compensate, as scholar Sidney Tarrow points out, "by assembling concentrated numbers at strategic places and times. . . . The antiwar coalitions of the late 1960s, the pro-abortion movements and the peace movement of the 1980s developed this technique of collaboration to a high level—in some cases forming quasi-permanent peak organizations to coordinate their efforts."[56]

What is new since the 1980s is the degree to which networks have been empowered by technology. That technology has made it far easier for new groups to coalesce and carry out collective action, and it removes any geographic constraint on their interaction. It enables diffuse groups united by shared principles or interests (rather than geography) to begin to carry out international policy making on a wide range of transnational issues, as is already evident in such fields as the environment, arms control, human rights, and, increasingly, economics.

Like transparency, the new capacity for networking has a dark side. The capacity to network globally benefits not only principled advocacy groups but anyone with an agenda to pursue, including, as is now all too clear, terrorists and members of organized crime syndicates. By drastically reducing the costs of communicating and organizing, the information revolution may lead to an excess of civil society: too many competing interest groups with little common space. Moreover, it can allow extremist groups, such as white supremacists and skinheads, to grow to critical mass in cyberspace and reinforce one another rather than be contained through local ostracism.

Making It Work

For good or for ill, the global spotlight is on. But there are reasons to believe it might lead to a more open, transparent system of global governance. First, the broad trend toward greater democracy brings with it a normative shift. When governments are seen as entities whose purpose is to serve the public interest, government efforts to keep secrets from the public face a higher standard of justification. Second, in issues from security to economics to the environment, as later chapters will show, many parts of the world have enjoyed much success in using disclosure to serve broad public interests, creating powerful models.

This approach to global governance will require that a broad range of people around the world become sophisticated consumers and analysts of information. It will also require that more people see themselves as having a stake in things that happen far away and act on what they see. Whether such visionary action is likely to become widespread depends on what kinds of connections people can and will form across borders—the subject of the next chapter.

3

The Global We

There was a man who died and was being taken to heaven by angels. Although he was happy to be going up, he was curious about what happened in hell, so the angels agreed to swing by hell on the way. They took him to a place where there was a great bowl, as big as a lake, from which emanated the tantalizing smell of a delicious, nutritious stew. Surrounding the bowl were hordes of people, emaciated, starving, miserable people, each holding an enormous spoon with a ten-foot handle, long enough to reach into the bowl. The trouble was that although they could scoop the stew into the spoon, they could not get it into their mouths because the handles were so long.

Then the angels flew the man up to heaven. To his great surprise, it looked much like hell—the same vast bowl, the same enticing aroma, the same enormous spoons. But all the people in heaven looked well-fed, happy, and content. Perplexed, the man watched to see what made heaven so much happier a place than hell. It didn't take long. In heaven, as in hell, no one could feed himself. But in heaven, people were feeding each other.

Short of paradise, people still manage to help one another out, even unrelated people, sometimes even total strangers. Why they do so can be something of a mystery. Religions teach that brotherly love is the motivation, as in the popular religious parable recounted above. Social scientists look more cynically toward explanations based on reciprocity—I will hold your spoon if you will hold mine. Both types of explanations are on to something important to the prospects for global governance.

We are a highly *social* species, strongly predisposed to belong to a group and contribute to its success. That desire is visible in everything from group action at its worst in al Qaeda or the former Yugoslavia to collective action at its best in the form of local community solidarity or transnational principled advocacy groups. Unlike solitary beings such as tigers, which in the wild do quite nicely while rarely seeing another of their kind, humans have to rely on other humans for protection, not least from one another. We thus evolved to live collectively rather than individually. That ability to cooperate (combined with our substantial brainpower) put men on the moon, allows symphony orchestras to perform, and enables groups of humans to kill other groups of humans on a scale no other species can approach.

In behavioral scientist Abraham Maslow's famous hierarchy of human needs, the need for belonging to a group comes right after satisfaction of the essential physical requirements of life and security.[1] It is easy to understand why belonging to a group may be beneficial—through such memberships, individuals gain the benefits of the group's solution to collective action problems. But very often, people are not driven to join or to act on behalf of groups by calm reflection about what serves their individual rational self-interest. Instead, they often seem to reverse the order: people find, or inherit, a group identity, and their strong sense of group loyalty motivates them to adopt the group's goals and interests as their own. One striking example lies in the infamous gangs of America's inner cities: young men and, increasingly, young women consign themselves to violent and often short lives in exchange for strong connections to the only significant group available. For reasons rooted deep in human evolution, belonging to a group feels good, right, and necessary.

In humanity's tribal past, it was easy for people to know which group they belonged to. They would interact solely with the same few dozen people, mostly relatives, throughout their lives. Now, however, we must construct identities within communities that in the larger countries may number hundreds of millions and that on global issues involve billions. All groups beyond small kin groups are social constructions to some extent, "imagined communities" in Benedict Anderson's evocative phrase.[2] In such communities, people who are not related and often do not know one another nonetheless assume they share an identity. These collectivities matter, and are able to act coherently, because the people inside and outside them act as though they matter. The power of the collective identity is so great that individuals shape their behavior and expectations according to their belief that they have *something* in common with people whom they will never meet.

Over the past few centuries, the most obvious form of group identity came from nation-states. Analysts of international relations treated group identity as a given rather than a question, looking at states—legally recognized countries—as the source of identity and assuming that people identified themselves primarily as citizens of the country where they lived. For a period after World War II, the equation of group identification with country seemed to work. As more and more former colonies became independent, it was thought, modernization would ensure that these new countries would overcome internal divisions to create workable civic identities. The new countries would follow the Western path of economic and political development, ending up with stable polities—political organizations—able to address internal problems and to serve as constructive members of the international community.

But in many places, that has not happened. Identity is in flux as major changes are occurring in the way people distribute their loyalties and the way they identify themselves. Nobody really has a clue what information technology will do to identity, but we are already seeing new connections made via the World Wide Web and electronic mail among people who used to be separated by distance. As the world undergoes simultaneous trends toward globalization, based on economic and technological forces, and on new divisions that draw ever sharper distinctions based primarily on ethnicity and religion, old certainties about identity are disappearing.

That leaves us all wondering: Who belongs to what groups? Who legitimately has a say in which groups' decisions? And, most important for the global governance debate, is it possible for there to be a group that encompasses the entire species?

Human Nature

Let us take a brief detour into history—prehistory, actually, via a new field of study that roots the human need for group identity in millions of years of evolution. The field of evolutionary psychology points out that the human mind, like the human body, evolved to serve certain functions: to deal with the plants, the animals, and, especially, the other people in the ancestral environment.[3] Natural selection shaped the human mind just as it shaped the body, over a very long period creating entities with the full range of mental abilities and physiological responses we perceive as emotions. Minds with characteristics that made them relatively more successful in getting genes into the next generation became, by definition, more widespread than those with less success. Much of what we experience as emotion may actually be our genes' grab bag of tricks to get us to do the things that get *them* passed on via reproduction—falling in love; sticking around to raise the kids; ensuring our own survival long enough to reproduce. Two key causes of group identity figure prominently among those tricks: kin selection and status seeking.

KIN SELECTION

Genes succeed if they reproduce themselves, and it does not matter to the genes what happens to any particular host. Since my siblings share half my genes, my genes do as well when I help siblings as when I help myself. My genes can also do well if I help a number of cousins, who on average share one-eighth of my genes. So it makes sense that we have evolved to promote the well-being of those we identify as close kin. Such kin selection may be the basis of the human propensity for self-sacrifice on behalf of the group. But of course people do not size up a dangerous situation, calculate which members of a threatened group share what percentage of their genes, and then risk life and limb to rescue only those who pass the genetic cutoff. Instead, we are emotionally equipped to sacrifice our own well-being for those we have identified as part of our group—who in the ancestral environment would have been our local tribe, most of whom would have been close relatives.[4]

STATUS SEEKING

High status has great reproductive rewards, especially for a male: it increases the chance that a female (or her family) will choose him as a mate, and in polygamous societies it raises the likelihood of having multiple wives. Moreover, for both males and females, high status helps to ensure access to resources, such as food. In the modern world, so very different from the ancestral environment, what constitutes status can vary wildly between or even within cultures, ranging from wealth to athletic prowess to high political position to artistic achievement. But no matter what guideposts exist to measure status, all human societies have some degree of hierarchy. Even small transient groups quickly develop hierarchies, as any group of schoolchildren demonstrates.

Status seeking would seem at first glance to involve the opposite of collective action. Since status is inherently relative, status seeking is a zero-sum game—if I win, you lose. But it is not necessarily an individual game. Coalitions of individuals can and often do work together to raise their status collectively vis-à-vis another group even in a state of nature, as research on the social organization of primates has shown.[5] And status seeking need not entail taking on other people in direct opposition. Symphony orchestras and teams of researchers can acquire high status through their works without ever "defeating" others directly. Either way, the sense of collective glory is a powerful source of social cohesion.

Thus, evolution has primed us for "groupness," making it at least plausible that a group of souls confronted with that tricky celestial soup kitchen would figure out a cooperative response. But let us complicate that scenario a bit by adding a chilling dose of realism. Let us say that around that big soup pot was a limited supply of saltines—not exactly the food of the gods, but enough to stave off starvation. Would people still risk taking the time and effort to feed someone else the good stuff, at the risk of missing out on even the chance to fill up with crackers?

For a group to cohere, to reap the full benefits of collective action, its members must trust one another to ignore the crackers and concentrate on the soup. What accounts for such trust? The simplest explanation is reciprocal altruism.[6] Friends engage in reciprocal altruism: I help you in the (often unconscious) expectation that you will help me. I do not think about contributing in those terms—I help you because you are my friend and I feel affection for you. If, over time, you repeatedly fail to reciprocate, at the very least I will stop helping you and stop feeling affection for you. More likely, I will not just stop helping you; I will get mad at you and express my outrage far and wide so that everyone around knows you cannot be trusted to reciprocate altruism. Such angry punishment of nonreciprocators seems just and natural to us because the genetic complexes that produce such sentiments are the ones that succeeded in getting reproduced—their hosts were not people to mess with.

These feelings of affection, anger, and outrage are the products of natural selection: the way evolution solved the collective action problem in the ancestral environment. As in all discussions of the evolutionary basis of human behavior, it is important to keep emphasizing that what we are talking about is propensities. Human behavior is enormously variable, not rigidly determined by genetics. Obviously, many people are never willing to sacrifice much of anything for anyone else. But such sacrifice on behalf of a group does happen quite often, particularly at the much less intense levels at which individuals provide money or resources for group goals rather than individual ones, and that self-sacrifice requires explanation. We are *able* to act altruistically, even if some individual members of the species rarely do.

Evolutionary psychology is a field very much in development. The account given here is a much-simplified overview of a few key ideas in a rich field. At its current stage, the field certainly does not explain everything about human nature, and it will never explain everything about human behavior. Evolution has merely provided us with certain very broad predispositions.[7] Much of what people actually do stems from culture and cognition. Even the feelings with which evolution has equipped us can serve broader ends than those of our selfish genes.[8] There is no obvious evolutionary advantage to the willingness many people have to care for elderly parents even when they become a burden and require resources that could otherwise be invested in the grandchildren. The human striving for meaning and purpose in life, the ability to experience the transcendent—indeed, much of what is most admirable in the species—would seem to have had little obvious utility in the ancestral environment. Such traits may simply be the lucky by-product of the evolution of brains that could thrive there—or they may reflect something deeper, something beyond the explanatory power of evolutionary psychology.[9] But understanding those broad predispositions helps us understand how likely people are to form groups that can stretch across political, linguistic, and cultural boundaries in pursuit of common ends.

The Consequences of "Human Nature"

Thanks to our evolutionary history as tribal rather than solitary creatures, humans are predisposed to cooperate within groups. Those emotions of affection, loyalty, and group pride can provide a powerful cement, helping to ensure that altruism is regularly reciprocated. And reciprocal altruism is the basis of social trust—the pervasive confidence among members of a group that other members will more often contribute than free ride. This social trust is in turn the basis of what scholars call social capital. Renowned social scientist Robert Putnam describes it as follows:

> By analogy with notions of physical capital and human capital—tools and training that enhance individual productivity—"social capital" refers to features of social organization such as networks, norms, and social trust that facilitate coordination and cooperation for mutual benefit. For a variety of reasons, life is easier in a community blessed with a substantial stock of social capital. In the first place, networks of civic engagement foster sturdy norms of generalized reciprocity and encourage the emergence of social trust. Such networks facilitate coordination and communication, amplify reputations, and *thus allow dilemmas of collective action to be resolved* [emphasis added]. When economic and political negotiation is embedded in dense networks of social interaction, incentives for opportunism are reduced. . . . Finally, dense networks of interaction probably broaden the participants' sense of self, developing the "I" into the "we."[10]

All this works readily on a small scale, where everyone interacts directly with everyone else. But for several hundred years, people have lived in communities too large for everyone to know one another; hence the importance of reputation. Even if you do not know me, you know somebody who does. Reputation is an effective mechanism for midsize groups. Once the chains get too long, however, the cement weakens. There is no absolute cutoff, but clearly the six degrees of separation that allegedly connect every person on the planet to every other is a few degrees too many.

So how do we develop social capital at a larger scale? One classic means is to define a community in opposition to other groups. It seems easy for most of us to see "our" group as superior and "them" as worthy of contempt.[11] "We" can be trusted to reciprocate cooperation among ourselves, but "they" cannot be trusted to reciprocate with us, since we do not know them. "We" can jointly achieve status, whereas "their" achievement of status pushes us lower down the hierarchy. And, most damning of all, "they" are clearly not our kin, not our family, not familiar.

Almost any basis for group identity, from nationalism to religion to principled social causes, *can* degenerate into us-versus-them hostility. Samuel Huntington's famous clash-of-civilizations thesis is based on a resounding assertion that group identity is inherently adversarial. People are groping for identities, and the dividing lines matter because those on opposite sides will hate each other, he claims: "For people seeking identity and reinventing ethnicity, enemies are essential."[12]

Not necessarily. Identity formation may require drawing distinctions—we are *X* and you are not—but it does not always require hatred and enmity. Although perceiving a common enemy is one effective means of cementing group ties, it is hardly the only one. Groups can bond in response to any kind of perceived danger, whether from war or flood or the spread of contagious disease. They can form in response to simple proximity: college fraternities and sororities, neighborhood communities. They can emerge from all sorts of social or professional interactions that over time lead to shared trust. And they can grow out of some rather peculiar shared experiences. Some of the people whose transatlantic flights were diverted to Canada on September 11, 2001, apparently formed close ties in the several days they spent together as involuntary guests of various Canadian communities—close enough that within a few months they were planning reunions.[13]

For all the attention that has understandably been focused on the dangers posed by intergroup hostilities, human history actually demonstrates a powerful trend toward larger, more inclusive groups. Robert Wright, in his fascinating book modestly titled *Non-Zero: The Logic of Human Destiny*, points out that the story of human history has been one long expansion in the size and complexity of human groups. Groups that can deal successfully with collective action situations have an enormous advantage over groups that fail to do so. The advantage is so great that a kind of "survival of the fittest" sets in, and the failures get swallowed up by those that succeed. That is why polities have grown bigger and more tightly integrated from the dawn of history right into the twenty-first century. There is nothing mystical about this. It is simply that social mechanisms that get big groups to engage in widespread reciprocal altruism (even when the reciprocity is quite diffuse) create societies that are stronger and longer-lasting than their alternatives.

In fact, the emotional proclivity for cooperation may be just as strong as the propensity to demonize the "other." As philosopher Richard Rorty points out, people have to play a psychological game with themselves to indulge in such nastiness. In playing this deadly game, members of one group assign less-than-human status to the other group:

> [Those who equate *human* with *people like us*] all think that the line between the humans and the animals is not simply the line between the featherless bipeds and the rest. Rather, this line divides some featherless bipeds from others: there are animals walking about in humanoid form. We and those like us are paradigm cases of humanity, but those too different from us in behavior or custom are, at best, borderline cases.[14]

There is nothing inevitable in such divisions. We may have evolved to hate on occasion, but we also evolved to love and to cooperate. We evolved with such a wide range of potential that we can re-create ourselves in any way we can imagine. Some groups get along peacefully for decades and then suddenly tear each other to pieces, as happened in Yugoslavia in the 1990s.[15] But in Europe as a whole, in the second half of the twentieth century, nations that had endured centuries of violent hostility came together to begin creating a new political and economic union. Definitions of who is included in the in-group and rationales for despising the out-group vary over time, and not every group's identity is dependent on the existence of an out-group.

The emerging global culture is now at a crossroads as to what kinds of group identity will dominate in the future. Will ties be based primarily on proximity, consanguinity, or shared interests? All are possible, although just what proximity will mean to those tied in to the information revolution is hard to predict. Calls for ethnic division and religious hatred seem always to find followers, yet at the same time growing numbers of people are deeply involved in pursuing principled causes around the world, broadening the scope of the moral community far beyond local tribes and national borders.

The starting point for understanding what kinds of group identity are likely to matter in the future is the present. And at present, the dominant form of group identity is national.

Nationalism

Nationalism is a very specific concept of group identity based on the idea that one's emotional identity (beyond the family) lies with the nation and that the nation should be congruent with the political unit that makes the rules, called the state.[16] That is why political scientists talk about nation-states instead of countries. International law and most thinking about international politics has taken for granted the idea that people's primary identity is their nationality. The idea of the nation-state has become so well entrenched that it appears to be the natural order of things.

It is not. Despite its current ubiquity, nationalism in the sense of a primary emotional identity matched up to citizenship in the place whose laws bind you turns out to be recent in its articulation and, say most scholars, in its existence.[17] Two or three centuries ago, if you had asked most people living in France or Russia who they were, the chances are that few would have described themselves as French or Russian. The answer would more likely have reflected a religious or local identity. Indeed, the French "nation" was still a collection of various ethnic and other groups within the borders of France as late as the 1850s.[18] Only by the end of the nineteenth century did most people within the borders of France perceive themselves as common members of a French nation. And France was not unusual. National myths and practices are relatively recent in most parts of the world and are often deliberately constructed by elites.[19] In other words, as scholar David Laitin puts it, nations "are not 'out there' to be counted; they are a function of social, political, and economic processes," most of which have occurred fairly recently.[20] Despite widespread use of the misnomer *nation-state*, almost no state is made up of a single nation in the ethnic sense.[21]

How and why did this happen? There are many possible explanations,[22] but a particularly compelling one comes from Benedict Anderson, who attributes the rise of nationalism in part to our old friend the printing press. He argues that nationalism arose first in the Americas in the series of revolutionary wars waged in the New World between 1776 and 1825. The American Revolution in the United States was the first (paralleled by the French Revolution). In Latin America, nationalist sentiments grew out of Spain's insistence on allowing only the Spanish-born to serve as viceroys in the Americas and to return to high positions in Spain. Those born in the Americas were consigned to lesser status. With the arrival of what Anderson calls "print capitalism" in the eighteenth century, the emergence of local presses printing provincial newspapers created an "imagined community" among readers, which in time served as the basis for the notion of a "national" community strong enough to liberate itself from Spanish power. Back in Europe, thereafter, popular nationalisms began proliferating, again driven by print capitalism and the unifying effects of newly shared language. The various dynasties responded by trying to merge their legitimacy with that of nationalism through a practice of "official nationalism" modeled on the American and French histories. This was not a straightforward process, Anderson notes: "a certain inventive legerdemain was required to permit the empire to appear attractive in national drag."[23]

But the focus on national identity as a deliberate political construction is only half the story. It explains why elites might want to use nationalism as a political strategy but not why they could do so, or why so many people have proven willing to die in defense of the nation. Nations cannot always be created, despite the most diligent efforts of political leaders, as the Soviet elites found to their dismay.[24]

In the search for explanations of the emotional power of nationalism, the evolutionary theory we traipsed through earlier proves illuminating. As American political scientist Walker Connor notes, despite the tendency of some scholars to define the nation as a community of people characterized by a common language, territory, religion, and the like, more is involved:

> How much simpler it would be if adopting the Polish language, living within Poland, and adhering to Catholicism were sufficient to define membership in the Polish nation— were sufficient to make one a Pole. But there are Germans, Lithuanians, and Ukrainians who meet these criteria but who do not consider themselves Polish and are not considered Polish by their Polish fellow citizens.[25]

Instead, Connor claims, the nation is a *perceived* kinship group. People respond strongly to the tie of "blood," even when the "national" group is not actually genetically related by any objective measure. There need not be, and usually is not, much factual basis to the claim of blood ties. Existing or emerging leaders need only convince a group of their consanguinity to provoke a powerful emotional response—one deeply rooted in the human psyche, as evolutionary psychology shows.

Israeli philosopher Yael Tamir agrees that "national continuity embodies a strong sense of genealogy" but believes that "kinship" is not all that matters.[26] She adds an emphasis on the importance of shared status in cementing loyalties:

> Members . . . see themselves sharing a common destiny and view their individual success and well-being as closely dependent on the prosperity of the group as a whole. They relate their self-esteem and their accomplishments to the achievements of other group members and take pride in the group's distinctive contributions. Consequently, they develop feelings of caring and duty toward one another. These feelings are exclusive and apply to members only.[27]

Both the kinship and the group-status explanations make sense in light of evolutionary theory and help us understand the enormous emotional power of nationalism.

The next question, then, is how it is decided who is a member of the nation and who is not. Nationalism has clearly changed over time. At least in the early to mid-1800s, nationalism appears to have been closely related to the development of nation-states. And writings on nationalism had a pragmatic cast: a nation had to be big enough to form a viable state—otherwise, it was of little interest.[28] By around 1880, the idea of nationalism was broadening, with the eruption of nationalist movements seeking self-determination for groups bound together by claims of ethnic or linguistic unity or both. Historian Eric Hobsbawm identifies three trends that drove the explosion, trends that seem eerily familiar to students of twenty-first-century identity politics:

> the resistance of traditional groups threatened by the onrush of modernity, the novel and quite non-traditional classes and strata now rapidly growing in the urbanizing societies of developed countries, and the unprecedented migrations which distributed a multiple diaspora of peoples across the globe, each strangers to both natives and other migrant groups, none, as yet, with the habits and conventions of coexistence.[29]

All this was exacerbated by the economic depression of the late nineteenth century and by the emergence of social Darwinism, a notorious corruption of the tenets of biological evolutionary theory used to justify claims of racial and national superiority. In this mélange, people proved susceptible to nationalist appeals at a time when the rise of mass politics was forcing political leaders to appeal to their populations as broadly, and often emotionally, as possible.

After World War I, the victorious powers tried both to clean up the mess left by the collapse of the Ottoman and Habsburg Empires and to stave off Russian-style socialist revolution through use of the principle of national self-determination in Europe, with nations defined in ethnic terms. It failed because people were far too intermingled for any policy of separating them into ethnolinguistically coherent states to be workable. Instead, the result was oppression of the minorities stranded within the borders of the new states, up to and including what we would now recognize as "ethnic cleansing." Nor was it clear that the people being separated into the new ethnic nations always wanted to be there. In some of the plebiscites conducted to determine to which states some regions of "mixed" nationality should be assigned, it was found that many people preferred to live in a state not of their "nation." Some Poles chose Germany over Poland; some Slovenes chose Austria over the new Yugoslavia.[30]

This "divergence between definition and reality," as one scholar calls it, recurred throughout the next several decades of the major anti-colonial independence movements.[31] Leaders speaking the language of nationalism often represented territories as ethnic, linguistic, or even political units even when these characterizations had little or no historical reality.

After World War II, most thinking about nationalism centered on state building, with the development of nationalism in the newly liberated colonies expected to parallel that of nineteenth-century Europe. Much of the early literature on development predicted that narrow communal, ethnic, and religious identities would fade away with modernization, done in as economic development, urbanization, education, and globalization broke down old barriers. In the wave of decolonization that followed World War II, westerners and the leaders of the new nations alike thought of nationalism in terms of a "modern," civic identity.[32] This modern, civic, secular nationalism would involve a strong personal sense of emotional identification, but one that was based on allegiance to a political system within a territory, not on ethnic, religious, or cultural affiliation.[33]

Throughout this period and up to the present day, governments have competed in the "market for loyalties," often deliberately creating or reinforcing national identities, using national media to foster either broad cohesion or the dominance of particular groups.[34] The Turkish government, for example, has used the monopolistic Turkish Radio and Television Corporation (TRT) to promote a vision of a secular state and to limit access to Islamic sects. When at one point the TRT seemed to be leaning too far toward legitimizing Islamic fundamentalism, its director was forced to resign.[35] Until the 1990s, Austria did not license any private radio or television stations, arguing that a small country needed a public monopoly to further democratic values.[36]

The Future of Group Identity

In many parts of the world, civic nationalism has yet to triumph or is facing new threats. The term *nationalism* now refers as much to ethnic or sometimes religious identities as to a broad, countrywide community. Although this can be good—a means of celebrating heritages and preserving cultural diversity—as a political development it has alarming implications. Nationalism gets nastier in times of stress, and much of the world is experiencing stress today. Even in relatively peaceful parts of the world, such as western Europe, massive population movements since the 1960s have sparked resurgent strains of xenophobia, a reprise of the tensions provoked by mass migrations a century earlier.[37] And everywhere, general feelings of disorientation and insecurity lead many to cling to the security of belonging to a common language and culture.

In other words, the stresses of modernization and globalization provoke nationalism, but of the ethnic rather than the civic kind. This causes political problems because ethnic group identities do not correspond to existing political boundaries. At least several hundred ethnic groups have some claim to nationhood, far more than the world's 200 or so states, and almost all states are "mosaics of distinct peoples," in Ted Gurr and James Scarritt's poetic phrase.[38]

But is the current visibility of ethnic identities temporary or long-term? Is the new "ascriptive" nationalism—based on ostensibly unalterable characteristics such as ethnicity or religion ascribed by others to an individual—a transient, indeed transitional, phenomenon, a set of bumps on the road to a more rational future? Or are "faith and family, blood and belief" the driving forces of group identity, immutable in essence even if malleable in specific application?[39] Is the major effect of globalization to create ever-broadening identities?[40] Or will it create a lasting identity-based backlash that will tear the world apart?

It is currently fashionable to see ethnic nationalism as a durable phenomenon that will eventually trump other bases for identity and that will plague the world into the indefinite future.[41] If ethnic nationalism has the emotional power described here, some writers argue, one can hardly expect it to go away. One describes such nationalism as a permanent force that has no rivals today as a collective sentiment, driven by psychological needs that it fulfills better than do other possible sources of identity.[42]

But such views go too far. Nationalism arises from the political manipulations of leaders or would-be leaders, not spontaneously from a deeply rooted sense of common destiny in any particular group. One partial explanation for the rise of ethnic nationalism is that there are simply more people now wanting to play the role of political entrepreneur. Levels of education have risen all around the world, and the resulting growth of the intelligentsia has created a considerable class of people wanting their turn in the political limelight.[43] And the uncertainties resulting from modernization and globalization create fertile ground for such manipulation.

Nonetheless, nationalism is no longer a *driving* force in the world in the sense of developing new, powerful, and sustainable polities than can solve the collective action dilemma.[44] Having created the European and American nation-states and undergirded the independence movements of colonial territories, nationalism in many parts of the world has mutated into a divisive response to uncertainty, providing no program for action, no sense of how society should organize and protect itself—in other words, no basis for sustained collective action. Because ethnic nationalism is merely a vague emotional appeal, leaders who invoke it can draw widespread support, but that support crumbles as soon as those leaders start proposing specific programs of action.[45]

This denigration of the importance of nationalism may seem hard to understand in light of the headlines since the 1990s. The newspapers and the nightly television news have been filled with descriptions of appalling slaughters. But that sense of incessant ethnic carnage is partly an illusion fostered by incessant reporting on some of the conflicts.[46] The number of major armed conflicts within countries, though still at an appalling level, is declining, not rising. A number of the prominent conflicts of the early 1990s turned out to constitute state-formation wars following the collapse of the Soviet Union and Yugoslavia. Violence in the formation of states is far from a new or surprising phenomenon. When states collapse, "ethnic conflict" frequently rears its ugly head, but as consequence, not cause, of the collapse of a state.[47]

Religion

Is faith the alternative? With thousands dead in the smoldering ruins of the World Trade Center, it would be hard to overlook the potency of religious fervor as a motivation for self-sacrifice on behalf of a group's goals, twisted as the goals of al Qaeda were. But the evil deeds of September 11 were not the inevitable result of an incomprehensible alien fanaticism. Religion provided the rationale, not the cause. Pundits and scholars will argue for years about the precise causes of Islamic terrorism, but the general recipe seems reasonably clear. Take incompetent, corrupt, and autocratic governments, throw in economic hopelessness (such as Saudi Arabia's rapidly declining per capita income), and add a large dose of unceasing anti-Western official propaganda meant to distract citizens from the failings of their own governments. It does not seem surprising that the resulting mixture produced some people susceptible to the blandishments of a relative handful of psychopathic fanatics. In no way are such phenomena unique to Islam. History is replete with examples of religions serving such roles. In this particular case, the Islamic revival seems far more important as a domestic political phenomenon in Islamic countries than as the core of a new transnational collectivity. In that domestic role, Islam provides "a powerful vehicle for expressing nationalist grievances against the West and for legitimizing opposition to oppressive domestic regimes."[48]

Nonetheless, religion clearly provides an important source of group identity that often spans national borders. The spread of religion, particularly Christianity in tandem with trade and colonization, has created ties that still bind millions in shared, non-national identities.[49] But the flows are changing direction and creating new types of transnational ties. This explosion of religious fervor comes both from the bottom up and from the top down, driven as much by migration and the information revolution as by deliberate proselytizing on the part of central church hierarchies.[50]

Evangelical Protestantism, for example, has swept much of previously Catholic Latin America and is now spreading rapidly in East Asia and sub-Saharan Africa. According to sociologist Peter Berger, its diffusion is creating a new international culture, inculcating a Protestant work ethic that carries with it the seeds of a pluralistic and modernizing culture favorable to democracy.[51] If Berger proves to be correct, and if the current fervent debate within the Islamic world over the appropriate nature of an Islamic identity were to lead to a similarly open worldview—both big ifs but not impossible outcomes—religion may in the end prove to be as much a source of global connections as of local division.

Even if that happy ending does not occur, religion will not necessarily shape group behavior. Strong religious identities that are shared across national borders do not always provide the basis for effective transnational collective action. Liberation theology in Latin America spurred the development of grassroots organizations (often Church-led) to provide services and to advocate for the poor, but these have not cohered into politically effective transnational actors.[52] The various religious revivals are creating transnational social capital, but we will most likely not face a future of theocratic dominance.

Rather, in the future no single form of group identity is likely to dominate. Group identity is becoming ever more a matter of individual choice. People participate in a large and growing number of systems and collectivities, each of which may recognize, or require, a different identity from the same individual. The political system may recognize a person as a citizen of a given country while his ethnic group sees him as part of a diaspora, for his on-line chat group he is a Netizen, and he sees himself primarily as an environmentalist. Identities have always been social constructions, but increasingly the constructors are individuals making deliberate choices rather than simply acceding to the weight of tradition. In modern societies, individuals must *choose* personal, professional, and religious identities.[53] Even so-called ascriptive characteristics in many cases are becoming optional, depending on what the individual in question chooses to emphasize. What is the identity of the daughter of a Chinese mother and an American father who attends a French school in Senegal?

Given that fluidity, it is perhaps not surprising that many different types of more or less coherent groups seem to be forming and trying to play various parts in global governance. Beyond the familiar groupings, such as business leaders (see chapter 5), a whole range of nonprofit activist groups, networked across national borders, is struggling to advance various causes, as discussed in chapter 6. These range from the tightly focused aims of the International Campaign to Ban Landmines to the diffuse, sometimes contradictory goals of the mislabeled anti-globalization movement. As later chapters will show, such groups concern themselves not (or not only) with the well-being of themselves, their neighborhood, or their ethnic group but with the global public good. And all sorts of unlikely people, from government officials to international bureaucrats to corporate executives, are participating in coalitions of change makers, spending considerable time on efforts to come up with ways of solving global problems. It is easy to be cynical and assume such efforts are motivated by crass considerations of personal profit or power, but not all of them can be so easily dismissed. A growing number of people around the world do seem prepared to think about the welfare of humanity as a whole.

Such globally minded thinkers may reflect a broader trend. Since all communities are now imagined, there is nothing that inherently prevents people from imagining broadly rather than narrowly. And there is some evidence that such broad imagining is beginning to spread around the world. Public opinion surveys find a steady increase in cosmopolitan attitudes across generations. Older people are far more likely to identify strongly with a country or locality, whereas those born more recently show themselves steadily more likely to claim a primary identity at the continental or global level. (Interestingly, the percentage claiming a primary territorial identity at the country level remains pretty consistent, in the range of 35 percent. The big shift over age cohorts shows up in the decreasing number claiming local identities and the increasing number thinking continentally or globally.)[54]

Even such a trend, if it continues, is not grounds for complacency. In too many places, the world remains riven by vicious hatreds and explosive conflicts, along with the persistent greedy shortsightedness that has always bedeviled humanity. But it does offer grounds for hope.

E Pluribus Unum?

What kind of celestial soup kitchen does the future hold? Will we all starve separately, feed one another plentifully, or subsist on crackers? Because we are not angels, the answer is likely to depend heavily on what kind of emotional connections people form and on what scale. Except for the occasional sociopath, all people need to feel a sense of identity with at least one group, and usually with several. We rarely consciously create these group identities. Instead, we choose from the available models.

Since we did not evolve in complex civilizations in which we chose our group identities, nature did not accustom us to making such choices. Rather, our evolutionary background provides us with many options for interacting within and across groups and for defining the groups to which we will feel loyalty. Thus, it is reasonable to think of this era of globalization as a time of searching for ways to create groups and networks able to handle global collective action problems, rather than assuming an inevitable splintering into hate-filled and violent rivalries.

Why Governments Won't Solve Everything

Picture yourself as the head of a government a decade or two from now. Technological transformation and economic integration have continued apace, leaving you subject to competing pressures your forebears never imagined when they designed your political system. If you wish to attain or maintain prosperity, you must make your country attractive to investors, often foreign ones, who can provide the capital and technology your economy needs in an increasingly competitive and integrated global system. The prevailing free market ideology and the ease of investing and operating overseas or in cyberspace make businesses unwilling to tolerate much regulation. But your increasingly educated and mobilized citizenry will not tolerate a free ride for business.

Other governments are bombarding you with demands that you lower your carbon emissions and other transnational pollutants and preserve your biodiversity. But the industries responsible for many of those emissions and much of the biodiversity loss threaten to move elsewhere—and take jobs with them—if your environmental restrictions get too onerous. Your country is facing the early effects of climate change, with increasing numbers of expensive natural disasters such as hurricanes and floods along with changing rainfall and temperature patterns that are wreaking havoc with agriculture and tourism.

Depending on whether you run a rich country or a poor one, you have either a large number of elderly, retired, and often ailing citizens or a lot of young, unemployed, and restive ones, all of whom demand that you provide them with a generous social safety net. (If you are really unlucky, you have both.) Your health care system is creaking under the strains imposed not only by an aging population but also by epidemics of resurgent virulent diseases that have become resistant to antibiotics. Huge numbers of people are on the move, either trying to cross into your (rich) territory, thus provoking your citizens to demand better border controls, or flocking into your (poor) cities, where infrastructure development lags far behind needs. You have to keep a wary eye out for terrorists and would-be extortionists who may be targeting you and your citizens with anything from conventional bombs to nerve gases to, conceivably, stolen nuclear weapons. And, by the way, watch out for international organized crime, which is addicting your citizens to drugs, laundering money through your financial system, and bribing your officials. Solving most of these problems will require close cooperation with numerous other countries, adding to the time and expense, particularly since most of those countries are too preoccupied with their own problems to care much about helping you with yours.

But when you look around for ways to pay for programs to deal with all these problems, you find money an elusive commodity, even if the national economy is booming. You have to keep taxes on capital low to prevent it from fleeing overseas. You cannot rely on sales taxes because so much retail commerce is now taking place in cyberspace, untraceable and thus untaxable, or in the "gray" informal economy, where nothing is ever declared. You cannot raise taxes on labor very much because so much of the labor force is in relatively low-paying service jobs, and people with high-paying jobs are internationally employable and thus able to move if taxes get too high. Your remaining option is to tax natural resources (oil, minerals, forests)—which, fortunately, are inherently immobile and thus firmly in your jurisdiction—but in most countries, these cannot by themselves provide a tax base adequate to support a government large enough to deal with all those demands.

And, perhaps most difficult, most of the problems with which you are grappling do not constitute the kind of urgent, dramatic threat that pulls a society together and makes people particularly willing to contribute, through taxes or other means, to the common weal. Indeed, your government is now stuck with these gradually worsening problems in large part because your predecessors mostly ignored them, instead following the political imperative to address only the most immediately pressing issues.

Of course, things may never get this bad. It is not certain that capital or skilled labor will ever become *that* mobile. And how much of commerce will move to cyberspace is unpredictable. But the dilemmas are real. Life in a globalizing world requires an enormous amount of collective action, but the same trends that create those needs make it difficult for national governments to solve the problems.

The assumption that governments alone will handle large-scale collective action reflects a habit of thinking deeply ingrained over the past century. Governments dominated most of the twentieth century for three powerful reasons. First, the twentieth century saw by far the biggest wars the world had ever endured, both hot and cold, and war on that scale is the forte of governments. For decades, many societies were consumed by preparations for, conduct of, and reconstruction after wars. These were *the* overriding collective action problems. Second, as democratic franchises spread, more and more governments found themselves under pressure to offer various kinds of services to their newly broadened constituencies. Thus was born the welfare state, with its high levels of taxation and big bureaucracies for transferring money from some people to others. Third, the combination of the apparent failure of capitalism in the Great Depression and the rapid economic growth of the USSR until the 1960s fostered a broad consensus that market economies could not work unassisted. That consensus led many governments to seize the "commanding heights" of those economies by operating state-owned versions of everything from communications and transportation companies to utilities.[1] (The United States did things a bit differently, regulating those industries heavily rather than owning them directly.) War, democracy, and ideology expanded the reach and power of national governments to unprecedented levels, creating new assumptions about the ability of governments to solve all problems and the appropriateness of expecting them to do so.

That power is waning. Although, as we were so shockingly reminded in September 2001, there is still very much a role for governments in protecting citizens and managing global issues, the factors that led to the extraordinary expansion of governments in the twentieth century no longer apply as they once did. War between countries has become rarer. States are no longer striving to seize the commanding heights of national economies—instead, they are scrambling down the slopes, selling off state-run enterprises as fast as they can find buyers. In many ways, states truly are in retreat, shedding many of the governance responsibilities they had taken on in the twentieth century.

So what can—and should—governments do about the growing need for global governance? Few national governments can individually do much, since by definition the problems require action across national borders. The real question is whether governments have the ability to reach effective agreements among themselves and then carry out those agreements.

Three factors influence the roles of national governments. The first is history—the reasons we live in a world divided into countries. The second is capacity—the ability of national governments to act effectively within their own territories and participate meaningfully in international negotiations. The third is the various ways governments have tried to cooperate in solving global problems, particularly through the institutions most people assume constitute the core of global governance: intergovernmental organizations such as the United Nations and the World Trade Organization. This last point merits a particular look at the role and extraordinary power of the United States, which, despite its enormous capacity to lead, has demonstrated an unfortunate proclivity to take its marbles and go home.

The Evolution of the State

Most of the works written on global governance, or any other kind of governance, do not actually discuss national governments at all. They discuss states. In bodies such as the United Nations, governments are not members; states are. For something so central to the workings of the world, the state is surprisingly ill-defined.[2] Under international law, the state is something more than the government because it remains beholden by its international commitments even when its government changes. Government can roughly be defined as the decision-making apparatus of the state. Formal definitions of the state (as opposed to the government) often concentrate on one key aspect—the state is that which legitimately, or at least successfully, claims a monopoly on the use of force within a demarcated territory.

But states are not divinely ordained, and possession of a monopoly on the use of force within a given territory is only one of several possible systems of political organization.[3] The national boundaries that now divide the world into legally equal, ostensibly sovereign entities did not come about through any systematic planning about how best to meet humanity's needs. The system evolved, driven by an inner logic that originally enabled it to wipe out feudalism in Europe and eventually made it the only conceivable form of political organization everywhere. Until fairly recently in historical terms, alternatives such as city-states, overlapping and nonterritorial authorities of the type seen in medieval Europe, and empires all flourished. To understand why they disappeared requires plunging back a few hundred years into European history.

The first states were not *nation*-states. Their inhabitants shared no sense of common or national identity, and their leaders were not particularly concerned with the welfare of most of the inhabitants. The leaders who consolidated the European states did not set out to create anything like the nation-state as we know it today. They were out for their own power: achieving power meant controlling territory, and controlling territory required overcoming the armed resistance of others who wanted to control it. State making was essentially an accidental by-product of the successful internal struggle for dominance because successful lords needed tax collectors, police forces, courts, and accounting systems to extract and manage the resources necessary for war.[4]

As technology advanced and as the increasingly unified European states fought one another, the resources needed to fight such battles grew. The growth of state power both depended on and spurred the expansion of a quasi-private economy, including banks from which the governments could borrow. In the face of these internal and external struggles, only those states that became relatively proficient at making war and suppressing competing lords survived. Not all made it. Poland disappeared from the maps for a while when its aristocrats fended off internal efforts at centralizing control, making it easy for outside powers, notably Russia, to grab slices of Polish territory. By 1795, Poland had vanished, not to reappear on the map of Europe until the end of World War I.[5] But for those that survived, proficiency at making war required building up the institutions of the state. The state form of political organization won out because states turned out to be the most efficient and effective polities at a certain point in European history, and shortly thereafter Europe came to dominate the world, spreading that particular form of polity.

Initially, the interests served by the state were primarily those of the rulers, the people who controlled the state apparatus, joined in time by their economic allies. To the degree that states succeeded in imposing domestic order and fighting off attacks from outside, the broader population benefited tremendously. But the centralized accumulation of power took centuries of violent elimination or subordination of other, previously semi-autonomous authorities.[6] And states made little effort to address people's collective needs beyond the central one of physical security.

Over time, as technology made war more expensive, the need to induce contributions from a broader range of the population introduced important constraints on the ways in which rulers could treat the ruled. Taxation at anything beyond minimal levels does not work well if it is wholly coercive: the monitoring and enforcement costs are too high. The rulers selectively extended protection to some groups in return for their support, agreements that made those rulers vulnerable to the withdrawal of that support.[7]

Until about the eighteenth century, states did not do much other than wage war. The local nobility, the churches, and other such entities carried out much of what collective action there was, and there was little beyond the village level. By 1700, according to one estimate, the European states "absorbed perhaps 5 percent of the GNP in peacetime, 10 percent in wartime."[8] At these levels, most people's lives were not greatly affected by the activities of the state. That is why most people within the territory controlled by a state did not think of themselves as a single group bound by a common identity.

Then came the explosion in central government power, fueled in part by the capacities made available by the industrial revolution. By the time of the Napoleonic Wars of the early nineteenth century, the state share of the national economy in Europe had risen to between 25 and 35 percent, and armies constituted about 5 percent of the total population.[9]

Accompanying and enabling the new dominance of the state were the first signs of nationalism: the feeling of shared identity among the inhabitants of a country that made them *willing* to contribute massively to the collective goals of their country, even to sacrifice their lives. As noted in chapter 3, this was no mysterious upwelling of fellow feeling. In an act of deliberate political creation, state authorities and the intelligentsia were striving to create a shared sense of identity to legitimize their demands that an increasingly wide swath of the citizenry fork over an ever larger share of the national income.

Over time, as the industrial revolution shook up European and other societies, increasingly representative institutions formed to incorporate those newly powerful social forces.[10] That ongoing political incorporation expanded the size and reach of the state in the twentieth century as governments instituted social security and welfare policies to benefit new groups of voters. And with such vast resources mobilized, large-scale collective endeavors—such as war—could flourish at a scale never before seen.

In the twentieth century, in addition to waging war and assembling police forces, states provided a vast array of collective goods and services. They developed communications and transportation infrastructure for both military and economic purposes. They became the channel for political representation. They guaranteed the rights of citizens vis-à-vis one another. And they invented and carried out macroeconomic planning.[11]

The state is not about to wither away. Government expenditures in many rich countries account for nearly 50 percent of gross domestic product.[12] In poorer countries, government expenditures are relatively lower, but they still average nearly 30 percent. But as the opening scenario suggested, governments of both rich and, especially, poor countries face rapidly growing demands to use their resources for purely domestic programs (pensions, health care, education) that leave little budgetary flexibility. Governments that fail to meet those demands face the very real prospect of finding themselves voted or forced out of power.

Whether even elected governments have the capacity to cope with the wide range of national and transnational problems they face is a topic of much debate. The World Bank issued a report in 1996 arguing that states need to redefine (meaning: shrink) their roles and focus on their core competencies.[13] That is part of what lies behind the waves of privatization sweeping the world: the consensus that the state should be a provider of a limited range of collective goods and services for the country and should not meddle in areas that the private sector can handle better.

But the privatization of state-owned industries still leaves governments facing big challenges that threaten their ability to manage the host of transnational collective action problems for which effective governance will be desperately needed in the first few decades of the twenty-first century.

Only relatively few states are currently in serious trouble, falling so short of fulfilling the basic functions of a state that, like Somalia, they effectively no longer exist as unified polities. But there are real, and increasingly widely recognized, reasons to doubt that the capacity of governments will be able to meet the demands for cross-border collective action in the coming decades.

Perhaps the biggest future danger to state capacity in general comes from a potential threat to the most basic requirement of statehood: the ability to tax. No matter how much people hate to pay taxes, it does not take much thought to realize that without taxes, a lot of the collective goods and services people want to have would not be available. In coming years, information technology may make it very difficult for states to collect taxes. The globalization of capital flows, itself a creature of information technology, has led many to question whether governments will be able to continue to tax capital. No matter how efficient and capable a state apparatus is, it cannot extract resources that are not within its territory. In the lingo of economists, states cannot tax a mobile factor of production beyond the level at which it is willing to be taxed, or, since it is mobile, it will get up and go. And the one absolutely indisputable consequence of the globalization of the economy is that capital has become vastly more mobile. Because capital is free to go wherever it can earn the highest rate of return, states can impose taxes only to the point that the after-tax return starts to dip below returns available elsewhere. If taxes get higher, capital may simply flow to jurisdictions with lower, or no, taxes.[14]

Governments are already cutting tax rates on capital. In 1988, the average statutory corporate tax rate among the member countries in the Organization for Economic Cooperation and Development (OECD, essentially the group of wealthy countries) was 44 percent. By 1997, the rate was down to 36 percent.[15] By 2000, the average was down to 33 percent.[16]

In the absence of global agreements regarding tax rates on capital, not exactly a prominent prospect, states may have to turn to other sources of revenue. For example, states can impose or increase income taxes to garner resources from labor, which is still relatively confined to national boundaries. But even here, as the most dynamic parts of economies become more integrated, the highest-paid workers are increasingly free to migrate elsewhere.

The emergence of electronic commerce raises the possibility that governments will also have trouble collecting sales taxes. It is already possible, though cumbersome, to conduct business over the Internet anonymously. As encryption systems become increasingly sophisticated, governments may find it increasingly difficult to know when economic transactions of any kind (from salary payments to commerce) are occurring in cyberspace, making it much harder to take a cut. Governments have some capacity to constrain levels of encryption technology, at least for a while, but constraining encryption may simply drive currently legitimate parts of the economy into the gray or black market. Agreement on international regulation of encryption levels is itself a massive global governance problem, but anything short of a truly global approach will not work, given the nonterritorial nature of cyberspace.

The tax problem is the most tangible way in which the information revolution may undermine state power, but it is not the only one. State power is based much more on voluntary—or quasi-voluntary—compliance with everything from tax requirements to criminal law to military drafts than on sheer coercion. Remember that the great rise in the nation-state occurred when European governments deliberately set out to create largely mythical "national" identities that made citizens willing not only to pay taxes but also, on occasion, to lay down their lives. These national identities, resting as they often did on distortions of historical reality and unfounded claims of kinship, were possible only because information and communications remained largely under state control. States have used their ability to regulate and control national media quite deliberately in their efforts to create and maintain national identities, a process that continues to the present day.

But partly as a result of the broad shift toward deregulation of everything, including media, and partly as a result of the new communications technologies, as discussed in chapter 3, states are finding it harder to maintain such national controls. Now all states face increased competition for people's loyalties as information technology connects people across borders, uniting dispersed identities and interests. The ultimate outcome of that competition is as yet unknowable.

It's Hard to Create a State

Of course, in a world so sharply divided between rich and poor, talking about the prospects for the state as a general phenomenon gets us only so far. Many countries are still working on basic tasks of constructing viable government institutions and national identities. When Europeans colonized the rest of the world, they brought with them the concept of the nation-state as the sole legitimate form of political organization. All other possibilities—empires, colonies, feudal arrangements—have faded from the scene, and their reintroduction is hard to imagine.[17] As countries broke free of the colonial yoke, they became states, often without having gone through the lengthy and violent process of state building that their European predecessors had endured. Even countries that had long existed as independent entities prior to colonization, or that escaped colonial subjugation altogether, often found that their political institutions fell far short of twentieth-century needs.

These countries have had to undertake state building under far more difficult circumstances than Europeans ever faced. Political scientist Mohammed Ayoob describes in detail just how hard state building is for the latecomers.[18] They face extraordinary time pressures that compel them to do in decades what European countries did in centuries. They must compete with existing and well-established states if they wish to participate in the increasingly globalized economy. If they cannot compete, they are left out of an economic system that seems to be far more productive than national autarky. And thanks to the information revolution, their citizens will know they are being left out.

At the same time, their governments are held to a much higher standard of performance than were the early European state builders. To make themselves legitimate, and thus able to extract contributions for collective action without relying solely on coercion, they must accommodate competing ethnic nationalisms and try to develop a sense of civic nationalism that overcomes existing ethnic and religious fissures. But they are expected to do so gently, including everyone in a democratic system that allows mass participation rather than simply subduing dissident groups through coercion. Establishing channels for mass participation while simultaneously building state institutions is no easy task. Some states (such as South Korea, Brazil, and Mexico) have made extraordinary economic and political strides, but many others have fallen far short. Given the difficulties, it is perhaps not surprising that some governments, such as that of Iran, have tried to legitimize themselves by claiming divine right, as European royalty once did.

As if these basic challenges to state building were not enough, the demands on national governments keep rising. They are now expected to participate in a bewildering range of environmental treaties and maintain the integrity of the environment within their borders while setting the correct macroeconomic policies to ensure successful and sustainable economic development. At the same time, states are supposed to provide for the basic needs of their peoples through social safety nets—something the early European states never considered trying to do. In short, as Ayoob puts it, the new states "are under pressure to demonstrate adequate statehood quickly, to perform the task of state making in a humane, civilized, and consensual fashion, and to do all this in an era of mass politics."[19]

It may seem peculiar, given the wretched circumstances with which new states must contend, that more and more states keep emerging. The number of states rose sharply over the past two centuries, particularly in the last half of the twentieth century. When the United Nations was founded in 1945, it had 51 member states (two of which were actually constituent republics of the USSR with no real autonomy). By the end of the century, the number was close to 200.

The reason is a combination of the end of empires (including the collapse of the USSR, a collapse that created fifteen countries out of what had been one) and simple self-interest. Now that the nation-state system is entrenched, the obvious way for an individual or group to gain political power is to represent a state. If you live in a state whose government is oppressing your group, one way to escape that oppression is to become a separate state. Or, more cynically, if you are an individual aspiring to power, one ready means to achieve power is to convince a set of people who share some common bonds, no matter how tenuous, that they are indeed a coherent group and you are their leader. In either case, the international norm of self-determination means that the world community may support your claim to statehood, particularly if you have the military capability to make the alternative a long and bloody civil war.

Contemporary state formation arbitrarily designates the inhabitants of a given territory as a collectivity, asserting that proximity confers common interests. Yet the borders of many states reflect historical accident and colonial caprice more than any logical division between well-established and stable groups. In states-in-formation, the inhabitants often do not see themselves as a coherent group. Even when national leaders aspire to act in the public interest, their lack of legitimacy forces them to rely on coercion to extract contributions to state-defined collective interests because they do not get the quasi-voluntary compliance common in more established states. But human rights norms do not allow much in the way of coercion, and the use of coercion further delegitimizes the state. At the same time, the norm of self-determination legitimizes an alternative collectivity: the ethnic group. Such groups find it increasingly easy to organize themselves to protest or fight, thanks to the communications revolution. But if they succeed in achieving political autonomy, they often find that they lack the capacity to carry out the much harder tasks of economic development and thus to redress what ails them: joblessness, perceived economic inequities, and the lack of a political framework within which to express themselves peacefully. Because many such states are falling short of the mark, their ability to participate meaningfully in intergovernmental problem solving remains open to question.[20]

The Rich States

Other countries, mostly in North America, Europe, and parts of Asia, are having a much easier time of it. These are the ones that have well-developed government institutions, well-educated populations, and reasonably stable politics, not to mention most of the world's money. But even these governments are not off the hook. In addition to the unknown long-term effects of the information revolution, they face some quite well known threats for which they are clearly unprepared, as well as the prospect of spillover effects (such as terrorism, economic volatility, environmental degradation, and the spread of new diseases) from what takes place in the poorer parts of the world.

One crucial change is in the ability of states to engage in macroeconomic planning. Even in the boom times of the 1990s, the stagnation in real wages of many Americans, stubbornly high unemployment in Europe, and the uncertain prospects of the Asian economies meant that large numbers of citizens did not enjoy rising standards of living. Economic integration exacerbates the apparent inability of states to manage their economies to the satisfaction of their citizens.[21] As chapter 7 will show, powerful forces are pressing governments to free up their markets in goods and capital to international competition. When things go wrong economically—when wages stagnate for the poor or economies encounter downturns—citizens find it easy to blame governments for developments that may be beyond government control.

The rich countries also face a demographic change that will absorb more and more of their political attention. Over the first few decades of the twenty-first century, the populations of North America, Europe, and, especially, Japan will become markedly "grayer" as the proportion of elderly inhabitants grows to historically unprecedented levels, thanks to both declining birthrates and rising life expectancies.[22] These societies have created social security systems that transfer vast amounts of money from the working-age population to the older retirees. Now the rapid drop in the ratio of young to old threatens to bring on a crisis over entitlements. The graying of the population will also bring soaring medical costs, given the greater health care needs of the old. The political leadership of these countries will increasingly be absorbed in domestic battles over allocation of resources, an increasing share of which will go to income transfers rather than to solutions for the new global agenda of collective action problems.

The elderly may not be the only ones who will demand a growing share of government resources. One possible effect of global economic integration is the loss of low-paying jobs to poorer countries as companies take advantage of the much lower costs of labor in the developing world. This has not yet happened on a large scale, but if the theory of comparative advantage on which trade is based holds up, it should. When capital is free to flow across borders, the returns to labor should equalize. Workers in rich countries tend to be better educated and more skilled, so they will still command the higher incomes warranted by their higher productivity. But the large group of relatively unskilled and poorly educated workers in rich countries will be stranded even if the rich countries benefit overall from the growing international economic specialization.

Such are the predictable difficulties facing the world's wealthier countries. Their greater challenges, however, may be harder to foresee. These societies are rich because they are complex and technologically sophisticated. But the very traits that account for their achievements may render them peculiarly vulnerable to some very nasty shocks.

Keeping these societies humming takes an extraordinary range of interlocking systems that provide energy, food, water, transportation, and information. Disruptions in any component of these systems can cascade into broader disasters. Canadian scholar Thomas Homer-Dixon paints a chilling picture of this potential for disaster in his account of one such incident in the United States in 1996, when the failure of one transmission line in northern Oregon caused overloading on a series of connected transmission lines, leading to blackouts affecting millions of people in the western United States.[23] If terrorists chose to exploit such vulnerabilities, they could wreak economic and social havoc—especially if they attacked several at once. Any country, no matter how advanced, would be hard pressed to deal with a cascade of power failures combined with releases of biological and computer viruses and a few explosions at chemical and nuclear facilities.

Even absent malicious intent, unexpected shocks may well create new stresses. One possible consequence of climate change, for example, could be alteration of the flow of the Gulf Stream, which currently provides northern Europe with a climate similar to that of more southerly latitudes elsewhere. If the region were suddenly to be plunged into a new ice age, the consequences would extend around the globe. No one really knows how the various forces at work in today's integrated global economies will interact over time, but contagion effects have already buffeted many poor countries, and there is little reason to assume that the rich are inherently immune.

The world's wealthy countries may be vulnerable, but they hardly face imminent collapse. They have demonstrated great resilience in the face of previous shocks. Clearly, however, they face challenges that may well strain their ability to participate effectively in demanding systems of global governance.

Cooperation among States

Even if every country enjoyed the blessing of legitimate, stable, and effective national government, they would still find it difficult to solve *global* problems. Governments have certainly tried, creating an enormous range of cooperative mechanisms, incorporating treaties, international organizations, and various formal and informal arrangements generally known as regimes.[24] Some accomplish the goals their member governments set for them. As chapter 7 will describe, world trade has been kept relatively open through a series of multilateral agreements, buttressed now by the existence of the World Trade Organization.[25] Chapter 8 describes the cooperation that led to the ozone regime, which is now reducing global emissions of chlorofluorocarbons (CFCs) and other man-made substances that threaten to destroy the stratospheric layer of ozone that protects Earth from harmful solar radiation.[26] And there are many other such cases. To take just one, the nuclear nonproliferation regime has successfully used a treaty, an international organization, and a number of other agreements to keep the total number of countries possessing nuclear weapons to a handful, much smaller than the twenty to twenty-five nuclear powers foreseen in the early 1960s.[27]

But although intergovernmental cooperation has worked in such cases, there is a whole host of reasons to doubt that states will be able to keep up with the growing needs they themselves have identified. In a series of treaties and declarations promulgated over the past few decades, most of the world's governments have committed themselves to cooperate to end a host of scourges that seriously threaten human well-being.[28] Yet they do not seem to mean it. They have promised, for example, to halve global poverty by 2015—but poverty rates have barely budged (except in China, where the reliability of the statistics is open to question). They have vowed to ensure that all people attain a level of health that permits them to lead socially and economically productive lives. They first promised, in 1977, to meet this goal by the year 2000. Instead, the proportion of children being immunized against basic childhood diseases has fallen from more than 70 percent to at best about 50 percent.[29] The United Nations was founded to protect the world from the scourge of war, but more than 20 million people, mostly civilians, have died in armed conflict since the end of World War II.[30] And despite the successes in trade liberalization and protection of the ozone layer, there is a litany of failures, as recorded in chapters 7 and 8. The global economy remains highly unstable and grotesquely inequitable, and the global environment continues to deteriorate rapidly.

What will it take to do better? One key to successful collective action is often leadership, especially in the anarchic environment of global politics. Treaties and intergovernmental organizations do not just happen; someone has to make them happen. For centuries, it has been the great powers, the countries with the richest economies and the strongest military forces, that created global rules. Sometimes they have operated through "clubs" that satisfied the needs of the member countries. But, as noted in chapter 1, often a single country has served as a "benevolent hegemon," bearing much of the cost of collective action in order to ensure benefits for all.

The leading candidate for that role remains the United States, which has had the part since the end of World War II. Since the end of the cold war, it has been called the last remaining superpower, even a "hyperpower," stronger than anything the world has ever before seen. Yet it does not always use its extraordinary strength constructively. It has also been called an arrogant bully that demands special treatment for itself wherever governments gather and pushes its desired rules down everyone else's throats.

When measured in traditional terms, claims of U.S. superiority are not exaggerated. The military expenditures of the United States dwarf those of any other country; they are roughly five times those of the world's second biggest economy, Japan. Indeed, for many years it has outspent all the other big spenders put together—most of which, like Japan, are close U.S. allies rather than potential enemies against whose military power the United States must guard.[31] Its economy accounts for approximately one-quarter of the global total, depending on what measurements are used.[32] And it even has the advantage of what Harvard University dean Joseph Nye calls "soft power"—the ability to influence the ideas and desires of others purely through the power of example and persuasion.[33]

Unfortunately, now that the cold war is over, the United States shows little inclination to use its dominance to act cooperatively rather than unilaterally, except when other countries seem prepared to do things the U.S. way. As analyst Stewart Patrick has concisely argued, the United States often asserts the right to tell others how they ought to behave and to punish them when they fail to do so:[34]

> Between 1993 and 1998, Congress either imposed or threatened unilateral sanctions some 60 times on 35 countries. Particularly galling to United States partners has been the extraterritorial extension of United States domestic law to restrict trade with so-called rogue states or states of concern, especially the Iran-Libya sanctions and the Helms-Burton law regarding Cuba. Both threaten heavy penalties against foreign enterprises doing business with these pariah states. Among the most vociferous critics of these laws have been close United States allies. "This is bullying," former Canadian Foreign Minister Lloyd Axworthy responded tartly to Helms-Burton. "But in America you call it 'global leadership.'"[35]

When it does participate in international negotiations, the United States has taken to using its substantial weight to shape agreements and then refusing to adhere to the resulting treaty (as it did regarding the Convention on the Rights of the Child, the Rome Statute of the International Criminal Court, the Convention on Biological Diversity, and the Kyoto Protocol to the

United Nations Framework Convention on Climate Change). And the United States has been known to refuse to honor clear and specific treaty commitments. The most notorious example of such free riding is the long-standing saga of the United Nations dues. Every member country is required under the Charter of the United Nations to pay dues annually to support the organization. The amount due is based on shares of the global economy and ability to pay. The United States' share has long stood at 25 percent, in line with its share of the global economy. Many countries lag in their payments, but starting in the late 1980s, the United States alone started refusing to pay on principle. It announced that it would withhold payment until the United Nations undertook serious administrative and structural reforms, an action clearly illegal under the Charter. By the late 1990s, the amount due topped $1 billion, and the United States faced the prospect of losing its right to vote in the United Nations General Assembly, as required by the Charter if members get too far behind in payments. In 1999, the United States Congress agreed that the nation would remit $926 million of the unpaid dues, but only if the United Nations agreed to cut the U.S. share to 22 percent. The United Nations, facing destitution, agreed, but as of September 2001, only $100 million had actually been sent.[36]

After September 11, it briefly appeared that the United States had been shocked out of its illusion of invulnerability. Suddenly Congress, recognizing that the United States would need the world body as part of its broad international anti-terrorism coalition, found more than $500 million to send to the United Nations.[37]

But on issues of greater concern to other countries than to the U.S. government, United States policy did not become more forthcoming. Indeed, the United States proceeded with its long-threatened abrogation of the Anti–Ballistic Missile Treaty, and as chapters 7 and 8 will show, did little in the economic and environmental fields to demonstrate greater willingness to take into account even the most reasonable concerns of others.

Most of this reflects domestic politics rather than any grand scheme to annoy the world. Indeed, it does not even reflect the broad preferences of American citizens. For decades, U.S. public opinion polls have shown that large majorities (usually 60 percent or more) support active U.S. engagement in the world in cooperation with other countries.[38] Even after the September 11 attacks, when one might expect a highly nationalistic response, some three-quarters favored including other countries' forces in a military action in Afghanistan even if that constrained U.S. freedom of action; even more wanted the United Nations to play a much-strengthened role in fighting terrorism. And 95 percent agreed that it was important "for the war on terrorism to be seen by the world as an effort of many countries working together, not just a U.S. effort."[39]

Should America run the world, deliberately using its enormous power to create a global empire? Some people think that is already happening, and some approve. *Wall Street Journal* editor Max Boot made "the case for American empire" in an article arguing that "the Sept. 11 attack was a result of insufficient American involvement and ambition; the solution is to be more expansive in our goals and more assertive in their implementation."[40] Boot and others portray America as an "attractive empire," one that uses "soft power" cultural and economic instruments as well as military tools to shape the world to its liking. But given the track record just described, there is little evidence that the United States is actually engaged in such an enlightened long-term strategy.

Joseph Nye provides a more realistic description of the challenges facing America's extraordinary power.[41] He describes the twenty-first-century world as a three-tiered chessboard. On the top, military, board, the United States is indeed overwhelmingly dominant. But on the middle, economic, board, the United States is only one of several important players, along with the European Union, Japan, and the quickly rising China. And on the bottom board, transnational ties allow everyone from bankers to terrorists to act largely outside any government's immediate control. The United States retains enormous influence and has the power to lead, but it cannot shape the world entirely to its liking.

Patterns of Cooperation

Even though systematic leadership of the kind that created the post–World War II institutions is lacking, sustained cooperation does take place, institutionalizing itself in all sorts of ways. Some consist of direct cross-border collaboration among government officials who have the same jobs. Supreme Court justices from different lands are researching one another's decisions as precedents and meeting to discuss how to promote judicial independence and the rule of law; regulators of all types are collaborating informally or concluding good-faith "memoranda of understanding" on how they will cooperate to achieve their similar ends.[42] Sometimes these collaborations merely help government officials do their jobs, as when law enforcement agencies share information about terrorists or organized crime syndicates. But sometimes they set rules, as when the central bankers of the world's big economic powers met in the Basel Committee on Banking Supervision in 1988 and agreed on capital adequacy requirements for all the banks they supervise.[43]

Much intergovernmental cooperation, however, takes place under the auspices of intergovernmental organizations (IGOs) that governments have created. These include everything from the sprawling United Nations system, with its multiple agencies and agendas, to the International Hydrographic Organization, established in 1921 to promote safety in navigation and protect the marine environment.[44] Many are highly controversial. Indeed, intergovernmental organizations seem to arouse a visceral reaction wildly disproportionate to their actual power. They draw the attention of everyone from one-world idealists to black-helicopter conspiracy theorists. They do have some degree of power, of course, and have done both good and harm, but they are neither saviors of humanity nor villains about to deprive the masses of life and liberty.

On the plus side, intergovernmental organizations are useful tools to help their member governments cooperate in ways that benefit everyone or at least leave no one worse off.[45] By monitoring compliance with international agreements, these organizations can help reassure states that others are not getting away with free riding. And by serving as a central point for collecting and disseminating information among states, they lower the costs of collective action and thus make cooperation more likely.

These dull and dry tasks are a big part of what these organizations do. Most international organizations are fairly boring bureaucracies plugging away at making the international system work. Globalization would not be possible without the rules of the road administered by an alphabet soup of organizations. If you want to take a plane flight overseas, you owe thanks to the International Civil Aviation Organization, and if you have pen pals abroad, you should be similarly grateful to the Universal Postal Union. This is pretty uncontroversial stuff, akin to making rules about which side of the road people should drive on. Most people do not much care which rule is chosen as long as *some* rule is.

Also on the plus side is the capacity of some intergovernmental organizations to exploit whatever wiggle room governments allow them in order to promote the global public good. The United Nations Environment Programme, for all its many problems, probably saved many of us from galloping cases of skin cancer by catalyzing formal and informal negotiations on ozone depletion (see chapter 8). These organizations also tend to be the keepers of the world's statistics, a not inconsiderable source of power. People are much more likely to talk about and take action on problems that seem precisely measured. The United Nations Development Programme created the Human Development Index to measure how well people are living. It provides an alternative to standard gross national product figures, which show only how much total economic activity is being generated in a country. Since economic activity can be destructive (clear-cutting of forests) or so skewed that most people do not benefit, an alternative was badly needed to provide understanding of whether humanity was in fact making material progress. The Human Development Index uses measures of longevity (life expectancy), knowledge (adult literacy and years of schooling), and economic standard of living to help provide that understanding.[46]

But that wiggle room does not amount to much in the way of independent power. Not only does the United Nations lack the black-helicopter fleet that conspiracy theorists claim it will use to subjugate all of humanity; it has no military resources at all. Every time the Security Council's member governments vote to require the United Nations to step in to stop a genocide or separate combatants, a wild scramble ensues as the Secretariat phones around the world, begging governments to spare a few troops for the exercise. Most intergovernmental organizations are similarly starved for resources to do the jobs their member governments have told them to do. It is true that these bureaucracies, like all bureaucracies, often entangle themselves in internal turf wars and budget disputes, becoming ineffective and inefficient. But given that no one has yet invented a perfect way to run a bureaucracy, such inefficiencies seem to be the inevitable and generally acceptable cost of attempting to act cooperatively.

There is a far bigger problem undermining the effectiveness and indeed the legitimacy of some intergovernmental organizations. Not all governments have equal roles in creating and running them. The highly visible protests around meetings of the World Trade Organization, the World Bank, the International Monetary Fund, and others reflect increasingly widely held views that these organizations not only reflect the global distribution of power but exacerbate it. Essentially, they are clubs of, by, and for the world's most powerful governments.

Why would less powerful governments join and stay in these organizations unless they saw real benefits to their membership? After all, it costs at least something in the way of time and money to send dues and representatives to participate in these institutions. And governments are not being coerced to join at gunpoint.

The answer, as political scientist Lloyd Gruber puts it, is that the less powerful governments "know the supranational arrangements they dislike are perfectly capable of functioning without them."[47] The bigger powers, such as the United States, European countries, and Japan, have a go-it-alone ability to write the rules for the world to their own satisfaction, even if that leaves other countries worse off than before. In such cases, joining organizations and signing on to global agreements become defensive ploys to mitigate the damage.

Do these organizations actually operate as clubs? In some cases, the answer is clearly yes. At the World Bank and the International Monetary Fund (IMF), voting power is allocated according to monetary contribution. The United States (with 17.20 percent of the votes) alone can block the most important decisions at the IMF, which require an 85 percent supermajority. Ten industrialized countries known as the Group of Ten (G-10) have 52 percent and thus can outvote the other 172 members.[48] The IMF was not designed to be so one-sided. It originally had only 29 members, mostly industrialized countries, and it played the relatively technocratic role of providing loans to members that were having trouble defending their fixed exchange rates. But now that the IMF's membership and influence have so drastically expanded, its structure raises serious questions about its accountability to the people affected by its actions.

The World Trade Organization (WTO) is ostensibly more egalitarian, with all of its 140-plus member countries entitled to equal voice. But the ability to exercise that voice varies widely.[49] Haiti, with 7 million people, has just one man in its delegation to the World Trade Organization—which makes Haiti better off than the 28 WTO member countries that cannot afford to keep even a single permanent representative at the WTO's Geneva headquarters. That one Haitian representative has the unenviable task of trying to attend the often simultaneous meetings of more than thirty WTO committees, subcommittees, and working groups. Japan, by contrast, has twenty-one diplomats and lawyers permanently on hand, supported by secretaries, technicians, and drivers. The rich countries also have large, well-funded trade bureaucracies at home to support their international teams.[50] And the WTO Secretariat has been kept too small and poor to provide all that much in the way of technical assistance, with a staff of only about 500 and an annual budget of about $80 million.

Such difficulties stem from a common conundrum that pops up in many efforts at governance. It is called the principal–agent problem. The principal–agent problem is a simple idea. One important way of overcoming collective action problems is for the group that has the problem to appoint an agent to solve it. That is what governments are—agents for the citizens. Managers of publicly owned corporations are the agents of the stockholders. But then the group, the principals, must make sure the agent is acting to serve the interests of the principals rather than those of the agent.

The principal–agent problem with intergovernmental organizations is particularly tricky. We know who the agents are in these cases. But who are the principals? These are, after all, intergovernmental organizations, established by and under the control of national governments. As just discussed, governments have wildly varied capabilities to exercise that control. Yet even if all governments were equal, the problem would not be solved.

The ultimate "principals" for intergovernmental organizations are not governments—they are the citizens those governments are supposed to represent. To the degree that governance gets done through such international institutions, they depend for their effectiveness, and arguably for their moral right to exist, on a broad sense among the world's peoples that they are acting appropriately. Look, for example, at the Charter of the United Nations. It does not say "We the governments of the world"; it says "We the peoples of the world." The World Bank may have been constituted by national governments, but its avowed goal is to help the world's poor, a group often ill-served by national governments. Governments have been known to use World Bank funds in ways that are not in the interests of their citizens. Those citizens on occasion complain loudly and clearly to the Bank about those misuses. Is the World Bank then answerable to the affected citizens or only to their governments—the supposed agents of those citizens? And what are citizens of relatively powerless countries supposed to do when more powerful governments create and enforce rules to which they object?

All these complications give one pause when thinking about how to use these institutions to improve global governance. How much power do we want international organizations to have? Do we want intergovernmental organizations to use enforcement capabilities, such as loan conditionality or the ability to authorize trade sanctions, in support of such goals as labor and environmental standards? Given the current inequities in institutional structures and practices, such steps seem a long way from democratic voice and accountability.

The problem is that when decision making reaches the rarefied level of intergovernmental organizations or even informal multilateral rule making, the threads of democratic accountability can be stretched very thin. It is often hard to see such decision-making systems as means by which the people of the world, through the instrument of their freely chosen governments, resolve their common problems. Often, they are means by which major powers—which may or may not be reflecting the wishes of even their own peoples—set the rules for everyone. Accountability to the general public is at best indirect, and often, for all intents and purposes, it does not exist at all. In the words of political scientist Robert Keohane, "If the terms of multilateral cooperation are to reflect the interests of broader democratic publics rather than just those of narrow elites, traditional patterns of delegation will have to be supplemented by other means of ensuring greater accountability to public opinion."[51]

What the Future Holds

All this adds up to an explanation of why a lot of thoughtful people hold somber views about humanity's future. It is not that we face some inevitable Malthusian tragedy. It is that the mechanisms we have put in place to deal with large-scale collective action problems seem so thoroughly inadequate when matched up against the scale of the problems. National governments face serious constraints. Where states are entrenched, their citizens expect the state to provide a large and growing number of collective goods. Where states are still being formed, they face enormous obstacles to the consolidation of their authority. For all states, some of the biggest threats to the security and well-being of their inhabitants come from outside their borders and are largely beyond their control. And all states face the prospect of steep declines in future revenues as economies become more virtual and less territorial and as their citizens become less nationalistic in their loyalties.

National governments will find that they are expected to meet growing demands for collective action to resolve transnational problems. They will frequently fail for a variety of reasons: lack of resources, a tendency to address urgent rather than incremental demands, lack of effective national institutions able to channel political participation, and incommensurability of the scale of the problems with the scope of national authority. Cooperation among states will not pick up the slack. Many states are currently unable to handle the onerous burden involved in negotiating, implementing, and enforcing the wide range of international agreements that would be needed, even if all states were willing to try. That leaves the bulk of global decision making to the handful of rich and powerful countries.

Does this mean we should throw up our hands in despair over humanity's future? No. It does require, however, that we seriously rethink what governments ought to be doing and how they cooperate. (We also need to think about the involvement of nongovernmental actors, but that is the subject of the next two chapters.)

There is no simple way to overcome the inadequacies of most national governments or the relative unaccountability of many intergovernmental organizations, no easy answer to the principal–agent problem that plagues any system of governance beyond small-scale direct democracy. But there is a way to give things a big push in the right direction.

To the degree that democracy and accountability exist in the world, they exist largely at the national level. Democratic countries have electoral systems. They also have civil society groups that provide channels for citizen input between elections. But their citizens rarely have access to the information they need to hold government officials fully accountable and to express informed opinions on what those government officials should be doing. Ever since democracies were first designed, their designers have grappled with that problem. One of the framers of the Constitution of the United States, James Madison, wrote: "A popular Government, without popular information, or the means of acquiring it, is but prologue to a farce or a tragedy, or perhaps both. Knowledge will forever govern ignorance; and a people who mean to be their own governors must arm themselves with the power which knowledge gives." Such sentiments are not confined to U.S. shores. Article 19 of the Universal Declaration of Human Rights, signed by almost all countries, explicitly recognizes the right to "freedom of opinion and expression: this right includes freedom to hold opinions without interference *and to seek, receive, and impart information and ideas through any media and regardless of frontiers"* (emphasis added).

A vast array of citizens' movements began seizing on such principles in the 1990s, trying to force information out of recalcitrant governments. At the beginning of that decade, only a few countries (notably Sweden, Finland, and the United States) had laws in place enabling citizens to demand disclosures. But over the decade, those demands grew. Many occurred in countries that were trying to make the transition from autocracy to democracy, particularly in central and eastern Europe. But many arose in countries long seen as well-established democracies, such as Britain and Japan, good at holding elections but not necessarily as good at keeping their citizens informed. Others arose out of extraordinary acts of determination on the part of some of the world's most marginalized people.

India's National Campaign for People's Right to Information, for example, was born in the mid-1990s in a mostly illiterate village in the state of Rajasthan, where the villagers had managed to get hold of local government accounts and were holding a public reading. As described by a professor from Delhi who had been invited to attend, the reading took place in the scanty shade of a roofless unfinished building in 120-degree heat:

> First came the muster roll, the list of names of those paid to work on the various road repair and building projects in the area. Everyone listened solemnly until about the fourth name, when chuckling broke out. The Delhi professor looked puzzled until someone explained that the person named had died three years before—"dead souls" littered the muster roll. Then the reader started on expenditures made: "30,000 rupees [about $800] to repair the roof of the school." The villagers guffawed: "This is the school building that we're sitting in!"[52]

By the turn of the millennium, some forty countries had freedom of information provisions in place or under debate in the national legislature. Many are not well implemented, and of course most countries still lack such provisions altogether. But the trend is encouraging.

Like national governments, intergovernmental organizations have been under severe pressure to join the transparency parade. Their rhetoric has become most impressive as their staffs vie to outdo one another in proclaiming their devotion to disclosure. But the new dedication to disclosure does not always extend to the member governments that control them.

Until recently, both the World Bank and the IMF were highly secretive, releasing virtually no information to the general public and sometimes not even telling their member governments everything about their policies and operations. When they negotiated loans with governments of poor countries, there was often no one present from those governments other than finance ministry officials and perhaps one or two people from the central bank. Not only were documents not published, they were often not provided to national parliaments or to officials in other government agencies, even after the loans were disbursed.

Not surprisingly, that kind of secretive decision making led to some very problematic policies and programs. Even the World Bank's own policies on subjects such as environmental protection and resettlement of displaced peoples were routinely violated in the projects it funded. The so-called structural adjustment lending, provided to help countries restructure their economies, was at least as bad, with the World Bank and the IMF imposing all sorts of conditions about how countries must run their economies. This represented an extraordinary loss of democratic power for the principals—the citizens—of those countries. In response, a whole host of civil society networks rose up to demand changes. And high on the list of demands was access to documentation about those projects and programs. Under intense pressure from a wide range of civil society groups, not to mention threats of funding cut-offs from the U.S. Congress, in 1989 the World Bank established a disclosure policy. For every project, it now releases a Project Information Document, and it also makes available various other documents. This is definitely progress, although many of those Project Information Documents are as notable for what they leave out as for what they include.

But the Bank still has far to go. In 2000, it revised its disclosure policy, and in the process the brass knuckles came out on both sides. On one side were a few governments and a great number of activists. They claimed that since the poor are the ostensible beneficiaries of World Bank loans and many IMF loans, and since national governments frequently do a very poor job of keeping their citizens informed, it is morally indefensible for the World Bank and the IMF to keep information about those loans secret. The problem is that the institutions attach conditions to many of their loans, conditions that essentially dictate how countries may run their economies. Many of those conditions have been highly intrusive, telling a country's leaders which companies to privatize, sometimes which individuals to fire, and so on. The recipient governments have little choice about accepting the conditions. Even though private capital flows now dwarf the size of the loans the World Bank and the IMF can offer, private creditors use those loans as a kind of Good Housekeeping Seal of Approval. Only when the World Bank or the International Monetary Fund signs off will other creditors fork over. And for the very poorest countries, Bank and Fund loans and other government aid remain essentially the only source of foreign capital.

Yet the negotiations were conducted in secret. Members of Parliament were sometimes unable to get access to the terms of the loans, even when they had to vote to approve the loans. They did approve the loans—their countries need the money—but not much democratic consent was rendered.

On the other side of the World Bank's transparency debate were many governments. Not surprisingly, the world's more repressive governments are singularly unimpressed by claims that they have a responsibility to be held accountable. But resistance also arose from a number of democracies, particularly the democracies of large developing countries such as India and Argentina. They argued that releasing sensitive information during loan negotiations could spook markets, driving off private creditors. And, more emphatically, they claimed that information would be used by the opposition for political purposes. Quite possibly they were right. That is, after all, the essence of democratic politics—open competition of ideas.

How much difference can stronger national and global transparency policies really make? In part, they can permit after-the-fact accountability. If people in intergovernmental organizations know that outsiders will know what they have done, presumably they will try hard to do things that will be publicly acceptable. This is the basic idea of representative government: you let your agents make the decisions, but then you get to evaluate your agents' performance and force changes, or change agents, if you do not like the performance.

But there is a broader purpose behind the many calls for greater transparency on the part of intergovernmental organizations, particularly the most powerful ones, such as the World Bank, the IMF, and the WTO. That is to make it possible for interested people to *participate* in the decision-making process. For those who believe that governments are not adequate transmission mechanisms between citizens and intergovernmental organizations, such direct participation is a key means of overcoming the principal–agent problem. When governments undertaking policy decisions must seek the approval of intergovernmental organizations before that of their own citizens, the assertion that citizens of developing countries enjoy adequate representation becomes difficult to sustain.

Thus, the World Bank, the International Monetary Fund, and others are talking about the need to involve citizens and nongovernmental organizations in open discussions of policy and projects. Civil society groups are demanding the same level of voice in other institutions, such as the World Trade Organization. But progress has been limited. The World Bank touts its greatly increased participation levels, but it turns out that the Bank is talking about involving local people in the implementation of projects that are supposed to benefit those people. They are still not allowing much public participation in the design of projects, and nobody is doing much to encourage public involvement in policy debates.

In short, some—but not most—national governments are opening up in recognition of their citizens' essential right to know, and some intergovernmental organizations are similarly heeding calls for greater transparency and broader participation. But progress remains slow. In any case, governments and the organizations they create to foster cooperation among themselves are not the only players on the global stage. The next chapter turns to another: the private sector.

Business

It must have seemed like such a good idea at the time. It was the 1980s. American corporations were vastly expanding their global reach while suffering intense and unaccustomed pressures from corporate raiders at home as well as competitors overseas. The chief executive officers (CEOs) of some of America's largest companies were getting tired of losing out on potential profits overseas, where their patents and copyrights were regularly ignored or violated. It probably seemed quite reasonable to turn to the United States government for help in protecting their "intellectual property." The corporations succeeded—all too well.[1] By the time the dust began to settle, they had found themselves vilified as callous profiteers willing to condemn millions to a miserable death for the sake of filthy lucre.

Intellectual property includes an enormous range of intangible products, from copyrighted computer software to patented pharmaceuticals—all the trademarks, patents, copyrights, and trade secret protections that companies rely on to earn a return on their investments in making those products. Like all property, the intellectual sort is defined by legal rules about who has control, on what terms, and for how long. But intellectual property is easier to steal than is the physical kind. If someone were to break into a Microsoft Corporation warehouse and take 1,000 boxes of Microsoft Word programs, the company would be likely to notice. However, if someone made 1,000 copies of the software and sold the copies in China, Microsoft might never find out.

Because American firms are the leading corporate creators of intellectual property, as global economic integration blossomed in the 1980s they found themselves particularly vulnerable to such losses. Arguing that foreign pirates were depriving them of royalties, the CEOs of such major companies as International Business Machines Corporation (IBM) and Pfizer Inc. lobbied the U.S. government hard to make other countries start enforcing those property rights. The government was more than receptive to their arguments, threatening to impose trade sanctions on countries that failed to crack down.

By the mid-1980s, the Office of the United States Trade Representative was asking U.S. corporations to help get intellectual property protection included on the agenda of the upcoming Uruguay Round of international trade negotiations. At that point, companies in the other major economies (Canada, Europe, and Japan) were paying little attention to the issue, so their governments were under no pressure to reach an intellectual property agreement. The corporations based in the United States set out to create that pressure. In March 1986, a dozen major U.S. corporations with strong international connections came together to create the Intellectual Property Committee (IPC).[2] Over the next six months, the IPC met with the major industry associations in Europe and Japan, persuading them to lobby their respective governments in favor of an intellectual property component of the upcoming round of the General Agreement on Tariffs and Trade (GATT). The lobbying paid off. When the Uruguay Round opened, in September 1986, just six months after the formation of the IPC, the governments of Europe and Japan joined the United States in supporting an intellectual property agreement.

As the Uruguay Round dragged on through the next several years, the so-called TRIPS Agreement (Agreement on Trade-Related Aspects of Intellectual Property Rights) became a major bone of contention. Developing countries hated the idea, arguing that TRIPS would impose heavy enforcement costs and would force poor countries to pay more than they could afford for essential goods such as medicines. But in the end, the corporations got most of what they wanted. TRIPS requires governments to protect intellectual property rights. It permits long-term patents, so patent holders are protected from competition for as long as twenty years.[3] It puts the burden of proof on alleged infringers of patents to show that their processes are different from those protected by a patent, imposing high legal costs on defendants.[4] The developing countries had to be satisfied with a provision giving the poorest of them ten years to phase in implementation of the rules.[5]

If the story ended there, it would be a familiar account of the rich and powerful writing rules to further their own interests. It is hardly new for big business to have a big influence on global rules. But subsequent years saw unexpected twists and turns.

What to pharmaceutical companies is intellectual property, to sick people around the world is the knowledge, transmuted into lifesaving drugs, that can end their woes. Because the generation of that knowledge is increasingly determined by the marketplace, it is highly skewed. Most medical research funds are applied to the diseases of rich people. The diseases of poverty—tuberculosis, malaria, and the like—get short shrift. Profit-seeking firms have little incentive to come up with medicines that will mostly help people who cannot pay. But one disease strikes rich and poor alike: acquired immunodeficiency syndrome, or AIDS. And while AIDS victims in the rich countries began benefiting from very expensive, patent-protected medicines that literally saved their lives, those in poor countries became grim statistics in an ever-mounting death toll, now in the tens of millions.

By any definition, AIDS constitutes a medical emergency. And TRIPS does allow for exceptions to its stringent protections of intellectual property. Most notably, in cases of medical emergency, countries can issue "compulsory licenses" allowing local firms to produce needed medical drugs even if foreign companies hold patents on those drugs. But in practice, poor countries that have tried to take advantage of such provisions found that their emergencies were somehow deemed less critical than they appeared to those who were dying.

In 1997, Nelson Mandela, then president of South Africa, signed into law the Medicines Act to ensure that the government could manufacture or import affordable generic drugs so as to improve access to medicines for the human immunodeficiency virus (HIV) and AIDS. Some forty international drug companies swiftly filed suit to block implementation of the law, claiming that it violated both the South African constitution and the TRIPS Agreement.[6] Thailand tried to take advantage of the TRIPS exceptions to get cheaper access to an HIV medicine that costs more than the average Thai income.[7] But the Bristol-Myers Squibb Company, a U.S. company, holds a twenty-year patent on that medicine, and the U.S. Trade Representative threatened trade sanctions against Thailand if it persisted.[8]

But the governments and companies turned out not to be the only players in this game. Nonprofit and advocacy groups in Thailand and abroad began rallying against what they perceived as unfair pricing and patenting policies for vital AIDS medicines, generating massive publicity.[9] The South African legal case soon became the focus of global opprobrium. An international humanitarian group called Doctors Without Borders launched a "drop the case" campaign, uniting with numerous human rights and advocacy organizations worldwide to accuse American pharmaceutical firms of participating in a "new global apartheid." They did not find it difficult to vilify the corporate lawsuit: in the more than three years that the legislation lingered in the South African courts, more than 400,000 South Africans died of AIDS, and the disease became the country's leading cause of death. At the same time, Oxfam International launched a campaign to pressure GlaxoSmithKline, the world's largest drug manufacturer, to provide necessary medicines at affordable prices to poor countries.[10]

The drug companies buckled. In April 2001 they dropped their legal challenge to the South African Medicines Act, even volunteering to pay the government's legal costs.[11] They also responded to a call by United Nations secretary-general Kofi Annan for private sector participation in the global response to AIDS. Five major firms (Boehringer Ingelheim, Bristol-Myers Squibb, Glaxo Wellcome, Merck & Co., and F. Hoffmann-La Roche & Co.) announced that they would work on innovative ways to ensure care and treatment for those suffering from HIV and AIDS.[12] Glaxo handed over the rights to its AIDS medicines to a South African generic drug company.[13] Merck & Co. took the lead in providing HIV-fighting drugs to eight poor Caribbean countries at heavily discounted prices.[14] Merck then announced it was cutting the price on two of its AIDS drugs. Brazil's health minister, Jose Serra, commented, "The price offered [was] lower than what we would get by breaking the patent and producing the drug in the country." The discount saved Brazil $38 million per year.[15]

TRIPS essentially constituted global policy made by the heads of a dozen major U.S. corporations to serve their commercial interests. These corporations worked legally through their designated political authorities. They did not set out to do harm or to provoke a global controversy. They continue to argue vehemently that protecting intellectual property is the best way to ensure that more intellectual property—such as new and better medicines—will emerge. The chair of the German pharmaceutical giant Boehringer Ingelheim argued that "more flexibility [a code word for less stringent patent protection] in TRIPS would be disastrous for continuing investment in research and development on AIDS."[16] And the director-general of the International Federation of Pharmaceutical Manufacturers Associations, Harvey Bale, contended that easing up on implementation of TRIPS could enable governments to abuse drug patents by declaring national health emergencies when none existed.[17] But such arguments are bound to look callous compared with the immediate reality of dying babies and decimated populations. And the fact that the corporations' behavior was perfectly legal proved no protection in the court of public opinion, which eventually won the day. At the 2001 ministerial meeting of the World Trade Organization, governments agreed to take more seriously the health exemptions contained in the TRIPS Agreement.[18]

The pharmaceutical corporations learned a painful lesson that is now registering with many other businesses. The TRIPS case is only one of the dramatic conflicts in which quite different conceptions of corporate rights and responsibilities are competing for public favor. Many corporate leaders see themselves as legally and morally obligated to strive for profits above all, with some concern for employees and maybe a bit of corporate philanthropy thrown in. Increasingly, however, corporations are being held to new standards of social responsibility that go far beyond legal requirements to enrich shareholders and obey the rules governments make. But what exactly should those standards be? And who should decide?

The private sector is both the beneficiary and target of an astonishing array of new global rules promulgated by governments, civil society groups, and businesses themselves. As the TRIPS case shows, those rules often emerge at the behest of the private sector, which needs rules to establish and protect property rights, to allow corporations to incorporate, to set technical standards so that related products can work together, and to ensure that contracts are enforced. Indeed, in a surprising number of areas (Internet governance, bond-rating agencies, some insurance markets), businesses have supplemented or even substituted for governments in the exercise of governance authority.[19] The only thing worse for business than too many rules is no rules at all.

But many of the rules aim to rein in or even transform the private sector, whose activities generate many of the problems governance is supposed to solve. Industrial activities cause much of the world's pollution. Businesses hire workers and want to spend as little money on them as possible, making it necessary for someone to protect labor rights. Someone needs to ensure that consumers get what they pay for and have redress if they do not. And many people object strenuously to the prominent role corporations play in shaping global rules such as TRIPS.

Now that socialism has demonstrated its inadequacies, few people are seriously suggesting we eliminate such problems by eliminating the private sector itself. However, the traditional counterpart to big business—big government—does not exist at the global level, and efforts to regulate business by global intergovernmental conventions have failed. Instead, the fight over the place of business in global governance is occurring largely in the realm of corporate codes of conduct—supposedly voluntary mechanisms for improving business behavior by getting firms to agree to abide by stricter standards of behavior than local law requires. Will they work?

The Short, Strange History of the Modern Corporation

Before getting to global regulations and codes, a quick look at just what corporations are, and how they got to be so powerful, is in order. Corporations are not, of course, the only kinds of entities that carry out for-profit activities. People can also organize themselves into family firms, partnerships, or purely informal associations. But it is the corporation, particularly in its large multinational guise, that most dramatically influences global rules and provokes the most consternation on the part of nonbusiness groups concerned with global governance. One best-selling book, for example, is titled *When Corporations Rule the World*.[20] Many of the more thoughtful protestors in Seattle, Prague, and Genoa argued that they opposed not globalization itself but the particular realities of "corporate-driven" globalization. The corporation matters to this discussion of global governance because, of all for-profit entities, it is the corporation that has proven itself most capable of exercising power on a large scale.

The basic idea behind the corporate form is simple: a group of people can collectively create a financial entity that governments recognize as a legal "person," with finances separate from those of the individuals who created it.[21] And for thousands of years, governments have understood that concept to be both economically useful and politically dangerous. In their masterful tome on the history of business and economic regulation, scholars John Braithwaite and Peter Drahos quote an exchange between the Roman emperor Trajan and Pliny the Younger:

> *Pliny:* A great fire has devastated Nicomedia. Would it be in order to establish a society of 150 firemen?

> *Trajan:* No. Corporations, whatever they're called, are sure to become political associations.[22]

Given that political sensitivity, it is perhaps not surprising that until recently, corporations were very different from the animal we know today as the pervasive organizer of economic life in most parts of the world. Governments chartered them, but usually for quite specific purposes and often with time limits attached. The British Empire chartered such corporations as the famed East India Company and Hudson's Bay Company to colonize much of the world. In the United States, state legislatures granted charters to construct public works.[23] The idea of a corporation as a potentially immortal for-profit entity entitled to seek its profits in pretty much whatever way it wants did not become widespread until well into the nineteenth century. That was when the demands of industrialization began to chafe against the size constraints of mere partnerships and family-run businesses.

In the late nineteenth and early twentieth centuries, the railroads, steel producers, and other great instruments of industrialization all fell under the sway of monopoly firms. They created extraordinary wealth, not only for their founders but arguably for society as a whole, through the vast economies of scale they were able to realize. But their extraordinary power had no checks. Unions were weak and in some cases were viciously repressed. And the government elements that later came to balance big business often supplied troops or police to do the repressing.[24]

The one counterweight available was our good friend transparency, in the form of what came to be called muckraking journalism. A growing number of mass-circulation magazines pounced on the opportunity to provide what American historian Jean Strouse calls a "literature of exposure" to an American public that was increasingly worried about the massive new firms.[25] A flood of exposés spurred the U.S. government to enact a spate of anti-trust legislation.

These reforms, which aimed to preserve competition, were not, of course, the end of the struggle over corporate power. The International Labor Organization, established in the aftermath of World War I and Russia's Bolshevik Revolution, was intended to fend off social upheaval by providing a legitimate channel for workers' protests. In the 1930s, under the agonizing social pressures of the Great Depression, the United States undertook reforms to protect workers and citizens from the vagaries of unregulated competition. In Europe, unions became part of official government decision-making bodies. The new burst of regulations that started in the 1960s added a host of new requirements intended to protect consumers, civil rights, and the environment.[26]

There were attempts along the way to establish global rules regarding cross-border business activities. When the victors in World War II set out to design the postwar international economic order, they intended to include some regulations concerning cross-border businesses. The treaty that would have created the planned International Trade Organization contained provisions to protect cross-border investment and to control restrictive business practices. But the United States Congress decided not to ratify the treaty. International trade instead fell under the aegis of the much less ambitious GATT, and no overarching international regulatory system governed the activities of international business.[27]

In the early postwar era, big American corporations came to dominate not just the domestic market but also the outside world. With the European and Japanese economies in ruins and the rest of the world too poor to offer much competition, for several decades American corporations had the field pretty much to themselves. Not surprisingly, that unchecked power corrupted some of its wielders, apparently leading some corporate executives to believe they were entitled to do virtually anything to advance their corporate interests.

From 1963 to 1973, International Telephone and Telegraph, Inc. (ITT) was preoccupied with more than just telecommunications. Developing countries had a habit of nationalizing private companies in key industrial sectors. In 1964, ITT was particularly concerned with its majority interest in the Chilean Telephone Company because Salvador Allende was running for the presidency under campaign promises to bring such service industries under Chilean ownership. Fearing an Allende-led Chile, ITT and other U.S. corporations with Chilean holdings approached the Central Intelligence

Agency with a proposal to provide campaign funds to the Christian Democratic Party, the party in opposition to Allende. Because it was official U.S. policy during that time not to support—however clandestinely—any political party in Chile, the CIA declined ITT's offer.[28]

Allende lost the 1964 election, but in 1970 he ran again. ITT funneled funds both to Jorge Alessandri, Allende's main opponent in the 1970 elections, and to the National Party. ITT eventually spent $350,000 on its anti-Allende political campaign, and assorted other U.S. companies contributed about the same amount. The CIA apparently learned about this "campaign assistance" but did not contribute to it. In fact, the CIA rejected ITT's offer to give the CIA $1 million to influence the election.

After Allende won the 1970 election, the CIA changed its tactics: political involvement was then more than permitted; it was welcomed. The CIA began actively seeking out ITT for more integral involvement in the U.S. government's policy of placing political and economic pressure on Chile. ITT responded by pouring money into a known anti-Allende publication, *El Mercurio;* this propaganda campaign continued even after Allende took office.

In 1972, relying on leaked documents, U.S. newspaper columnist Jack Anderson exposed ITT's shenanigans. Such brazen corporate infringement on national sovereignty spurred developing countries to fight back in the only way they knew—through the United Nations. In 1974, the United Nations established the Center on Transnational Corporations and began negotiations on a code of conduct for multinational corporations. The code would have laid out standards requiring companies to respect national sovereignty and human rights, disclose information about their operations, and generally redress what many governments saw as an imbalance of power between the corporations and themselves.[29] In that same decade, the International Labor Organization issued its Tripartite Declaration of Principles concerning Multinational Enterprises and Social Policy, and the United Nations Conference on Trade and Development (UNCTAD, which despite the name is an organization, not a conference) proposed codes on restrictive business practices and on the transfer of technology. The rich countries, home to the multinational corporations that wanted to fend off such global regulation, fought back with a declaration issued by the Organization for Economic Cooperation and Development (OECD, essentially the club of rich countries) on international investment and multinational enterprise, which would have established purely voluntary standards.[30]

The rich countries, and the multinational corporations, need not have worried. The various negotiations faltered in the changing climate of the 1980s. Ideology and technology changed. Developing countries stopped nationalizing foreign firms and instead started encouraging them to invest. Rich countries privatized their state-owned enterprises and eased up on regulation. By the 1990s, international discussions of the role of multinational corporations tended to focus on expanding their rights—such as intellectual property rights—rather than their responsibilities.

Corporations beyond Borders

At the same time international regulation was failing, the dominant U.S. firms found themselves facing new competition from revitalized industries in Europe and Japan, and firms from all parts of the world began to encounter strong incentives to go global. Cheaper and better transportation and communications technologies began making it easier and more profitable for corporations to operate simultaneously in several countries, a trend with no end in sight. Indeed, the new economies of scale are making it ever harder for national-level operations to compete with global enterprises for anything other than niche markets.[31]

Technology, however, is only part of the reason corporations began expanding massively beyond their accustomed national borders. Ideological changes played a big part, too. Through much of the twentieth century, centrally planned economies from the Soviet Union to China to Cuba saw government control of literally everything. And some of those countries initially enjoyed great economic success—the Soviet Union industrialized extraordinarily quickly. Between that and the searing experience of the Great Depression, which convinced governments that markets could not be trusted, even free market governments around the world operated vast swaths of their economies directly, owning everything from mining companies to energy utilities to telephone companies.

In the 1980s and 1990s, that changed. The Soviet model failed spectacularly. And Ronald Reagan and Margaret Thatcher were in power, bringing with them a mind-set strongly favoring the private sector over government. Corporations became the beneficiaries of the late twentieth century's ideological shift from favoring government as economic arbiter to seeing market forces as the road to prosperity. The resurgence of pro-market fervor led to a massive wave of privatization of the enterprises governments had owned.[32] Many of the newly private operations were snapped up by foreign buyers. As countries started worrying less about capturing territory and more about capturing global market share, their attitudes toward foreign-based corporations changed. Governments of poor countries now seek out the investment, technology, and managerial expertise multinational corporations can bring. Formerly viewed as exploitative agents of neo-imperialism, these corporations are increasingly seen as much-needed providers of capital, technology, management skills, and access to export markets.[33]

Not only are there more multinationals; some of them are much bigger. Deregulation in both the rich countries and emerging markets has laid the groundwork for a vast wave of mergers and acquisitions, creating sometimes enormous corporations. At first glance, the mega-mergers and acquisitions of the 1990s (such as Exxon and Mobil in the oil industry, Travelers Group and Citicorp in finance, and Daimler and Chrysler in the automotive industry), costing some $20 trillion, would seem to be creating the same kind of enormous monopolies at the global scale that the United States faced nationally a century earlier, when corporations so effectively squashed rivals that competition essentially disappeared.[34] Not only has the total value of worldwide mergers and acquisitions soared since the 1980s—from a few tens or hundreds of billions of (constant 1998) dollars in the early 1980s to several trillions per year by the late 1990s—but by 1999 more than a trillion dollars in such deals represented *cross-border* mergers and acquisitions.[35]

Only a handful of corporations are truly transnational entities lacking a clear national base. But a much larger number engage heavily in cross-border activities even if they have strong ties to one particular country. The figures are impressive and growing. At the beginning of the 1990s, there were perhaps 35,000 parent multinational corporations with about 170,000 foreign affiliates.[36] By the end of the decade, this had jumped to some 60,000 parent companies with more than 500,000 foreign affiliates.[37] These companies are investing huge sums in foreign countries—some $300–$400 billion in foreign direct investment each year in the mid-1990s.[38] All that accumulated investment pays off in market share. More and more of what the world buys is sold by transnational companies, which are reorganizing the production of goods and services, making production global rather than merely national in structure. Parent companies and foreign affiliates together accounted for one-quarter of global output in 1998.[39]

Can Colossus Be Constrained?

Does economic size translate into political power? Can national governments make these elephants abide by national rules and regulations? The problem is more subtle than the old danger of monopolies overcharging consumers. Because the corporations are competing at the global rather than national level, they still may well face enough competition to keep them economically efficient. But governments find it increasingly difficult to rein them in. Mega-banks cannot be allowed to fail because their failure could cause the collapse of the global financial system. The huge amount of resources available to mega-companies dwarfs the resources of prosecutors, making legal control difficult—not to mention that it would take one whopping big fine to constitute a serious penalty to companies with such enormous revenue.[40]

Sheer size, however, is only one of the factors that make it increasingly difficult for governments to control corporate behavior. At least as important are global changes in the ways goods are produced. Many relatively small companies, such as Nike, Inc., contract with suppliers in far-flung parts of the world. Big companies do the same—Disney reputedly has some 300,000 separate suppliers. In these cases, a company with a brand name, such as Levi Strauss & Co. or Wal-Mart, effectively controls a long chain of frequently shifting suppliers based primarily in low-wage countries. The "branded" companies control much of what the supplier does: what product quality standards and schedules must be met, what products will be produced. But for the most part, control over such matters as working conditions in and environmental spillovers from those suppliers' facilities remains in the hands of the national governments where those suppliers are located. Since enforcement of labor and environmental standards in those low-wage countries is often, to put it mildly, less than fully effective, this pattern of production enables firms in rich countries to reap the benefits of low production costs without paying attention to the associated social costs.

Even at the national level in countries with well-established regulatory systems and effective courts, a determined company can flout the law extensively. Some eventually get caught, but only after doing extensive damage. In the United States, the Louisiana-Pacific Corporation was recently assessed the largest criminal fine in the twenty-eight-year history of the Clean Air Act. The company employs approximately 13,000 people in the United States, Canada, and Ireland and grossed $2.49 billion in sales in 1997.[41] The corporation pleaded guilty to eighteen felony charges and agreed to pay $37 million in penalties and $5.5 million for criminal violations of the Clean Air Act. Moreover, the corporation was fined an additional $31 million for other offenses including doctoring reports, tampering with monitoring equipment, and lying to inspectors. The company was also ordered to donate $500,000 to environmental groups.[42]

The corporation was caught only because a former supervisor filed a lawsuit against the company alleging that he had been fired because he refused to tamper with one facility's pollution-monitoring equipment.[43] That is a rather haphazard way to catch a company responsible for such egregious offenses with such significant potential costs to human health, but federal and state environmental regulators cannot possibly supervise closely the vast array of firms operating in the United States.

If ensuring that companies behave themselves is difficult in the rich countries, with their well-developed legal, regulatory, and political institutions, it does not take much imagination to see how much more harm misbehaving corporations could do elsewhere. In other parts of the world, complaints abound of human rights abuses and environmental devastation on the part of large multinationals:

- In 1998, a union official in Honduras, Medardo Reyes, was murdered, along with his son, after leaving a meeting at which workers employed by the Standard Fruit Company (a subsidiary of the Dole Food Company) were organizing against the use of harmful pesticides. Even though Reyes had received death threats warning him to abandon his fight for workers' rights, local police reports attributed the killings to robbers.[44]

- Chiquita Brands International evicted 123 families from a plantation in northern Honduras in April 1994, bulldozing all buildings and gardens, on the grounds that the land was becoming infertile and no longer produced commercially viable quantities of fruit. But the company then rented the land to so-called independent—that is, nonunionized—producers.[45]

- Shell has come under widespread attack for its alleged connection to Nigerian troops who committed serious abuses in the course of protecting Shell personnel and equipment. Shell paid transportation costs and salary supplements to troops living outside their barracks, a practice Shell called normal. Although the company said it had no control

over the troops, the *New York Times* reported that an internal memorandum indicated Shell specifically requested the "mobile" police, who
were locally known as the "kill and go" mob.[46]

In short, international regulation by governments, where it exists, mostly
addresses corporate rights (such as intellectual property rights) rather than
corporate responsibilities. Many national governments seem unable or
unwilling to ensure that national standards exist and are adequately
enforced. No matter how much corporations may complain (sometimes jus-
tifiably) about the heavy hand of government regulation, in the ongoing see-
saw between government and market, it is currently the market side, not
government, that predominates. Thus, it does not seem wise to rely exclu-
sively on government regulation, either national or by intergovernmental
agreement, to set the rules by which corporations will operate.

Because intergovernmental cooperation falls so short of what many people think is needed to keep the private sector under a reasonable degree of
control, an extraordinary variety of nongovernmental groups dedicated to
filling the governance gap has sprung up. Activist groups are proving ever
more adept at shaming or coercing corporations into paying attention to
what the activists say are the broader social responsibilities of the private sector. And some in the corporate world seem to be listening.

Corporate Codes: Cover-Up, Tryout, or Buy-In?

In 1977, the Reverend Leon Sullivan undertook the task of helping to
dismantle South Africa's notorious apartheid system. As an American, he had
little direct influence on South Africa, so he went after a more readily available target: the multinational firms based in the United States that had operations there. As first formulated in 1977, his Sullivan Principles merely
specified the workplace conditions American corporations should provide,
including integrated and racially unbiased employment practices.[47] The
principles said nothing about making any broader commitment to social justice or to changing the overall South African system. Sullivan argued that the
principles were just a starting point, given that corporations would not yet
accept anything broader, and he did get a dozen major corporations to sign
on. In keeping with the ideas about the relative rights and responsibilities of
corporations and governments prevailing at that time, nobody thought it

odd that Sullivan and the corporations first presented the principles to the South African ambassador to the United States before implementing them.

The South African government had no objections to the Sullivan Principles. Indeed, it welcomed them. The more dire alternative, promoted by the Interfaith Center on Corporate Responsibility, based in the United States, was corporate withdrawal until such time as the apartheid system was dismantled.

Over the course of the next decade, as the South African government became more bloodily repressive, U.S. universities and others began selling off stocks of corporations that had operations in South Africa, and the Sullivan Principles became more demanding. In 1984, Bishop Desmond Tutu won the Nobel Peace Prize, which gave global prominence to his campaign for economic sanctions against the South African government, and in 1985 the South African Council of Churches called for foreign divestiture. With more and more universities selling off stocks and hundreds of shareholder resolutions demanding an end to corporate operations in South Africa, the pressures were becoming intense. Many of the multinational corporations that remained used their adherence to the Sullivan Principles as a defense, arguing that they were doing everything they could to improve the situation on the ground and that leaving would hurt the innocent most of all.

In 1985, Sullivan issued an ultimatum. South Africa had two years to do away with its apartheid laws or he would disavow his own principles and call for divestiture. He was not bluffing. In 1987, with apartheid still in full bloom, he did exactly that. But in the intervening two years, business leaders who a decade before would sign on only to principles approved by the South African government found themselves calling for massive political change. In March 1987, shortly before Sullivan gave up on his principles as an instrument for ending apartheid, a new principle was added. It went far beyond standards for corporate behavior in the workplace and community. Instead, it called on the signatory corporations to use their influence to press for the abolition of essentially all apartheid laws and practices—an enormous change in the type of activity corporations believed themselves entitled to undertake.

Having gone so far to change the way they saw their role in South Africa, corporations soon faced pressures to change the way they saw their role in the world. Other principles and codes of conduct began appearing in the late 1970s, mostly among U.S. companies responding to waves of bad publicity from the ITT scandal and from revelations that companies had been paying bribes overseas. Most were formulated after the U.S. Securities and Exchange Commission began investigating such payments, followed by passage of the Foreign Corrupt Practices Act of 1977, which banned overseas bribery.[48]

As the sheer scale of corporate cross-border activity blossomed, a new set of campaigns emerged, aimed at demanding that corporations change their practices on everything from workers' rights to environmental sustainability. By the 1990s, a new "corporate social responsibility" movement was in full swing. Corporations began learning the hard way that failing to comply with consumer and investor preferences about corporate behavior can be costly. The chair and chief executive of Nike commented as follows when his company faced accusations of tolerating horrendous working conditions in its manufacturing facilities:

> It has been said that Nike has single-handedly lowered the human rights standards for the sole purpose of maximizing profits . . . the Nike product has become synonymous with slave wages, forced overtime, and arbitrary abuse. I truly believe that the American consumer does not want to buy products made in abusive conditions.[49]

The Nike example is no fluke. In response to such pressures, Nike and other companies are creating codes of conduct stating that they will meet environmental, labor, or human rights standards that go beyond what local laws require. The codes are meant to protect companies' reputations and to reassure consumers that the products they buy come from environmentally benign production processes in which workers enjoy decent working conditions.

Sometimes governments encourage the code-of-conduct trend. In the United States, the White House set up the Apparel Industry Partnership, which put forward a code of conduct setting standards for working conditions applicable not only to participating companies but also to their foreign contractors.[50] The United Nations has established a code called the Global Compact. Business associations have also gotten in on the act. In 1990, the International Chamber of Commerce put forward its Business Charter for Sustainable Development, which has since been signed by more than 2,500 companies worldwide.[51]

But the big push for such codes has come from civil society organizations, whose intense public criticism of corporate behavior can, as Nike found, drive away customers and investors if left unanswered. Their spotlight has shone even on firms that consider themselves socially progressive: the Starbucks Corporation, faced with intense picketing by activists denouncing conditions at the Guatemalan coffee plantations from which it purchases beans, eventually issued a code of conduct and action plans for all its suppliers.[52] There is little doubt that the public protests had an effect. In April 2000, just days before a scheduled nationwide series of demonstrations, Starbucks agreed to sign on to a Fair Trade certification project to sell coffee independently certified as having been bought from small farmers for a fair price—that is, a price that enables the farmers to earn a decent living. Consumers can now purchase Fair Trade certified coffee on request at any Starbucks outlet. The planned demonstrations were canceled.

Corporate codes of conduct may matter to everyone, not just to the corporations relying on them to salvage reputations and sales. Indeed, they may be essential to the future of globalization. United Nations secretary-general Kofi Annan pleaded with corporate leaders at the World Economic Forum in 1999 to enter into a "global compact of shared values and principles, which will give a human face to the global market":

> Globalization is a fact of life. But I believe we have underestimated its fragility. The problem is this. The spread of markets outpaces the ability of societies and their political systems to adjust to them, let alone to guide the course they take. History teaches us that such an imbalance between the economic, social and political worlds can never be sustained for very long.
>
> The industrialized countries learned that lesson in their bitter and costly encounter with the Great Depression. In order to restore social harmony and political stability, they adopted social safety nets and other measures, designed to limit economic volatility and compensate the victims of market failures. That consensus made possible successive moves towards liberalization, which brought about the long post-war period of expansion.
>
> Our challenge today is to devise a similar compact on the global scale, to underpin the new global economy. If we succeed in that, we would lay the foundation for an age of global prosperity, comparable to that enjoyed by the industrialized countries in the decades after the Second World War. . . .

National markets are held together by shared values. In the face of economic transition and insecurity, people know that if the worst comes to the worst, they can rely on the expectation that certain minimum standards will prevail. But in the global market, people do not yet have that confidence. Until they do have it, the global economy will be fragile and vulnerable—vulnerable to backlash from all the "isms" of our post-cold-war world: protectionism; populism, nationalism, ethnic chauvinism, fanaticism and terrorism.

What all those "isms" have in common is that they exploit the insecurity and misery of people who feel threatened or victimized by the global market. The more wretched and insecure people there are, the more those "isms" will continue to gain ground. What we have to do is find a way of embedding the global market in a network of shared values. . . .

Let us remember that the global markets and the multilateral trading system we have today did not come about by accident. They are the result of enlightened policy choices made by governments since 1945. If we want to maintain them in the new century, all of us—governments, corporations, non-governmental organizations, international organizations—have to make the right choices now.

We have to choose between a global market driven by calculations of short-term profit, and one which has a human face. Between a world which condemns a quarter of the human race to starvation and squalor, and one which offers everyone at least a chance of prosperity, in a healthy environment. Between a selfish free-for-all in which we ignore the fate of the losers, and a future in which the strong and the successful accept their responsibilities, showing global vision and leadership.

I am sure you will make the right choice.[53]

Can corporate codes of conduct make the necessary difference? Such codes have now proliferated to the point that almost every self-respecting large corporation has one. But they are highly controversial. Proponents generally see them as a valuable means of getting corporations to buy into new norms of behavior without government intervention, making them attractive to corporate leaders who want to fend off government regulation. More ambitious proponents see them as a means of gradually achieving consensus on standards of behavior that can be tried out voluntarily and then eventually adopted and enforced by governments. But detractors portray them as mere fig leaves with which uncaring corporations can wrap themselves, allowing private enterprises to enjoy unblemished reputations while they sell out the public interest.

Corporate codes come in two quite different models. Model A types are aspirational codes—statements of what companies aim to do. The Model A versions usually have fairly general terms. They assume that corporate leaders would happily do the Right Thing if they knew what the Right Thing was and how to accomplish it. The Caux Round Table Principles for Business provide a good example.[54] Put forward by the Caux Round Table, a regular meeting of senior executives from leading firms based in Europe, Japan, and the United States, the principles lay out both general principles and some slightly more specific stakeholder principles. The general principles are broad to the point of mushiness: corporations should operate in a spirit of honesty and fairness, should contribute to the economic and social development of the communities in which they operate and the world community at large, and so on. The stakeholder principles are nearly as broad, essentially consisting of promises to obey the law and not to cheat. Human rights gets a brief mention (a promise "to respect human rights and democratic institutions, and to promote them wherever practicable"). But the formulators of the Caux Principles point out one big selling point: because the document was formulated by business leaders, its ethical norms are more likely than those from other sources to be broadly accepted by the business community.[55] And a number of firms are now using the Caux Principles as the basis for their own corporation-specific codes of conduct.[56]

Model B is more demanding. It requires specific commitments regarding labor standards, environmental standards, or both, along with independent confirmation of whether corporations are meeting those commitments. The Model B assumption is that corporations either want to or should have to prove that they are doing what they say they are doing. Under Model A, it would be easy for firms to free ride on the codes, promulgating them but avoiding the costs of compliance. Because the codes are arising piecemeal, the thousands of codes have different specifications, making it hard to compare what various firms are promising to do. Moreover, many codes, especially those designed by the firms themselves or by business associations, rely on internal monitoring of compliance, a difficult task for a large firm that may have subsidiaries and suppliers around the world, and one that lends itself all too easily to cheating or to slipping through the fingers of already overburdened staff. And many firms do no monitoring at all. Monitoring and enforcement are key elements of such collective action, goes the Model B argument, because without them firms will be greatly tempted to free ride—to gain the benefits of good publicity (or avoid negative coverage) without making meaningful and sustained changes in behavior.

The growing answer is certification: once a code is established, an independent external auditor comes in, assesses whether a company is in full compliance, and if so certifies the firm as being in compliance. The firm can then advertise its compliance and display the stamp of approval on its products to differentiate itself from competitors whose degree of social responsibility has not been so certified. The nonprofit Council on Economic Priorities, in collaboration with human rights organizations, businesses, and auditing companies, devised a code of conduct called Social Accountability 8000, intended to become the global standard on workers' rights. Companies that adopt the code permit outside auditors to inspect every facility and assess practices on child labor, health and safety, freedom of association, collective bargaining, discrimination, disciplinary practices, working hours, and—a matter excluded from most corporate codes—whether compensation provides workers a living wage. The idea is that just as firms and consumers now often demand that producers be certified as meeting international quality standards, in the future both firms and individual consumers will choose to buy only from producers certified as being in compliance with SA8000.

Compliance with SA8000 and other externally monitored codes of conduct is completely voluntary. No government enforces them. Instead, the assumption is that corporations will want to be so certified because they will find it good for business—because consumers will prefer to buy certified products.

Such codes seem a promising step in solving such global problems as environmental degradation and cross-border exploitation of workers. But how well they will work in practice remains unclear. A few big companies, including Toys "R" Us and Avon Products, Inc., have announced they will buy only from SA8000-certified suppliers, and Avon is the first to be so certified. But some industry groups have objected strongly to the whole approach, arguing that the ever-mounting costs of certification with the growing array of standards are too great and that industry should set and monitor its own standards.[57]

They have a point. Certification *is* expensive. Corporations are being flooded with demands to meet standard after standard. Some of those demands come from groups whose claim to represent a broad public interest seems dubious. It is not at all clear who should decide exactly what standards the codes should uphold.

And there is another question: *Quis custodiet ipsos custodes?*—Who guards the guardians? The complexities show up in the current competition over who should monitor the treatment of overseas labor forces by U.S. garment manufacturers, who have often been accused of subjecting their workers to sweatshop conditions. On one side is the Fair Labor Association (FLA), the outcome of a presidential task force that included both human rights groups and major corporations. On the other is the Worker Rights Consortium (WRC), a university coalition formed by the United Students Against Sweatshops (USAS). The two groups hotly contest each other's motives, methods, and primary goals. FLA member companies agree to have conditions in their overseas contractors' factories monitored by independent agencies, but the companies hire the monitors and the reports are not made public. The USAS says this is not good enough, and it set up the WRC to inspect factories that are licensed by American colleges and universities to produce goods bearing the trademarks of these institutions. The WRC is not yet carrying out inspections, but the USAS has already persuaded some colleges to withdraw from the FLA and join the WRC. In response to growing pressure from the USAS, in October 1999 Nike disclosed the locations of 42 of its factories, making it possible for outsiders to look for abuses. And in April 2000 it announced that it would release the audits of all 600 plants that manufacture its shoes and apparel, despite its earlier protests that those contractors should first have a chance to address any issues raised by the audits.[58]

The certification approach is running into difficulties because it is essentially an effort to replace a government function that even most governments have had difficulty carrying out: discouraging people from behaving the way they want to behave if they can be sure no one is watching. If corporations do not want to improve working conditions, or simply do not want to bother keeping a close eye on working conditions in their suppliers' factories, it would take an army of dedicated, well-trained inspectors to force a change in behavior. There is no particular reason to think private inspectors will systematically do better than public ones or that private resources will readily be found to pay for all the necessary inspections if public resources are unavailable. By default, many of the private inspections are being carried out by big accounting firms, whose expertise lies in a very different kind of inspection. And the results are not promising.

PricewaterhouseCoopers (PwC), which has become the leader in so-called social accounting, allowed Massachusetts Institute of Technology professor Dara O'Rourke, who has conducted many such inspections, to accompany its auditors on inspections of labor practices in factories in China and Korea. Both O'Rourke and PwC were hired by the Independent University Initiative, a research project supported by Harvard University, the University of Notre Dame, Ohio State University, the University of California, and the University of Michigan. O'Rourke's report is disturbing.[59] In one inspection, the PwC auditor found some of the questions she was supposed to ask of workers embarrassing and skipped them, and she filled in answers to other questions without bothering to ask the workers being interviewed. In another, the factory president selected the workers to be interviewed, and the auditors skipped all questions about freedom of association, collective bargaining, child labor, and forced labor, claiming that since the factory had no union, the questions were not relevant. In both cases, the auditors, financial specialists who had received only a crash course in social and environmental monitoring, missed major health and safety violations and reported that the factories had only minor violations of labor laws and codes of conduct.

Model C: The Global Compact

After Annan's 1999 speech to the World Economic Forum, his office promulgated the Global Compact agreement, which corporations are asked to sign to indicate that they will voluntarily adhere to nine principles drawn from the 1948 Universal Declaration of Human Rights, labor standards contained in International Labor Organization conventions, and the Rio Declaration on Environment and Development, signed by most governments at the 1992 United Nations Conference on Environment and Development in Rio de Janeiro, Brazil. Signatories are supposed to report annually on how well they are doing in implementing these widely accepted principles. The Global Compact thus combines Model A's broad aspirations and assumption that most corporate leaders are basically decent human beings with Model B's belief that corporations should make a public accounting of their efforts to live up to those aspirations. But it does not insist on hard proof. Instead, the Global Compact relies on self-reporting. It is what political scientist John Gerald Ruggie, who was instrumental in its creation, calls a "learning model" approach.[60]

As is the case with all compromises, there is something in the Global Compact to displease everyone. Activist groups around the world claim that notorious corporate bad guys will now be allowed to wrap themselves in the halo of the United Nations logo while nefariously refraining from any real change. On the other hand, the head of the International Chamber of Commerce, Maria Livanos Cattaui, wrote the following in response to Annan's speech:

> Business accepts the challenge and is eager to cooperate with the UN and other public sector bodies to enhance all three [sets of environmental, labor, and human rights standards]. Alongside them, however, we must place a fourth value—the economic responsibility incumbent upon any company to its customers, to its employees and to its shareholders.
>
> Fulfillment of that responsibility is the key to the other three, for without it companies cannot remain in business. . . .
>
> Business should not be called upon to meet demands and expectations that are properly the preserve of governments. The private sector cannot, for example, ensure that the rule of law reigns in a given country, that all citizens have access to education and enjoy freedom of speech, that wealth is fairly distributed, and that there is an adequate social safety net for the old, the sick and the jobless.
>
> And it is for governments, with the help and advice of business, to negotiate and perfect global rules in areas like investment, intellectual property protection, competition and the suppression of corruption, without which competitive enterprise cannot achieve its full potential.[61]

Despite the skepticism on both sides, voluntary corporate codes may indeed improve corporate behavior even without the coercion that backs up government regulation. The reason is that companies care about their reputations. In small societies where everyone knows everyone, concerns about reputation alone may be enough to ensure that everyone abides by contracts, respects property rights, and accepts standards: if I renege on my contract with you, you will tell all our mutual acquaintances, and then no one will do business with me. Until recently, reputations depended mostly on personal contact to generate the degree of knowledge necessary to generate confidence. Only that firsthand knowledge would allow a customer or another firm to feel safe in signing a contract or could assure a local community that a firm was not exploiting its workers or polluting the local water supply. The information revolution is reducing the need for firsthand information. Reputations are increasingly global, and that leaves corporations increasingly vulnerable to new pressures. One commentator gleefully crowed after Nike announced in 1998 that it would raise the minimum working age (that is *age,* not wage) and impose American air quality standards on its contractors around the world:

> Consumers and workers of the world unite. . . . Just do it? If you do, you can affect the behavior of manufacturing giants like Nike, for whom image is everything. . . . It turns out that public shaming and consumer pressure can have a mighty impact on mighty manufacturers.[62]

Even self-reporting systems such as the Global Compact may turn out to be reasonably effective. The kicker is those annual reports the corporations are supposed to file. Self-reporting may not be the ideal sort of monitoring, but it has two potentially beneficial effects. First, it forces the corporation to take a look at its own practices, if only to justify them. Although many corporations will undoubtedly seize the opportunity to exercise the art of spin, the first step in changing behavior is self-awareness, and some businesses will just as undoubtedly discover things about themselves they had not previously known. Second, the activist groups will not accept those reports at face value. Several groups have already promised to scrutinize them carefully. By signing the Global Compact, the corporations agree that they should be held to standards of behavior beyond what government regulations require. The activist groups fully intend to provide the fire to hold to the corporations' collective feet.

Who Knows?

Whether they can do so depends on whether they can amass meaningful information about the degree of corporate compliance. Given that the effectiveness of corporate codes depends so heavily on public exposure, the big missing piece in the code puzzle has been how to get the necessary information out in some systematic fashion. The mishmash of existing principles and reporting systems makes it impossible to compare organizations across time or with one another and makes it hard to evaluate claims of good or bad behavior.

Into the morass has stepped the Global Reporting Initiative (GRI), which has developed a framework for voluntary reporting on corporate economic, environmental, and social performance.[63] The brainchild of the Coalition for Environmentally Responsible Economies (CERES), a nongovernmental organization that itself promulgated one of the leading codes on environmental conduct, the GRI was formally inaugurated as a permanent institution in April 2002. It now includes a polyglot array of corporations, accounting firms, and environmental, human rights, and labor organizations. Its Sustainability Reporting Guidelines, tested in draft form on twenty-one companies in the late 1990s, have gone through two rounds of revisions. Already, companies are using the GRI framework to report on their compliance with the United Nations' Global Compact.

Who Cares?

All disclosure-based "regulation" depends on the assumption that someone somewhere cares about the information that is released. The usual argument, especially by certifiers, is that consumers care—that is, consumers in rich countries, who are the ones with the buying power that corporations care about. Unfortunately, the percentage of consumers who actually demonstrate a preference for "certified" goods is substantially lower than the percentage who claim in marketing surveys to be willing to pay a bit more to be sure that the products they buy are being produced by happy workers in ways that do not despoil the environment. This is not surprising. If a pollster asked you whether you would spend an extra dollar on your jeans to help prevent the exploitation of children, would you say no?

The assumption that consumer power can drive improvements in social

justice is an old one. Consumers leagues were founded as early as the 1880s
to press for social justice for workers. Their founders argued forcefully that
"it is the duty of consumers to find out under what conditions the articles
they purchase are produced and distributed and to insist that these conditions shall be wholesome and consistent with a respectable existence on the
part of the workers."[64] But consumer pressure has had far more effect in
improving product safety. It took unions—workers looking out for their
own interests—to address labor conditions.

In other words, trying to regulate corporate behavior by mobilizing consumers can be remarkably effective—but only in limited circumstances.
Only "branded" companies such as Nike and Starbucks, which care about
their reputations with consumers, are vulnerable to such pressures. They
in turn can pressure their suppliers. This is not a trivial part of the global corporate network, but it is far from the whole thing.

Fortunately, consumers are not the only source of funding that corporations need to satisfy. They also have to please investors. And a rapidly growing number of investors are adding social responsibility to their criteria for
picking companies to invest in.

The focus on investors first became prominent as part of the anti-
apartheid campaign that took off in the late 1970s. But rather than declining after apartheid ended, it turned out that the habits of screening and
shareholder activism had taken hold. The trend is most striking in the
United States. In 1984, according to the Social Investment Forum, which
tracks such matters, a total of about $40 billion in assets under professional
management had undergone some sort of social or environmental screening.[65] By 1995, the total was $639 billion. Two years later, social investing
had cracked the $1 trillion mark, and by 2001, it had more than doubled,
reaching $2.34 trillion. This is a notably faster growth rate than that of the
total universe of professionally managed investment assets. Even in the
downturn of 2001, socially responsible mutual funds did relatively well at
attracting and keeping investor assets, seeing much less of a decline than
some other types of mutual funds.

What constitutes socially responsible behavior varies according to who is
determining which firms to include in or exclude from investment portfo-
lios or mutual funds. The single most widely used criterion is simple: no
tobacco. Screens can include everything from environmental sustainability
to treatment of workers to animal rights. Religious mutual funds and indexes

have sprung up that use the beliefs of specific faiths as criteria. And religious organizations concerned with determining where to invest their own, often substantial, resources have sought to establish appropriate standards. In 1998, three Western religious coalitions released a document titled "Principles for Global Corporate Responsibility," which proposed standards for corporate social and environmental performance and suggested ways to measure that performance.[66]

That $2 trillion–plus figure, impressive as it is, may represent just the beginning of something much bigger. More than $6 trillion is locked up in U.S. pension funds.[67] Until recently, the trustees who managed those enormous funds rarely paid much attention to social and environmental criteria, believing that screened investments would underperform the market.[68] But evidence is mounting that screened investments do just as well as the market and may even outperform it.[69] If the people who control those assets start taking social and environmental screens seriously—and people who control workers' pensions just might find themselves under pressure to take workers' rights seriously—what is already a powerful trend could become a tidal wave. And focusing on investors addresses one of the key legitimacy questions about the whole approach. Even in the most conservative perspective on the social role of the corporation, those who own a corporation are entitled to a significant say in what goals it should be trying to achieve.

But corporate codes, even if certified, and social screening of investment seem unlikely by themselves to ensure that corporations will do all they might to alleviate the many urgent problems that require global governance. Not all corporations are vulnerable to concerns about their reputation. Many around the world are not publicly traded, getting their financing primarily in the form of bank loans.

Even if all corporations could be reached via pressures from consumers or investors, the existing codes and screens do not go nearly far enough. They call for incremental changes. The efforts of Nike and others to reduce sexual harassment at their suppliers' facilities are commendable, but those efforts do not get to the fundamental gender inequities that underlie such harassment. The Fair Trade living wage clearly brings about an enormous improvement in the lives of the small farmers who participate, but these farmers are and will remain a tiny share of coffee producers. Obviously, it is desirable to reduce pollution by increasing the efficiency with which corporations operate, as many environmental screens require, but such reductions fall short of the fundamental redesign of industrial systems that, as chapter 8 will show, is really needed.

The Corporation's Role in Running the World

The Roman emperor Trajan was right. Corporations are inherently political. They are chartered, directly or indirectly, by political bodies. They pay taxes and, at least in the United States, are considered legal persons with the rights of citizens. They generate spillovers that require collective action to redress. And as cases such as the TRIPS Agreement make abundantly clear, they participate vigorously in political processes by lobbying to protect their interests.

These are, in many ways, halcyon days for business. The halls of the United Nations used to ring with calls for regulation of those dreaded evildoers, the multinational corporations. Now, secretary-general Kofi Annan has launched the Global Compact, imploring business to join with the United Nations in ensuring respect for internationally agreed environmental, labor, and human rights standards. A few decades ago, governments often seized the assets of private corporations and turned them into state-run businesses. Now governments are engaged in a frenzy of selling their state-run entities back to the private sector.

Yet the struggles over corporate political power that have persisted for more than a century are not nearly over. Corporations may be increasingly off the hook with governments, but they face growing pressures from other sources. The lack of effective national or international regulation leaves workers, communities, and the environment inadequately protected. Nongovernmental activists and the United Nations are working frenetically to try to fill the gap, promoting a social responsibility agenda that puts more and more corporations under the spotlight. And because unregulated business activities can cause societies to question the legitimacy of corporations, corporate leaders themselves are struggling with fundamental questions about how far their social responsibilities extend: to shareholders, employees, local communities where they operate, humanity as a whole, future generations.

And the stakes are higher than ever. As chapter 7 argues, future global prosperity depends in part on whether private investment and labor practices encourage a widespread sharing of the benefits of economic integration to prevent what otherwise threatens to be a serious political backlash against the disruptions such integration causes. And as chapter 8 will show, that prosperity, and human well-being more generally, also depends on a significant transformation in the way industrial societies produce and use all the goods that make life so pleasant—a transformation that is essential if we are to avoid committing collective environmental suicide.

The private sector could decide of its own volition to behave with the necessary degree of social responsibility, either out of altruism or from an enlightened view of long-term self-interest. Some firms will, but most will not. Nor will governments be able to regulate them into compliance with such high standards of behavior, given the lack of capacity of many governments and the growing ability of corporations to pick up and leave any too-effective jurisdiction.

Thus the need for *credible* regulation by revelation, using transparency to determine whether corporations are adhering to codes of socially responsible conduct. This approach differs from traditional "hard law" thinking about how to ensure that corporations solve some of the problems they generate. Those who distrust corporations on principle will not be satisfied with such "soft law," and no one can yet be sure it will work on a large scale. The new, softer approach is an evolving process, as indicated by the continuing revisions of the Global Reporting Initiative's framework, and in some ways it has already gotten better. The growing tendency to use standards set by legitimate national governments in international declarations and treaties as the bases for codes is particularly promising.

In the corporation can be seen all the themes of this book: the need for new global rules, the growing participation of nonstate actors in the various phases of collective action, and experimentation with new transparency-based solutions to the collective action dilemma. Nothing is yet working perfectly, or even very well. But there has been an enormous evolution in thinking about the appropriate role of the corporation. Some still claim that corporations should simply make money (within legal limits, whatever those might be), but the growing acceptance of broader ideas is more than just lip service. Corporate motives may be pure, or the corporations' executives may simply want to protect their companies' bottom lines, fend off possible government regulations, or both. But what matters is their behavior.

Civil Society

The collapse of Soviet-bloc governments at the end of the 1980s raised questions about how to reconstitute societies where the state had long insisted on doing everything itself. That collapse made it suddenly necessary for the citizens and the new governments of the former Warsaw Pact countries to think anew about how modern societies engender the extraordinary degree of social cooperation needed in democratic society to cope with the many problems inherent in the increasingly complex life of the modern age. Part of the answer, as discussed in earlier chapters, was assumed to be privatization—redefining collective problems as private ones. But the other major assumption (particularly dear to the hearts of American funding agencies, both government and private) was that new democracies could flourish everywhere if sufficiently vigorous civil societies—nongovernmental organizations (NGOs) and other nonprofit associations—were created.[1] At the same time, people around the world were organizing themselves into an extraordinary variety of advocacy coalitions linked across national borders.

This flurry of activity has created high hopes that all this nongovernmental, nonbusiness activity could solve the world's pressing problems. The rosy scenario in chapter 1 imagined a world rendered just and prosperous by hordes of concerned activists and citizens.[2] Groups of such people already do everything from delivering services to the poor to confronting corporations to pressuring governments about every cause on the global agenda—indeed, such groups are often the reason causes get on the global agenda. With groups of people in every corner of the world linking up to demand change and arouse the public, we have a picture of a path that *could* lead to the optimistic scenario of chapter 1. What would it take to turn such a possibility into reality?

The Deep Roots of Civil Society

What we today call civil society has existed for all of human history, but the term arose out of the Scottish Enlightenment, when the religious basis for morality was fast disappearing and philosophers were seeking an alternative.[3] The Scottish Enlightenment thinkers found that alternative in what they called civil society, "a realm of solidarity held together by the force of moral sentiments and natural affections."[4] They thought the "natural sympathy" of civil society was enough to overcome the collective action problem because it would root individuals in a community and so "present a coherent vision of society beyond its individual members."[5]

This optimistic view of civil society was strongly disputed. Thinkers such as David Hume dismissed it as wishful thinking that ignored the degree to which individual interests dominate group goals. Others saw civil society not as a solution but as a major source of the conflicts of interest between groups that have to be overcome. The philosophical furor was never resolved, and in time the term faded away. Later in the nineteenth century, the focus shifted from civil society to citizenship.[6]

But even as the concept of civil society dropped off the radar screen for many decades, the groups that constitute civil society proceeded to organize themselves apace. Their rise was made possible, ironically enough, by the growing power and penetration of nation-states. The state building described in chapter 4 demanded an industrial base, a legal infrastructure, and a citizenry "with the skills necessary to staff the armies, pay the taxes, and turn the wheels of industry," as sociologist Sidney Tarrow noted.[7] The communications and transportation infrastructure created by the emerging states made it easier for widely separated individuals and groups to recognize and act on common interests. By such means, states inadvertently created social groups able to carry out collective action in support of goals other than those of the state. The rise of the territorial state also provided groups within a national society something to mobilize *against*. Much of state building consisted of raising taxes and conscripting soldiers, both unpopular expansions of state authority against which civil society groups formed social movements in protest.

Although most civil society ties in the eighteenth and nineteenth centuries were domestic, some connected people across national borders. The first of these long predated the Scottish Enlightenment—missionaries and monks created webs of transnational communities for centuries before anyone thought of giving those links a label.[8] Religious organizations provided the impetus for the first modern transnational policy campaign: the nineteenth-century campaign to end slavery. That campaign took on a well-entrenched and profitable practice and put an end to it. Quaker, Methodist, and Baptist groups made up the core of the campaign. In what would come to be a familiar pattern, they made common cause with sympathizers elsewhere, notably in the British government, which used its dominant naval power to constrict trade with slaveholding countries.[9] Such national organizations as the Pennsylvania Society for Promoting the Abolition of Slavery (established in 1775), the British Society for Effecting the Abolition of the Slave Trade, and the French Société des Amis des Noirs (these last two established in the mid-1780s) found their effectiveness enhanced by the establishment in 1839 of the British and Foreign Anti-Slavery Society, in one commentator's view "the first transnational moral entrepreneur—religious movements aside—to play a significant role in world politics."[10]

The anti-slavery campaign gave birth to what would prove an increasingly vigorous transnational civil society in the 1800s and early 1900s. Peace groups based in Europe and the United States lobbied at various international peace conferences. Governments began to use nongovernmental technical experts as delegates to international conferences. A variety of civil society associations formed around trade issues, including the International Association for Customs Reform. Such groups as the Institut de Droit International and the International Law Association, both formed in 1873, contributed substantially to the development of international law.[11]

Most noteworthy of all the new groups was the International Committee of the Red Cross (ICRC), born in the mid-1860s.[12] A Swiss banker, Henry Dunant, happened to find himself down the road from the bloody battle of Solferino in 1859. As thousands upon thousands of wounded soldiers streamed, or crawled, off the battlefield and into town, Dunant saw them die in agony, with no medical assistance whatsoever from anyone other than Dunant himself and a handful of townspeople. After a few days of offering water and tearing shirts into bandages, the shaken Dunant returned to Geneva, where he wrote *A Memory of Solferino*. The book called for the establishment of volunteer aid societies to follow armies around and care for the wounded, and it argued that international treaties were needed to confer noncombatant status on those agencies and the wounded.

Military leaders were remarkably uninterested in the proposal. Medical care at the time was not good enough to return many wounded soldiers to combat, and military commanders were reluctant to have civilians cluttering up the battlefield and possibly looting the wounded and dead. Even Florence Nightingale objected, arguing that the proposal would absolve states of their responsibility to care for their own wounded. But the book caught on with the royalty of Europe and with a number of private associations dedicated to human welfare. By 1864, the first Geneva Convention for the Amelioration of the Condition of the Wounded in Armies in the Field was in existence, and over the next 130 years the convention was repeatedly revised and expanded. The ICRC, still a privately operated Swiss organization, has become the core of a vast transnational network of national Red Cross and Red Crescent societies dedicated to offering assistance to the world's wounded, imprisoned, and distraught.[13]

Following the establishment of the ICRC, a steady trickle of cross-border connections formed, and these grew steadily over the next century (with interruptions for the two world wars). The post–World War II period saw an explosion in the number of formally constituted NGOs with members and activities in more than one country, accompanied by uncountable numbers of less formal cross-border ties.

For the most part, behind those numbers lie powerful stories of people who saw something wrong with the world and set out to right it. But a caveat is in order: people who work via civil society groups to achieve their goals are no more paragons of enlightened virtue than are people who work in corporations or governments. There are incompetent and greedy and downright malevolent civil society groups. Al Qaeda fits the definition of a civil society organization—it is not primarily motivated by profits, it is not a government, and its members seem to think they are working in a righteous cause. Other less vicious groups are undesirable fronts for other interests or exist merely to do the bidding of governments or funders. A whole lexicon of pejorative terms has sprung up to describe such groups, terms such as DONGO (donor-organized NGO), GONGO (government-operated NGO), QUANGO (quasi-governmental NGO), and my personal favorite, MANGO (Mafia-run NGO). And even activists truly motivated by what they see as the global public interest face increasingly tough questions about whose interests they represent, how they should be held accountable, and what power they are entitled to have.

Saving Life and Limb

In 1991, an American veteran of the Vietnam War sent a fax to a German psychologist. Six years later, a nonexistent group won the Nobel Peace Prize and 122 governments signed a treaty. Here is the story of how the former led to the latter.[14]

Bobby Muller, an American whose spinal cord was severed by a bullet in the Vietnam War, went to Cambodia in 1987, where he saw a disturbing sight—large numbers of men, women, and children whose limbs had been blown off by anti-personnel land mines left over from long-past conflicts. In April 1991, while working for the Vietnam Veterans of America Foundation (VVAF), Muller sent a fax to Thomas Gebauer, a psychologist at Medico International who had been helping similar victims in Central America. Muller suggested they cooperate on mine victim assistance projects. But over the next few months, the two men came to agree that something a lot stronger was called for. Something on the order of 100 million mines lurked underground in scores of countries, and they were injuring or killing more than 25,000 people every year. The victims who survived—usually poor people—faced enormous financial burdens, often having lost limbs and needing prostheses that cost $1,000 and needed frequent replacement. Muller and Gebauer agreed that anti-personnel land mines had come to constitute a humanitarian catastrophe raging largely unnoticed and that the only solution would be a complete ban on their production and use.

At the time, the prospects of success seemed at best remote. An international treaty dating from the early 1980s purported to prohibit the indiscriminate use of land mines, but it was so weak and riddled with loopholes as to be essentially meaningless, even for the relative handful of countries that had bothered to sign on.[15] The treaty's weakness was no accident. Land mines were an important part of many countries' military strategy. Cheap (costing as little as $3) and widely perceived as a defensive weapon, they had become widely used without anyone paying much attention to their horrific consequences after conflicts had ended.

Knowing their work was cut out for them, Muller and Gebauer rolled up their sleeves and got going. They hired staff, starting with Jody Williams, who was then working on medical projects in El Salvador, and a German former member of Parliament named Angelika Beer. By October 1992, four other NGOs—Handicap International, Human Rights Watch, the Mines Advisory Group, and Physicians for Human Rights—had joined the VVAF and Medico International in launching the International Campaign to Ban Landmines (ICBL). Their goal was simple, if audacious: to completely eliminate the use, production, stockpiling, sale, transfer, and export of anti-personnel mines.

Following a second conference that brought 50 groups together in London in May 1993, the anti–land-mine movement spread to include more than 1,000 NGOs in more than sixty countries, combining loose transnational coordination with a dazzling array of national campaigns. The coordination was loose indeed, especially in the early days—more along the lines of "let a thousand flowers bloom" than any tight strategy. And bloom they did. Handicap International–Belgium scored an early success, working with members of Parliament on national legislation, enacted in March 1995, that banned the production, storage, and export of anti-personnel mines. Groups in the Netherlands and Ireland flooded the media. Mines Action Canada launched a letter-writing campaign until a government official protested that the letters were taking up too much space in the offices of government agencies. In the United States, Human Rights Watch put together a report for the U.S. campaign to use in lobbying companies involved in land-mine production. Various groups experimented with vivid ways of capturing public attention. One effective technique was to strew a sidewalk with circles of cardboard. On the side facing up were printed the words *Pick Me Up*. When pedestrians complied, they found written on the other side *Congratulations. I am a land mine.* Underneath that message was an Internet address indicating where people could get more information about the campaign.[16] In Japan, the Association to Aid Refugees (AAR) simultaneously worked with the ICBL and targeted local public opinion through a variety of efforts: publishing a picture book titled *Give Me Not Land Mines, But Flowers,* which sold more than 200,000 copies; opening an office in Cambodia in October 1996; and sponsoring a concert, which raised enough money to remove eighty land mines from a school for the blind in Sarajevo.[17] The International Committee of the Red Cross joined in with an influential international media campaign in October 1995.[18] Thanks to new information technologies, campaigners were able to instantaneously transmit information and coordinate their efforts in all parts of the globe. According to Steve Goose of Human Rights Watch, an active figure in the campaign, "e-mail made this campaign work."[19]

While all this was going on, campaigners had their eye on the existing treaty, hoping governments would upgrade it to a meaningful ban. Since France was one of the forty or so parties to the treaty, Handicap International and French groups lobbied the French government for a review conference of the parties at which the governments could negotiate an upgrade in the treaty's terms. France agreed, and the conference convened in Vienna in September 1995. But the governments found themselves sharply divided over everything from the legitimacy (or lack thereof) of land mines as a defensive weapon to the very definition of an anti-personnel mine. Britain and the United States were willing to ban all but "smart" mines—the kind that turn themselves off after a set period so they do not lie in wait indefinitely to maim unwary passersby. Poorer countries such as China, India, and Russia were not enthralled by the idea of paying $300 for a smart mine instead of $3 for a conventional one, arguing that such a ban would unfairly benefit richer countries. Although the conferees agreed to meet again the next year, it was clear that not much could be expected from the standard intergovernmental route. Indeed, in May 1996, the final session of the review conference closed with an improved treaty that was still far from a comprehensive ban.

One of the Dutch campaigners, Pieter van Rossem, decided to try something different. In January 1996, he called a meeting of the twenty or so governments that had announced support for a land-mine ban to brainstorm with the NGOs. Eight countries sent representatives, and the attendees, encouraged by the highly constructive atmosphere of the discussion, found themselves beginning to believe that a ban could be achieved. The Canadian delegate went home and asked Canada's newly appointed foreign minister, Lloyd Axworthy, whether Canada might take some initiative. Axworthy responded vigorously with an official call for a fast-track strategy to bring about a total ban on all anti-personnel land mines. In October 1996, Canada hosted a conference in Ottawa, attended by representatives of some fifty governments and many NGOs, to work out a strategy for achieving the ban. On the last day, Axworthy shocked the conference participants by announcing that Canada would host a treaty-signing meeting by the end of 1997—lightning speed by the standards of international negotiations. The NGO representatives in attendance gave him a standing ovation.

The resulting "Ottawa Process," driven by a coalition of like-minded states and civil society organizations, proved strikingly successful. The various groups, connected under the umbrella of the ICBL, held meetings around the world and carried out public relations campaigns aimed at building government and popular support for the ban. In October 1997, when it had become clear that a substantial number of governments would sign a ban treaty by the December deadline, the Nobel Peace Prize committee announced it was awarding that year's prize to the ICBL and its coordinator, Jody Williams, in recognition of the campaign's creative diplomacy. The committee expressed its hope that the campaign to ban land mines and the working partnership that had been created between governments and civil society would become a diplomatic model for the future.[20]

In December 1997, a second Ottawa conference produced the Convention on the Prohibition of the Use, Stockpiling, Production and Transfer of Anti-Personnel Mines and on Their Destruction. It was not a complete victory for the campaign—a number of countries did not sign the treaty, including the United States, Russia, China, Israel, and several Arab nations. The United States cited the need to protect American soldiers in South Korea as its reason for not signing. Nevertheless, a number of the more powerful nonsignatory states, including China, Russia, and the United States, agreed to work with the Convention in removing mines and providing assistance to victims. The United States has since said it will sign in the year 2006 if (and only if) the Pentagon has by then devised an effective alternative weapon.[21]

Although the treaty went into effect in March 1999, the story is far from over. The ban will be effective only if the major producers of land mines adhere to it and if the countries that have ratified the treaty live up to its terms. As reported in the *Ottawa Citizen,* "there is no firm blueprint for action on how governments and non-government organizations will co-ordinate their mine actions or how priorities for spending will be determined."[22] The ICBL still exists—in fact, it legally came into existence only after the treaty was signed, when it had to transform itself from an amorphous coalition into a legal entity with a bank account so it could receive its Nobel Prize money. It is expanding into new realms, monitoring compliance and pressing for ever more ratifications. But how effective all this will be in saving civilians from pointless death and mutilation remains to be seen.

The one indisputable lesson of the ICBL experience is that a civil society network, working with the governments of relatively weak countries, was able to bring about a disarmament treaty to which the major military powers vehemently objected. As Lloyd Axworthy noted, the Ottawa Process "worked because new synergies were created. This was not simply a question of consulting NGOs or seeking their views. We have moved well beyond that. What I am talking about is a full working process between governments and civil groups."[23]

Was this a one-of-a-kind occurrence, or does it represent the wave of the future? On the "it was a fluke" side, land mines are a problem in nearly every region of the globe, which makes it easy to drum up worldwide support for their removal. Their indiscriminate nature—victims are usually innocent civilians caught at the wrong place at the wrong time, often years after the mines were planted—makes it easy for John Q. Public to understand why they are morally objectionable. And the anti–land-mine campaign was able to build on the publicity following both the awarding of the Nobel Peace Prize and the death of Diana, Princess of Wales, who was an active and visible campaigner for the ban—not the kind of events transnational activists can generally count on for support.

And even though an impressive number of nations have signed the ban, a number of the world's most powerful nations have not. One official of the U.S. Department of State, Jim Bishop, told the Gannett News Service that he wondered whether more traditional diplomacy would have brought President Bill Clinton to the table. He claimed: "If there had been a little more diplomacy than confrontation, it might have been possible to bring in the United States. . . . The NGOs are advocates who are used to pounding the table and taking confrontational approaches."[24] Other skeptics have questioned whether the much-heralded cooperation between NGOs and governments was really a global phenomenon. Philippe Chabasse of Handicap International claimed that in France there was no real partnership between the two. He argued that "in certain countries—Canada, Austria and Belgium—you can trust some people, develop a partnership with the government, but not in other countries."[25]

Perhaps most important, most issues on the transnational governance agenda lack the compelling imagery of mutilated young land-mine victims. It is relatively easy to agree to rid the world of such a repugnant weapon. Civil society campaigns on issues such as global finance and climate change have a harder time generating the strong visceral responses that motivate public outcry. And clarity of message is harder to achieve when what is needed is something more complex than a straightforward ban.

On the other hand, campaigns always look implausible when they begin. When the anti–land-mine campaign started in 1991, very few people dreamed that more than 100 governments would adhere to a total ban within a mere eight years. And the activists who were instrumental in the campaign have learned an important lesson along the way. The NGOs that drove the campaign learned how to effectively shape and mold public opinion. These activists proved that it is possible to mobilize a transnational coalition on the grassroots level, providing a model for other efforts. The anti–land-mine campaign got activists around the globe excited about their success and eager to capitalize on the momentum. And the technological revolution in global communications that aided this campaign continues to reduce the costs of communicating and organizing.

Human Rights

Despite the vast amount of attention the anti–land-mine campaign received in the press and in the policy community, it is not the progenitor of a new type of global governance. It is just one in a series of myriad such campaigns, many equally successful. We have already seen older versions, dating back to the anti-slavery movement of the 1800s, that successfully mobilized activists around the globe. These early human rights issues, however, were ordinarily tied to religious beliefs. The twentieth-century human rights movement had different roots: the Holocaust.[26]

Before World War II, nothing in international law prohibited governments from abusing their citizens. Governments legally could and did protest if the rights of their own citizens were violated abroad, but rare indeed was any effort to stop even the most outrageous abuses at home, so long as they involved no foreigners. Under the doctrine of national sovereignty, states had the legal right to do virtually anything within their own territory, including torture and murder. And although the losing side in a war might be forced to pay economic reparations to the victor, even the losers were not held criminally accountable for the human suffering they had imposed.

Revelations about the Holocaust and the Nuremburg trials changed all that, creating for the first time a standard that governments could be held broadly accountable for the way they treated their citizens, at least in some cases. But except in the postwar trials, it was not governments that took the lead. It was groups of citizens, often quite ordinary people. Civil society groups pressed for the inclusion of human rights as a founding principle of the United Nations at that organization's founding conference in San Francisco in 1945. NGOs then set out to strengthen human rights standards by drafting an international bill of rights, which became the 1948 Universal Declaration of Human Rights, affirming a number of political and civil rights. The Declaration is, of course, a toothless document utterly lacking enforcement provisions. But as we will see, "toothless" statements of human rights standards have been known to develop some real bite.

It took a while for these human rights activists to coalesce into a powerful force.[27] One step forward came in 1961, when a group of lawyers in London appealed in the *London Observer* for the release of two Portuguese college students who had been sentenced to twenty years in prison after toasting to "freedom" in public. The lawyers' "Appeal for Amnesty" called on all governments to release prisoners of conscience—people imprisoned for the peaceful expression of their beliefs. The response surprised even the founders of the effort: the appeal was picked up by newspapers around the world. Carefully neutral, what would later become Amnesty International organized its members in local groups that campaigned for the release of three prisoners, one each from what were then called the First, Second, and Third Worlds. As Amnesty's credibility grew, so did its membership, reaching more than a million by the end of the century.

Through the 1960s and 1970s, governments did their best to further the human rights cause by demonstrating just how badly a human rights campaign was needed. First came the Greek colonels' coup of 1967, accompanied by widespread reports of torture, which spurred European activism. Then came Augusto Pinochet's coup and subsequent repression in Chile, sparking an outpouring of activism in the United States in a backlash against the active support for the overthrow of democracy on the part of the administration of President Richard Nixon. South Africa helped by carrying out an apartheid policy so abhorrent that people around the world found themselves united in protest.

The final straw came in the form of treaty language that was intended by most of its signatories as mere rhetoric rather than an expression of sincere commitment. In 1975, members of the North Atlantic Treaty Organization (NATO) and the Warsaw Pact signed the Helsinki Final Act of the Conference on Security and Cooperation in Europe. It included human rights language, language that both the Soviet Union and the United States clearly saw as meaningless boilerplate meant only to assuage the concerns of a few western Europeans. But Soviet-bloc dissidents took it seriously, founding organizations that legitimized their demands as simply calling for compliance with the agreement their governments had signed. This mobilization, linked in time to human rights groups elsewhere, contributed in no small part to the collapse of one repressive regime after another in the late 1980s.

Civil society networks were certainly not the only proponents of human rights—the administration of U.S. president Jimmy Carter was one notable example of a government playing a big role in promoting the cause. But not much would have happened without them. From the 1948 Declaration to the 1987 Convention against Torture and Other Cruel, Inhuman or Degrading Treatment or Punishment (primarily the outcome of a campaign by Amnesty International and other NGOs), most governments have now agreed to be held to demanding standards with regard to the way they treat their citizens. Although many governments clearly sign with little expectation of honoring the terms, the same groups that have pushed for the creation of standards have often proved useful in shaming governments into better behavior. Through a repeated "boomerang effect," local groups that arise in protest against government repression find support from overseas NGOs, which pressure their own governments to pressure the offending governments to shape up.[28] The overseas NGOs sometimes also manage to inflict economic pain, persuading big corporations not to invest in countries with repressive regimes. The process is long, arduous, and often marred by violent setbacks and protests (by the repressor) that all these human rights claims are just Western imperialism in a new guise. But in an extraordinary range of cases—in South Africa, Chile, Guatemala, the Philippines, Uganda, and Poland, to name a few—countries that once were synonymous with vicious repression have become full-fledged members of the community of human rights–observing states. They all underwent their transformations at roughly the same time, in large part influenced by the maturing of the transnational network of human rights advocates.

As in the land-mines case, the human rights network faces major challenges. It still has its traditional work to do—there still are some severely repressive governments around, and even the ostensible good guys suffer serious lapses from time to time—but increasingly the problems lie elsewhere. Addressing problems in economic and social rights often requires getting corporations rather than governments to change behavior, and that is a massive number of targets for NGOs to grapple with. And given the lack of central government control in many civil conflicts, it is often not even clear who should be targeted.

And More, and More

There are plenty of other stories to choose among, so many that this discussion must now be restricted to a few quick snapshots from a broad range of issues. One is by itself a whole range of issues—environment, economic development, the rights of indigenous peoples—that come together in a misleadingly short word: dams.[29] For decades, large dams were built to provide water, irrigation, electricity, and flood control in scores of countries. Such needs remain unmet in many places. A billion people still lack adequate access to water, some 2 billion lack reliable electricity, and massive floods in China and elsewhere point to the still-unsatisfied demand for flood control. But the number of dams under construction has dropped precipitously, representing a 74 percent decline from the 1970s to the 1990s. Given that the demand for water, irrigation, electricity, and flood control has not lessened, and potential sites for large dams remain plentiful in many countries, something else must account for the decline.

That something else is, as you might guess, civil society. Opposition to large dams first arose in the 1950s through the 1970s in separate campaigns in Europe, the United States, India, and many other parts of the world. In rich countries, opposition came from conservationists who were trying to preserve nature. In poor countries, opponents tended to be those who stood to be flooded out of their homes and livelihoods, along with environmentalists. In the 1980s, these domestic groups began linking up across national borders. Groups in Europe and the United States, enjoying increasing success in halting and reforming dam building in their own countries, saw equally objectionable projects sprouting in the Third World, along with vigorous but often ineffective domestic opposition. At the same time, a number of environmental organizations based mostly in the United States initiated a campaign against the World Bank and other multilateral funders of large infrastructure projects such as dams. By the end of that decade, the loose anti-dam network was holding international meetings, issuing declarations and publications, and bringing massive publicity to protests that made it difficult for dam construction to proceed. By the mid-1990s, this movement had forced substantial changes in World Bank practices, a crucial point because the World Bank was for decades the most important source of funding for dams in developing countries.

In 1997, the broad anti-dam network accomplished something it had long pursued: agreement on an independent and comprehensive review of big dams. At a workshop sponsored by the World Bank and the World Conservation Union (IUCN), representatives of governments, international development agencies, transnational civil society, and private sector dam builders agreed to establish the World Commission on Dams. This commission was most unusual. Its twelve members included four each from government, the private sector, and civil society, who somehow overcame years of vituperative hostility to produce a consensus assessment of dams and their alternatives, along with criteria for the making and decommissioning of dams.

Even nuclear arms control, a preserve one might expect governments to guard with special vigor, has fallen prey to transnational activism.[30] Since the dawn of the nuclear age, a motley array of activist groups has campaigned long and hard for a complete ban on nuclear testing. They have argued that such a ban would be the one sure way to halt nuclear arms races. It is, after all, hard to have a race if the runners have no way to know whether they are passing the right milestones. At first, back in the 1950s, the peace activists, scientists, and doctors who constituted the early protestors focused their appeals on the health risks posed by radioactive fallout. The governments dealt with that by agreeing on the Partial Test Ban Treaty in 1963, which banned nuclear tests in the atmosphere and under water (and also, for good measure, in outer space). But moving the tests underground helped put them out of sight, out of mind.

Over the next few decades, a whole range of civil society groups tried to get governments to negotiate a *comprehensive* test ban treaty. The activists had a couple of legal legs to stand on. The parties to the partial test ban accord had agreed in a preamble to seek the "discontinuance of all test explosions of nuclear weapons for all time." And a few years later, when governments signed a nonproliferation treaty aimed at stopping the spread of nuclear weapons beyond the five countries (Britain, China, France, the Soviet Union, and the United States) that had already acquired arsenals, the five weapons-possessing countries explicitly agreed to seek an end to all their nuclear testing in exchange for everyone else's commitment not to start. But those five governments apparently did not mean it, and they never got much further than a few desultory discussions.

This made some people angry, and some groups came up with creative ways of expressing their discontent. Greenpeace started off as a group of Vancouver-based Canadians and expatriate Americans who decided one day in 1971 to sail an old fishing boat to the U.S. island of Amchitka, off the Alaskan coast, to protest U.S. nuclear testing. Within a few years, what had become Greenpeace International was using some of its multimillion-dollar budget to send protest ships to French nuclear testing sites in the South Pacific Ocean. The organization struck a nerve. When French secret service agents bombed and sank the Greenpeace flagship *Rainbow Warrior* in 1985 in Auckland Harbor, killing a photographer on board, the massive publicity made Greenpeace a household name.

After a two-year hiatus, Greenpeace was at it again, sailing a ship to a Soviet test site, hanging banners from London's Tower Bridge, and sending a group of activists to the U.S. test site in Nevada to stand on the spot of a planned test, which was halted just in time. At the same time, the winding down of the cold war and the growing environmental movement created new opportunities for groups within each of the testing countries to cause their own ruckus. In the late 1980s, Kazakh nationalists launched a powerful campaign to end Soviet testing at the main Soviet test site at Semipalatinsk in what is now Kazakhstan. (In honor of their strong transnational connections with other opponents of testing, they named themselves the Nevada-Semipalatinsk movement.) Members of Les Verts, France's Green Party, who put an end to nuclear testing near the top of their list of priorities, scored well enough in elections in 1992 to pressure the government of François Mitterrand to do something about French nuclear tests. In the United States, NGOs launched an effort to get Congress to force the administration of President George H. W. Bush to stop testing.

Governments caved. In short order, first the Soviet Union, then France, and finally the United States announced unilateral moratoriums on their testing programs. Then, motivated in part by lobbying on the part of NGOs, some of the countries that had earlier agreed to renounce nuclear weapons started arguing that the price of their continued renunciation would be agreement on a permanent comprehensive test ban. In September 1996, the Comprehensive Test Ban Treaty (CTBT) was opened for signature, and since then more than 150 countries have signed.

Unfortunately from the point of view of the activists, that is not the end of the story. During the negotiations, Russia, Britain, and China wangled a provision naming 44 countries that must sign and ratify before the treaty could come into effect. This was a showstopper because India was on the list. Far from being prepared to renounce forever the possibility of acquiring its own nuclear arsenal, in May 1998 India conducted a series of nuclear tests. Its regional arch-rival, Pakistan, quickly followed suit. Then, in October 1999, a sharply divided United States Senate refused to ratify the treaty on a highly partisan vote. The CTBT is not quite dead, but it is on life support.

What It All Means

There are books filled with case studies of civil society networks that have crossed national borders to bring about transnational collective action by governments or, as discussed in the previous chapter, by corporations.[31] Clearly, a great many people are not inclined to leave global governance to the mercies of governments and corporations. But their growing role raises a host of questions.

The conventional wisdom about democracy generally says that societies need ways to organize interests outside the channels provided by governments. Civil society embodies the social trust that provides the essential basis for sustained collective action. You may remember from chapter 3 that social scientists call this social capital: the habits of trust within a society. At the national level, the interlacing network of civil society organizations that exist within a country well endowed with social capital is the necessary complement to democratic government, providing the broad societal values that make sustained and effective democracy possible. As the scale of collective action problems goes global, we need the same creation of trust at that level.

But there is an enormous difference between the national and global levels. National civil society functions in a context set by national government. Political mechanisms exist to work out competing interests and set requirements for standards of behavior, such as libel laws, requirements for disclosure of funding sources, and the like. Those mechanisms do not always work well, but the principle is clear. There are few global counterparts to these political processes.

Transnational civil society connections may be able to create global patterns of trust and cooperation. But they can also make things worse. Some of these transnational webs contain nasty spiders spewing venomous hatred, propagated effortlessly across the Internet. And given that with most important issues there is no consensus on the details of what constitutes the collective good, the growing power of even the best-intentioned networks raises serious questions about the appropriate role in global governance for those who are largely unaccountable to anyone.

Those questions loom ever larger as the number and power of transnational civil society groups grow, driven by everything from technology to globalization to changes in ideas about what behavior is acceptable in the world. Information technology has provided powerful new means for transnational civil society both to organize itself, as seen in the land-mines case, and to get its message out. The process began with the Western social movements of the 1960s, which were transformed by television. Television made mass social organization cheap. The social movements of the 1960s needed only to attract a fairly small number of activists who could appeal to a much larger number of sympathizers. A few mentions on the evening news could do much of what earlier had required massive organizing.[32] This had been somewhat true in the age of print, but visual imagery is so much more compelling that it fundamentally shifted the repertoire available to nonstate collective action entrepreneurs. The effects were national because television at that time was a national medium. Now, however, new media such as the Internet are free of such geographic constraints.

But information technology is only a part of the story. Another key element is the growing availability of targets around which transnational coalitions can coalesce. Just as national civil societies arose partly because of the infrastructure provided by nation-states and partly in reaction to the activities of states, transnational civil society is benefiting from the development of even relatively feeble intergovernmental bodies such as the United

Nations and its associated agencies. Although civil society groups can become proactive, providing solutions as well as complaints, they often start off in reaction to something people do not like.

The series of United Nations conferences on global issues that began in the 1970s were meant primarily to draw governments together to consider how to deal with everything from housing to population to food to the environment, but as it turned out, the most important role of the conferences was to provide a focal point around which global civil society could coalesce. Nongovernmental groups appeared in force at the 1972 United Nations Conference on the Human Environment, with accredited NGOs outnumbering government delegations by two to one. Over the next twenty-five years, the United Nations hosted more than a dozen conferences on everything from food to population to the role of women.[33] Each stimulated a flurry of networking among the nongovernmental groups working on the issues.

The most conspicuous targets of civil society activities are, of course, the intergovernmental organizations that have real economic clout: the World Trade Organization, the World Bank, and the International Monetary Fund. These enjoy the unceasing attention of a smorgasbord of NGOs and assorted protestors. So it appears that, thanks to the meetings and activities of governments, intergovernmental organizations, and corporations, transnational civil society is in no danger of running out of targets. These focal points are part and parcel of the processes of globalization. Unless global integration comes to a screeching halt, the targets of opportunity will proliferate.

At the same time, thanks to higher levels of education and material standards of living, more and more people from all parts of the world have entered the middle class, with the skills and leisure time to participate in civil society.[34] Once civil society puts down roots within a country, it tends to mushroom. Although Robert Putnam has famously argued that we are seeing a decline in such participation in America, his findings are hotly disputed by other scholars who see a change in patterns of participation rather than an overall decline. And in other parts of the world, participation in civil society seems to be noticeably on the rise. People who become accustomed to acting in local civil society are more likely to be drawn into broader networks. Movements and coalitions often recruit their members from existing organizations that serve a different purpose. Churches, for example, were the springboard of both the early American women's movement and the more recent civil rights movement. But we seem to be reaching a self-sustaining cascade as so many people have become involved in some form of civil society organization that vast numbers are available for recruitment. As Sidney Tarrow points out, with so many organizations providing "reservoirs for recruitment into a wide spectrum of movements, we may be witnessing the foundation for a movement society."[35]

All this activity takes money. That money generally comes from three sources: governments (which are the largest contributors, especially to non-profit service providers such as hospitals, educational institutions, and various charities); voluntary contributions from individuals, corporations, and foundations; and fees charged for services rendered.[36] To a substantial degree, the global rise of the kinds of civil society groups that can contribute to global governance reflects the policies of Western governments and foundations, stemming from a Western worldview that emphasizes the importance of civil society to good governance. The World Bank estimates that in the early 1970s, 1.5 percent of income for development NGOs came from outside donors; by the mid-1990s, this figure had reached nearly 30 percent. In some countries, including Bangladesh, Sri Lanka, and Kenya, the level of dependence on donor funds is as high as 90 percent.[37]

The first few decades of the twenty-first century are likely to see even more money available to support civil society. Some scholars have projected that in the developed countries, the first half of the century will witness a huge transfer of wealth from one generation to the next, totaling well more than $10 trillion for the United States alone. Since bequests often provide a means to channel large amounts of money from private hands to civil society organizations, a fair chunk of this money may go to support civil society. The examples of Bill Gates, George Soros, and Ted Turner, whose donations are in the hundreds of millions, or billions, of dollars, may spur other members of the world's growing group of extremely wealthy individuals to follow suit.

Such dependence on outside funding raises the hackles of many people in both rich and poor countries who question whether groups funded from abroad reflect local people's needs and desires. If money drives the agenda, civil society in non-Western parts of the world may not play the truly democratic role it does in the West. The Western governments providing much of the funding are accountable only to their own electorates, not to the people whose lives are most directly affected.

But the reliance on Western funding is not necessarily bad, especially if some of it is directed toward building up local sources of philanthropy. Social capital, like any capital, takes time to accumulate, and a little seed money can help a lot. Effective and sustained civil society organizations rarely arise spontaneously at the grassroots level, even in the West. As anyone who has ever participated in a homeowners' association, parent-teacher association, or book club knows, it is exceedingly difficult to keep a quorum of members showing up at meeting after meeting. The successful new civil society organizations usually have links to established organizations that provide materials, ideas, and organizational structure. Given the nascent level of civil society organization in many parts of the world, it is perhaps not surprising that Western dominance currently looms so large. There are benefits: NGOs frequently assert that an attachment to donors helps them learn effective methodologies and acquire technical training.[38]

Because all people live in territorial states, "transnational" civil society consists of networks of individuals and groups that are located within individual states. And government willingness to tolerate, or even foster, nongovernmental associations varies wildly from one country to another.[39] The United States has long made it fairly easy for organizations to establish themselves, and it is one of the few countries that encourage contributions to a wide range of civil society organizations by making these contributions tax-deductible. Many Asian governments, in contrast, strictly regulate which organizations can be legally registered or allowed to exist at all.[40] China, for example, has about 200,000 registered "mass organizations," but given the obstacles to gaining official recognition, it seems likely that many more remain unregistered or slip out of existence. Under State Council Order No. 43, no group can legally exist if it duplicates any function ostensibly filled by a government-registered organization, whether or not the function is actually carried out.[41]

But attitudes and policies are beginning to change. Until quite recently, Japan made it very difficult for NGOs to incorporate, requiring, for example, that an organization have 300 million yen (about $3 million) in "basic capital" permanently in the bank and severely limiting tax incentives for contributions. In March 1998, however, Japan promulgated a new law dispensing with the cumbersome and arbitrary approval process and the basic capital requirement. The law still puts some obligations on civil society organizations (requiring them, for example, to submit all accounting documents and annual reports to local government administrative bodies each year), but it is expected to bring about the addition of some 10,000 non-profit organizations in Japan.[42]

Donors and governments may make civil society possible, but they cannot create it out of thin air. Some glue must bind together the participants in any collective endeavor—shared interests, feelings of solidarity, or, most likely, some combination of the two. The cosmopolitanism described in chapter 3 provides a basis, but not by itself a motivation, to act—just as a feeling of national loyalty may not inspire everyone to pay all their taxes and join the army. What glue exists that can bind together transnational civil society groups tightly enough to provide the basis for effective collective action? What, in other words, is the identity that the members of such groups perceive themselves as sharing?

Religion and nationalism, as discussed in chapter 3, are strong cements, but they are not the only causes in which people believe strongly enough to join together. One of the most striking developments of recent decades is the emergence of those coordinated nongovernmental campaigns described earlier in this chapter. These campaigns bring together individuals and groups from many parts of the world on the basis of shared principles and causes.[43] Some participants in such networks are motivated by religious views. Many others, however, seem to have adopted a cosmopolitan perspective, viewing victims of faraway disasters or repression or exploitation as being fully as human and deserving of protection as people close to home.

In short, it seems likely that the explosion of transnational civil society is still in its infancy. Targets of opportunity will continue to proliferate, and groups will come together to try to devise solutions to global problems. More and more people will be able and willing to participate. Advances in information technology will continue to lower the cost of staying connected to distant regions. Money, though not plentiful, will be available. And governments will accommodate the growing pressures for participation in civil society by providing the legal conditions under which civil society groups can exist, and perhaps even flourish.

New Rules for New Rule Makers?

Is all this newfound power and influence a good thing? Civil society *within* countries is widely lauded as the essential intermediary between the state and the citizen. Transnational civil society is different—there is neither a true global state nor a true global citizenry for civil society to mediate between. So ensuring that the sector does its share of pulling humanity up the road to our rosy future rather than pushing us down the gloomy path takes some careful weighing of the pluses and minuses of the roles these groups can play.

On the positive side, these groups often speak on behalf of the global future. They provide a kind of competition for the public conscience, a means of requiring that government officials consider broader perspectives than the immediate bureaucratic turf battle or the next election, or even the immediate national interest. Many of the pressing transnational issues, particularly the environmental ones, worsen slowly and incrementally, undergoing just the sort of barely perceptible change that ordinarily does not register on the political radar screen. Like the proverbial frog in the pot of water, which, if the temperature is raised slowly enough, is not alerted to jump out before the water has boiled, governments may not be prompted to act until serious damage has occurred. Civil society groups can provide the political spark that triggers action.

Civil society can offer a choice of venue, as both the human rights case and the land-mines case make clear: people dissatisfied with available government channels turn to existing NGOs or sometimes acquire outside help to create their own.

Intergovernmental negotiations on most issues drag on for years as negotiators seek agreements acceptable to both their home countries and the other negotiators. In the land-mines case, governments first negotiated an agreement in 1980 that, by 1995, despite being revised, still had not managed to ban the things. The Ottawa Process, driven as much by the International Campaign to Ban Landmines as by governments, got the job done in a year.

Probably the single most important role of transnational civil society organizations is as setter of standards of behavior. In the networking that occurs among themselves and in their interactions with governments, intergovernmental organizations, and the private sector, these nongovernmental and nonprofit groups convey norms regarding both the means and the goals of collective action, just as domestic civil society organizations do within national borders. In so doing, they may be creating the basis of a global polity: not a world government, but a common culture with enough in the way of shared values to seek broad agreement on issues that merit collective action on the global scale.[44] Some common values are already widely recognized, such as the universality of basic human rights and the need for economic development to be environmentally sustainable. The insistence of transnational civil society on these values holds governments and corporations to international standards that are high aspirations, not lowest common denominators.

But there can be big drawbacks to leaving global governance in the hands of unelected, often unaccountable, and sometimes fanatical activists. Not all campaigns are motivated by the pursuit of truth, justice, and equity. These problems arise at the national level, too, but at that level, governments—supposedly—can override the distortions of special pleaders. Transnational civil society networks can and do operate anywhere. They often consist of people in one place claiming to speak for people in another. To date, they have remained relatively immune to the growing pressure for transparency that governments and businesses face. Most of the groups that participate in transnational networks have become adept at gathering and disseminating information about their targets and their causes, yet few show much inclination to disseminate information about themselves. Unless that immunity is revoked, transnational civil society could exacerbate, not alleviate, the democratic deficit in transnational governance.

For the most part, this is not deliberate secretiveness. Staffs of NGOs are usually poorly paid and badly overworked, and those who have dedicated their lives to saving the world from some terrible menace may find the prospect of spending precious time releasing information about themselves irritating at best. For some groups, such as those working on human rights in repressive countries, secrecy is often vital to the survival of the organization, not to mention the survival of staff members. But most groups have no such need for secrecy. In the long term, the credibility of transnational civil society may be at stake. The best way for civil society groups to allow others to hold them accountable is to take the time to explain their mission, goals, funding, and information sources. Groups that believe they deserve a place at the global governance table, on the basis of their expertise or their ability to represent voices otherwise unheard, will have to accept others' demands for accountability. Since they are not subject to elections or market pressures and do not want to be closely regulated, accepting transparency is their best bet.

The Future of Transnational Civil Society

To return to the question that opened this chapter: Are the hopes for a world saved by civil society merely a bad case of the "warm and fuzzies," or are there real grounds for optimism? There is good news—actually, quite a lot of it. Transnational civil society has become a self-sustaining phenomenon, spurred on by the globalization of many of the same factors that drove the evolution of Western civil societies at the national level. At its best, it can build that foundation of trust, that sense of community, that is essential to the definition and resolution of collective action problems even at the global scale. Only through civil society can the world develop the habits of extensive cooperation, across cultures and issue areas, that constitute social capital. But this can happen only if donors, governments, and civil society organizations themselves recognize that transnational civil society needs to go beyond its typical role as advocate for single issues and special causes. Its success in the long run depends increasingly on its own willingness to be held accountable. Those who have designated themselves the guardians of a global public interest must now make it much easier for others to watch them. They must recognize that their growing power brings with it increased responsibility, and they must shine their powerful spotlight on themselves as well as on governments and corporations. The public whose interests they adamantly claim to defend has the right to see what they are up to in the public's name.

7

Economic Integration

The Raging Grannies were not accustomed to facing tanks. But on that bleak December day, they found themselves standing silently in a crowd and watching a tank roll slowly toward them.

The setting was Seattle, Washington, not a place normally associated with tanks in the streets. The time was late 1999, during the now notorious meeting of the World Trade Organization (WTO). Most news reports concentrated on the violence perpetrated by a handful of self-described anarchists. But the Raging Grannies, a group of mostly older women who sing at all sorts of local political protests and rallies, were much more typical of the tens of thousands of protestors who filled Seattle's streets that week. Their mission, as described on their World Wide Web site, is to "promote global peace, justice, and social and economic equality by raising public awareness through the medium of song and humor." They took to the streets not to smash windows or get themselves arrested. Instead, they went out of a strongly held conviction that the WTO was acting to benefit the world's big corporations at the expense of ordinary people. They saw the Seattle meeting as a major opportunity to draw attention to what they feared was being done to ordinary people in the name of globalization.[1]

On December 2, spooked by the inability of the police to control the violence, Seattle officials declared a state of emergency and cordoned off the

section of the city where the WTO meeting was taking place. The Grannies
had an engagement to sing at a church just outside the cordoned-off area as
part of a daylong conference on globalization. The church was packed.
(Imagine the scene: a group of mostly grandmother-age women wearing big
hats and performing an anti-WTO diatribe[2] in rap-song style.) After the
Grannies' performance, one of the conference coordinators proposed that
everyone form a human chain, linking hands, and walk to the police line
demarcating the cordoned-off area. The idea was not to break the blockade
but merely to silently protest it. The resulting crowd filled the block, standing there quietly for perhaps half an hour. On the next block, inside the cor-
don, was a tank pointing in the direction of the protestors.

Then—nothing. The tank moved toward them and then stopped. After
a while, some of the crowd started softly singing protest songs. Eventually,
everyone went home.

That dramatically unsatisfying denouement notwithstanding, the protestors had accomplished their main goal. They had forced awareness of the
WTO onto the front pages and into evening news broadcasts. The meetings,
and the protests, continued for a couple more days with massive media coverage. Unfortunately, that media coverage focused on the sporadic instances
of violence, leaving most observers scratching their heads about just what the
WTO really does, what the protestors were protesting against, and why.

But as massive anti-globalization protests have continued to dog most
meetings of global leaders in recent years (protests that were temporarily
scaled back in response to the attacks of September 11, 2001), the issues
raised by the protestors have become part of the debate over globalization.
When most people talk about globalization, they are thinking about economics. Vast quantities of capital and jobs now flow across borders. Multinational corporations such as McDonald's and Microsoft market their products around the world. Swings in stock prices and interest rates ripple from
one country to the next. A single car or computer may be manufactured,
component by component, in half a dozen countries. The level of trade
across national borders is growing substantially faster than is the total global
economy.

Some people believe this impressive degree of economic integration is
leading us straight to the rosy scenario presented in chapter 1. If governments will just continue to lower barriers to the flow of goods and capital,
the argument goes, their citizens will reap extraordinary benefits: more

choices for consumers, higher returns for investors, greater efficiencies from competition, possibly even perpetual peace in a world so tightly tied together that war would never pay. "On the eve of the 21st century the world stands on the threshold of a long, strong surge in economic growth and living standards unprecedented in world history," argues one true believer, Knight Kiplinger.[3]

Others see economic integration as the road to ruin, leading straight to the gloomy scenario. Many people, particularly poor people, find their lives disrupted and sometimes devastated by the decisions of faraway investors and international institutions. Even if many gain, others lose, and the losses can spark political instability—such as riots in the streets. Economic integration may create pressures within a country to lower health or environmental standards because domestic producers must compete with imports that do not have to meet those standards. And with border controls weakening, all sorts of nasty things are leaking or sneaking across borders, from the laundered profits of drug kingpins to the weapons of terrorists to non-native species of insects that wreak ecological havoc in their new homes. The customs posts that once might have sufficed to separate the bads from the goods now have about as much effect as a feather in the path of a fire hose. The United States alone saw some 500 million people, 100 million vehicles, and $850 billion worth of imported merchandise passing its borders in 1999—and that is just what went through legally.[4] Economic integration, says this view, is not the road to a prosperous nirvana. Instead, in the words of one wary voice, it has "the potential for destroying society."[5]

Why do so many people so passionately believe that economic integration is humanity's great hope for the future, and why do so many others condemn it? Both outcomes are plausible. Neither, however, is inevitable. The problem is not with the fact of integration itself; the problem is with the manner in which that integration is being carried out. Economic integration is a messy, complex process that requires an enormous number of difficult policy choices. Making those policy choices well requires a wide-reaching debate about the broad goals to which economic integration should contribute and about what rules and processes will get us to those goals. That debate needs to encompass more than protestors in the streets shouting at "experts" who closet themselves in private and listen only to one another. The rules that govern economic integration—globalization—are not technical matters to be settled by small committees of mandarins. They are fundamental questions about prosperity, democracy, and global stability, about who will—and who will not—benefit.

Despite the confident (and frequently contradictory) assertions of a host of economists and policy mavens, no one really knows how to devise an economic system that is broadly beneficial and reasonably equitable. We clearly are not there yet. The current global economy is deeply unjust, and in some ways it is becoming more so. Eighty percent of the world's people live in countries that produce only 20 percent of the world's total income. A century ago, the average person in the richest country was only nine times richer than the average person in the poorest country. Now, the disparity is sixty to one.[6]

Given the wildly divergent paths the richer countries have followed in achieving economic development, the continuation of extreme inequality between rich and poor, and the succession of financial crises from Europe to Mexico to Asia to Russia to Brazil just in the 1990s, one might expect policy makers to evince a certain humility and openness to debate. Adherence to the notion of democratic discourse would require wide-ranging debate both within countries and at the global level.

Reality is far from these ideals. To date, the rules of the newly global economy are being made primarily by a relative handful. The resulting rules largely reflect the interests of the governments of a few rich countries, in particular the United States. This is no great surprise to students of power politics. The seven richest countries, known as the Group of Seven, or G-7, dominate the global economy, and the United States, which by itself accounts for more than one-fifth of global gross domestic product (GDP), is the 800-pound gorilla in economic negotiations.[7] Given that virtually all the world's largest multinational corporations are based in G-7 countries and that most foreign direct investment originates there, it is hardly surprising that those governments promote corporate freedom of action. But that leaves most other interests, including those of the vast majority of national governments, relegated to the sidelines.

Not only is the decision-making process exclusionary, it is often unduly secretive. When the International Monetary Fund (IMF) offers a loan to a developing country, until recently the terms were negotiated between the IMF and one or two ministries of the national government, usually the finance or planning ministry. There was little scope for public debate.[8] When the WTO considers whether one country's environmental legislation constitutes an illegal barrier to another country's exports, it does so in closed hearings using confidential documents.

This is an unsustainable approach to global economic decision making. A process that lets the few make the rules for the many stands a good chance of resulting in mistakes and provoking a backlash. The photogenic protests at the WTO meeting in Seattle in late 1999, the protests in Washington, D.C., against the IMF and the World Bank in April 2000, and those in Genoa against the G-7 in 2001 represent just the most dramatic component of a widespread set of often reasonable objections to economic rule making. But little real dialogue is occurring. Instead, the general response has been vituperative dismissal. And that is unfortunate because only if it is handled properly can global economic integration help to create and sustain a long boom.

Back to the Future?

This is not the first time the world has tried globalizing its economy; it is the second. The first began in the late 1800s and ended abruptly in 1914 with the outbreak of World War I. That earlier incarnation of globalization saw massive flows of goods and money across borders, just as is happening today. But the rules were quite different.

In those days, the global economy operated according to the simple, and fatally flawed, rules of a system called the gold standard. Under the gold standard, countries held gold in national reserves and issued currency only in a fixed ratio to their holdings of gold. The point of using gold to back currencies was to ensure confidence, the most fundamental element of a modern economy. Any economy that has gone beyond the primitive barter stage needs money to serve as a store of value and a medium of exchange. But money is not a physical, tangible thing with inherent value. Instead, it is quite literally a confidence game. Because we all agree that those little pieces of paper or metal have value, they do. If confidence in the value of money disappears, so does the value of money, which can lead to the kind of hyperinflation that brought Weimar Germany crashing down. Since the belief in the inherent value of gold was considered to be much stronger than the belief in the value of little pieces of paper, having a gold-backed currency meant having a "sound" currency, one that would not collapse at the first sign of financial difficulties.

Because the gold standard dictated a country's money supply, it also regulated how much international trade could occur. Ships carried gold back and forth across the Atlantic Ocean in payment for imports. If a country imported more than it exported, it would have to send out more gold than it received in payment, its money supply would contract, interest rates would rise, economic activity would slacken, and it would import less.[9]

The gold standard system was so simple in essence that a child could understand it. Indeed, one of the world's best-known children's stories may actually be a parable about monetary policy and the gold standard.[10] When L. Frank Baum wrote *The Wonderful Wizard of Oz* at the end of the 1800s, the American dollar was pegged to gold. In 1896, with the economy in bad shape and looking likely to get worse, the hard-fought presidential campaign between Democratic candidate William Jennings Bryan and Republican William McKinley hinged on whether the United States should start backing its currency with silver as well as gold. The "bimetallic" standard, argued the "free silver" advocates, was desperately needed to increase the money supply so that banks could lend, so that businesses, which were failing at an alarming rate, could hire (making a dent in an unemployment rate that stood at more than 14 percent), and so that farmers could refinance their crushing debt loads.[11]

What does all this have to do with the Land of Oz? Start with the name. Oz is the abbreviation for ounce, the unit in which gold and silver are measured. Dorothy is carried to Oz on the cyclone of the free silver movement and lands on the Wicked Witch of the East, who leaves behind only her *silver* shoes. (The moviemakers, uninterested in the monetary allegory of the story, apparently thought ruby slippers would look better on the screen.) Dorothy gets the slippers but has no idea of their power. Neither, apparently, do most denizens of Oz, except for the Wicked Witch of the West (who may represent the Ohio-based Republican McKinley, defender of the gold standard). She is desperate to get the silver slippers before Dorothy, or anyone else, recognizes their power. But Dorothy heads off down the Yellow Brick Road (the gold standard) to the Emerald City (Washington, D.C.) in the company of a scarecrow (small farmer) and a tin man (small business) in search of the solution to their problems. None of them realize that they have the answer—silver—with them all along.

Baum never said whether the story was actually intended as a monetary allegory. But the wizard truly was a fraud. The gold standard was a good system for inspiring confidence, but confidence is not the whole story for an international monetary system. There must also be means to pump up the money supply when recession threatens or to reduce it to bring inflation under control.[12] As economies grow, they need to have more money sloshing around to handle the growing number and size of transactions. But under the gold standard, growth in the money supply was limited by the quantity of gold that happened to be mined each year, so the money supply ended up depending on the vagaries of gold discoveries rather than on the needs of an economy. And on that score, the gold standard failed.

But it is not easy to figure out how else to run a global economy. The lack of an effective alternative became evident at the end of the 1920s. When stock markets fell, governments did all the wrong things. They frantically devalued their currencies, each trying to make its own the cheapest currency so that demand for exports would rise. This obviously could not work—it is not possible for everyone simultaneously to be cheaper than everyone else. Governments also raised tariffs sharply, trying to protect domestic business from outside competition. The resulting closure of markets had devastating effects around the world, helping to spark economic depression that contributed to the outbreak of World War II. By the mid-1940s, Europe lay in ruins and the world's economies were in tatters.

Determined to avoid the mistakes of the 1930s that had led to such catastrophe, the economically dominant United States (with much help from British economist John Maynard Keynes) set out to establish three intergovernmental organizations. The International Trade Organization was to serve as the forum in which governments would reduce trade barriers. The IMF was to control exchange rates, to avoid those catastrophic competitive devaluations. The World Bank was to provide capital to rebuild Europe's devastated economies. In all three cases, things did not work out exactly as planned.

Trade

Policy makers recognized that if they wanted to promote free trade, with its attendant economic efficiencies and broad societal gains, they needed global rules in place to overcome the domestic political pressures they would inevitably face. The gains from free trade may be considerable, but they are diffuse. Everyone gains, a bit, from lower costs that result from higher productivity. But some people, those employed in low-productivity industries that cannot hold their own against foreign competition, lose a lot—their jobs. The losers have far more incentive to mobilize politically in favor of protections than the winners do to mobilize in favor of openness.

Internal U.S. politics derailed the planned International Trade Organization, but the General Agreement on Tariffs and Trade (GATT) quickly filled the breach. It evolved from a treaty establishing rules and principles for periodic multilateral trade negotiations into something resembling an international organization, with its own secretariat and director-general to oversee the implementation of GATT rules.[13] From 1947 until the formation of the World Trade Organization in 1994, GATT provided the forum for eight rounds of multilateral trade negotiations aimed at reducing tariffs, quotas, and other barriers to trade.

The first few rounds of GATT negotiations, held in the 1950s and 1960s, were relatively straightforward, involving some twenty to thirty major economies and lasting less than a year each. In those early rounds, the task was clear—to lower tariffs on manufactured goods. These rounds mostly liberalized trade among the rich countries, not between rich and poor. This is because GATT depended on reciprocal lifting of barriers, and poor countries had little to offer to entice the rich into specific bargains.

Over time, however, the number of countries participating and the range of products covered under the negotiations soared. By the 1980s, a hundred or so countries were involved in negotiations that covered trade worth hundreds of billions of dollars.[14] The subject was becoming far more complex. Governments that could no longer use tariffs to protect their domestic constituencies were devising a remarkable range of "nontariff barriers"—clever ploys such as quotas and government procurement policies that could quite effectively discriminate against imports or promote exports. At one point, for example, France reacted to a flood of Japanese videocassette recorders (VCRs) by requiring that all shipments go through a customs post in Poitiers, hundreds of miles from their ports of arrival—a truly peculiar bout of protectionism, given that, as the *Economist* reported, "France had no VCR industry to protect; its government simply found all those imports annoying."[15] Japan banned rice imports on the grounds that foreign-grown rice would upset Japanese stomachs.

But not all nontariff barriers were protectionist—that is, aimed at keeping out foreign competition. They included such measures as health and safety standards established in response to domestic demands for noneconomic quality-of-life improvements. These standards could not simply be eliminated, but they differed so widely from one country to another that they had the effect of impeding trade. At the same time, under intense pressure from the United States, GATT negotiators began trying to free up trade in politically sensitive and highly protected agricultural products and in services, involving a hugely increased number of economic actors, and began trying to deal with thorny issues of intellectual property rights.

The final set of GATT negotiations (called the Uruguay Round, after the location of the opening session), originally scheduled to last from 1987 to 1990, dragged on for year after weary year. Agreement was finally—barely— reached in December 1993, making some progress toward liberalization of agriculture and services and establishing that highly controversial intellectual property regime discussed in chapter 5.[16] And GATT members agreed to create a permanent World Trade Organization with a dispute settlement mechanism that could rule decisively on whether member governments were complying with the rules. The WTO has some 140 member countries, with more lined up at the door.

The creation of the WTO did not end controversies over trade. Instead, trade policy is becoming an ever more fierce battleground. Contending camps readily wrap themselves in self-righteous proclamations of moral superiority.

The most powerful weapon of the pro–free traders is a logically compelling idea: comparative advantage, which holds that all countries benefit from free trade because trade allows each country to specialize. Some countries have lots of workers but not a lot of capital and therefore are relatively more efficient at making widgets that require lots of labor but not capital. Rich countries with plenty of money but labor shortages should make other products, those that require lots of capital but not so much labor. If everybody does this and then trades, each country will be better off because all countries will be producing as efficiently as possible and everyone will end up with the maximum number of products at the lowest cost. Thus, economists often argue, governments should make trade as easy as possible, keeping barriers to a minimum.

So why were all those people in the streets of Seattle trying to stop the WTO's member governments from launching another round of trade negotiations? One big contingent was labor, which does not like agreements that threaten existing jobs. But many other protestors favored reasonably free trade. They just did not think that was what was being negotiated.

If comparative advantage explained trade, most trade should take place between countries that are capital-abundant and labor-short (characteristic of the world's rich countries) and those that are capital-poor and labor-abundant (the poor countries). That would lead to convergence of wages—workers around the world with similar skills and productivity would receive similar wages—which is exactly why that kind of trade is still relatively restricted. The rich countries impose high tariffs and other protectionist measures on everything from textiles to sugar from poor countries because allowing truly free trade would be too painful to many domestic labor and business groups that could not compete with cheaper producers overseas. Although it is theoretically possible in rich countries for the winners from trade to compensate domestic losers through progressive taxation and redistribution using the gains from trade enjoyed by consumers as a whole, this is practically and politically difficult to do. It is easier to keep the trade barriers up.

Although those barriers are coming down to some extent, at present most trade takes place within the rarefied confines of the triad made up of North America, western Europe, and Japan, all of which are by global standards capital-abundant and labor-short. It turns out that comparative advantage is only one reason countries engage in trade. Another is economies of scale.[17] When it is cheaper to make a product by the million than by the dozen, it makes sense for a company to increase the size of its market by selling overseas as well as at home. That creates an industry with a few big producers rather than many small ones, exactly the pattern of trade increasingly seen among the rich countries. This kind of trade also benefits consumers, economists say, because it enables companies to make their products efficiently, and that keeps prices down.

But those big companies are almost all based in the rich countries, which are accustomed to working out trade deals among themselves, with everyone else getting only the chance to sign on to the package deal. Only gradually are negotiations beginning to involve the broader WTO membership. At Seattle, delegates from developing countries contended that the rich countries were "keeping us like animals, keeping us out in the cold and telling us nothing," in the words of Egyptian trade negotiator Munir Zahran.[18] When President Bill Clinton made a speech suggesting that future trade agreements might include labor standards, developing countries were furious at what they perceived as a direct attack on their comparative advantage in trade—cheap labor. And remember that lone Haitian trade representative mentioned in chapter 4? As long as the world remains inequitable, so will trade negotiations.

Moreover, as economies become ever more deeply integrated, trade rules can no longer be just about trade. It has stopped making sense to think of international trade as a distinct issue that can be dealt with separately from others. Yet that isolation is exactly what the current system for regulating trade requires. The WTO's mandate and procedures are meant to promote free trade, not to balance among competing concerns. And there are no equivalent international institutions standing up for those competing global values. That is why networks of nongovernmental organizations (NGOs) are demanding that environment, labor practices, and human rights considerations be included within the WTO itself. They claim that previous rounds have sacrificed environmental and safety standards and lowered workers' wages.[19] They want a place at the bargaining table to ensure that does not happen again. And to make sure they get it, or at least that they are not ignored, they have organized public opposition to trade liberalization in a range of countries around the world, and they are demanding that the negotiations be transparent so deals cannot be cut in secret.

The current system of trade rule making elevates concerns about the efficiency gains from trade above all others, and it has the muscle to make its priorities stick. Unlike GATT, the WTO can authorize members to impose sanctions on other members that refuse to abide by WTO verdicts in trade disputes. Those verdicts are based on the rules laid down in a series of international trade agreements, including GATT itself and the Uruguay Round accords. The WTO dispute resolution procedure puts three trade experts on a panel to adjudicate trade disputes among member governments. If the panel decides that a country is engaging in a practice that contravenes the rules, that country must choose between being hit with trade sanctions or changing its practice.

This sounds straightforward, but the application decidedly is not. Which practices actually contravene the rules, and who decides, have proved to be highly problematic issues. One famous dispute exemplified the fears that WTO decisions would put trade liberalization ahead of all other concerns.[20] In the late 1980s, the United States began requiring its domestic shrimp industry to use a simple metal grid called a turtle excluder device to keep endangered sea turtles from being entangled and killed in shrimp trawler nets. The problem was serious—sea turtles are threatened with extinction, and 100,000 adult turtles were being killed each year around the world. But when the United States required foreign shrimp trawlers to use the same device if they wanted to sell shrimp in U.S. markets, four Asian countries complained to the WTO that this constituted an unfair trade practice—and won.

The initial WTO ruling was truly appalling. On April 6, 1998, a WTO dispute settlement panel ruled that the U.S. requirement violated the terms of GATT. The panel ruled that *any* unilateral environmental regulation that restricted trade constituted unjustifiable discrimination because such regulations violate rules that allow countries to keep out only harmful products.[21] Countries are not supposed to ban imports on the basis of the way those products are made. The ruling seemed to be based on a fear that allowing any distinctions based on method of production would allow countries to develop all sorts of new barriers to trade on the basis of environmental claims or other concerns, such as labor standards.

The rejection of any possibility of imposing production process requirements on imports ignores the basic nature of environmental and social policy making. Those policies are *about* production processes. To argue that countries must accept imports irrespective of the process by which they are made is to force countries to reward foreign practices that may damage the environment on which we all depend, even if they have banned those practices at home.

Fortunately, the story does not end there. The United States appealed the ruling to the WTO appellate body, which also ruled against the United States—but for very different reasons. It flatly rejected the original panel's reasoning, arguing instead that there is no reason to assume in advance that environmental restrictions on imports are unjustifiable. GATT does allow states to have nontariff barriers such as environmental regulations on imports if "necessary to protect human, animal, or plant life or health" or if the regulations relate to "the conservation of exhaustible natural resources." The regulations just have to be nondiscriminatory, applying equally to domestic and foreign producers. The appellate body also reprimanded the panel for refusing to allow NGOs to submit briefs directly, pointing out that WTO panels can accept whatever submissions they believe would be helpful to their analysis. It then found that endangered species are certainly included in the "exhaustible natural resources" that GATT allows its signatories to protect.

So why did the WTO appellate body rule against the law? The problem, it found, was not with *what* the United States had tried to do but with *how* the United States had tried to do it. It had required all other countries not merely to protect sea turtles but to do so by the methods dictated by the United States. It had made few efforts to reach multilateral agreements on the subject with other countries. It had not made use of existing forums to raise the issue, and it had not become a party to several multilateral treaties that aimed to protect turtles and other endangered species. It insisted that other countries put turtle excluder devices on *all* their shrimping vessels, not just the ones whose catch was sold in the United States. Its certification process for determining whether countries complied with this requirement relied on bureaucratic judgments not subject to appellate review. And it had given some countries three years to install the devices but others (including the four Asian states that filed the complaint) only four months. All this, ruled the WTO body, amounted to unjustifiable and arbitrary discrimination, illegal under trade rules.[22]

This decision still assumes that promotion of free trade deserves at least equal footing with prevention of extinction of a species, an assumption many people would hotly dispute. After all, if countries take the time to comply with all the procedural niceties, by the time they reach agreement, the species in question may already be gone for good. But it does open the door to a broader range of considerations in WTO dispute resolution procedures in the environmental arena. And the decision raises valid points about what kinds of considerations should go into global policy making. Poor countries argue, with substantial justification, that if the rich care so much about environmental public goods, then the rich should help the poor defray the costs of making the transition from environmentally destructive to more environmentally benign production methods.

Other issues may be more intractable. Labor groups and human rights advocates in the rich countries claim that their hard-fought improvements in working conditions are threatened by the loss of jobs to workers in countries that maintain lower standards and that often do not permit workers to unionize. They demand that global labor standards be enforced through the WTO, a prospect that horrifies governments of developing countries, which see their cheap labor supply as their major competitive edge. It is hard to tell whether labor groups from poor countries agree with their governments' assertions, since workers in many poor countries lack the right to organize independently and speak out freely. The standards themselves already exist. They were negotiated through the International Labor Organization (ILO), a body representing governments, employers, and workers set up after World War I, when the great threat to economic prosperity was seen to be labor unrest. The WTO and most governments argue that labor issues are properly still the province of the ILO. Workers' rights advocates have no interest in allowing their concerns to be sidelined to the toothless ILO when the real power lies with the WTO.[23]

Finance

Global finance sounds—and in its details is—intimidatingly complex, but the basics are simple. At the heart of capitalism is the need for sources of capital—that is, money. The system works when people can invest some of their money in businesses that can use it to make profitable goods and services.[24] The financial system has to be regulated so that people have confidence in the banks, mutual funds, and stock markets and are willing to put their money there. Otherwise, people will stuff their mattresses with cash and the capitalist system will grind to a halt. But for capitalism to work well, the financial system also has to be flexible and efficient, with firms competing to provide the best returns on capital. Thus, regulators are always trying to strike a balance between ensuring safety and creating the right incentives for firms to achieve the desired efficiency and flexibility.

In contrast to trade, capital flows remained relatively restricted until recently. World War II led to tight government controls on securities markets and banking systems as governments directed credit in order to channel financial resources to where they would do the most good for the war effort. "What was bequeathed by the War," economist Barry Eichengreen noted, "was thus not just controls on international financial transactions but tightly regulated domestic financial markets which made feasible effective enforcement of those controls on international financial flows."[25]

After World War II, the world experimented with variants on the gold standard, trying to find ways to fix exchange rates to avoid the competitive devaluations that had so badly undermined the world financial system in the 1930s. Under the system devised at the famous Bretton Woods Conference in 1944, the U.S. dollar was pegged to gold and other currencies were pegged to the dollar. But that system could work only as long as countries imposed tight restrictions on the amounts of currency that could cross their borders in either direction. Without those restrictions, speculators could buy or sell large quantities of a country's currency, forcing the government to choose between buying or selling large quantities of foreign exchange to defend the pegged exchange rate or changing the value of the currency. The Bretton Woods conferees established the International Monetary Fund to monitor and guide any adjustments of exchange rates.

The pegged system fell apart in turn in the early 1970s, when inflation drove the United States off the gold standard.[26] Since then, countries have tried all sorts of strategies to ensure confidence in the value of their currencies, such as pegging them to strong currencies such as the dollar. Argentina did this to conquer persistent hyperinflation until its ongoing fiscal problems made the peg too expensive to maintain. More and more, however, currencies are floating freely as the costs of trying to defend a fixed value for a currency prove unbearable in an era when capital is allowed to go wherever it wants.[27]

All the rich countries and a growing number of developing ones have deregulated their financial markets substantially, agreeing that markets are better than governments at figuring out where capital should go. From domestic financial liberalization flowed international liberalization. Once those with capital, such as banks and investors, are free to do as they please domestically, it is virtually impossible to prevent them from acting internationally as well, particularly in the era of advanced information and communications technologies.[28]

As a result, very large amounts of money now flow across national borders, primarily passing through private, rather than government, hands. Anyone with money to invest can put it anywhere in the world. The fluid transfer of funds across national borders is the single most dramatic element in global economic integration. Securities markets, banks, and insurance companies all operate increasingly in cyberspace, instantaneously anywhere. Capital floods across borders at a breathtaking pace in a bewildering variety of forms—more than $1.5 trillion in foreign exchange transactions every day. Capital is increasingly concentrated in large multinational corporations and in pension funds, mutual funds, and insurance companies, whose professional managers have proved quite willing to cross borders in search of better returns.[29]

That has advantages in that the capital concentrated in the handful of highly industrialized countries can readily flow to other countries, presumably to be put to its most efficient possible use. But it causes problems, too, sometimes severe ones. For one thing, what is most efficient from an investor's perspective—the highest possible rate of short-term financial return—is not necessarily the best use of resources for a country's long-term development. Moreover, this system of freewheeling capital flows is prone to very high levels of volatility—waves of capital flooding in and out unpredictably. In the last two decades of the twentieth century, some 100 countries experienced financial crises, and such crises are becoming both more frequent and more harsh.[30]

The biggest problem lies with short-term capital flows, which create huge problems for people who in no way benefit from, or have any voice in, capital market transactions. Investors know that there is no reliable international financial architecture to support the increasingly globalized economy, so they are easily spooked when markets in a country or region appear to be turning downward or even appear likely to do so. And because much capital is held in the form of short-term investments or liquid instruments, crises of confidence are easily triggered. In those crises, large numbers of foreign investors quickly pull their money out of a country, not because there is suddenly something wrong with that country but because it seems likely that everyone else will pull out their money, thus undermining the national economy.

Robert Solow, a Nobel laureate in economics, explained what can happen:

> In a world characterized by easy mobility of capital and the existence of enormous pools of liquid funds willing to go anywhere, anytime, in search of a few basis points of advantage, speculative bubbles can easily form and burst. Herd behavior on this scale can easily overwhelm national regulatory institutions, and may be more than a match for some international institutions. The result can easily be instability. Moderate amounts of speculation are often stabilizing: if interest rates are higher here than there, funds will flow from there to here, pushing down the yields here and raising them there. On a larger scale and at higher speeds, however, overshooting in one direction can turn into panic flows in the opposite direction, and then somewhere else, until whatever orderliness there is crumbles. . . . When Russian bonds collapsed in value, the lenders were subject to margin calls; they naturally sold off the least promising assets they had, which turned out to be Brazilian paper; so the panic was transferred to Brazil.[31]

That volatility has nasty consequences for ordinary people, especially people in poor countries. When foreign investors decide to pull their money out, countries can find themselves financially crippled, pressured to raise interest rates to astronomic levels to lure foreign investors back. If they fail to raise those rates, the IMF will not provide the loans they need to tide them over. But with interest rates so high, local businesses cannot afford to borrow to finance expansion, and the whole national economy plunges into recession, or worse.

This happens only to poor countries. When rich countries find themselves in similar difficulties, they are free to cut rather than raise interest rates to boost their economies because they are not so desperate to attract foreign capital or IMF loans. Only poor countries face pressures to adopt austerity policies to reassure foreign investors that they have the capacity to pay their debts. Since poor countries are far less likely to have social safety nets such as unemployment insurance to protect their most vulnerable citizens, the ultimate effects of financial volatility can be truly devastating for workers and their families.

The downsides of financial globalization showed clearly in the aftermath of the Asian financial crisis, as revealed in a series of reports from the Asian Development Bank. Korean unemployment tripled from 1997 to 1999, worsened by the conditions of the IMF emergency bailout, which initially required very high interest rates that sparked mass bankruptcies.[32] Indonesia suffered most, with the poverty rate nearly doubling, food prices rising sharply (exacerbated by drought), and school fees escalating beyond many family budgets.[33]

And it is not over yet. Although the headlines have cheered Asia's rapid recovery, the picture is actually quite mixed. In April 2000, the Asian Development Bank released another report. It showed what on the surface was a robust economic recovery, with GDP growth averaging 6.2 percent across the region in 1999 and expected to continue at the same pace in 2000. Foreign capital was flooding back in, raising stock market values by more than 25 percent in dollar terms.[34] But there are more people living in poverty in the region today than there were in the mid-1990s, at least 10 million more.[35] Indonesia remains a basket case.

Even if unrestricted capital flows were an unambiguous good and volatility could be somehow managed and contained, most people would not benefit from them. The degree and consequences of economic integration are, to put it mildly, uneven. If you are reading this, you are, by global standards, wealthy and well educated, and almost certainly tied relatively tightly to world markets. Most people are not. In fact, almost half [36] the world's population gets by on an income of less than two dollars per day. [37] Both economic growth and economic integration have occurred primarily among the already rich triad of North America, western Europe, and Japan. Fewer than twenty developing countries, such as Taiwan, Korea, and Brazil, have large trade and capital flows.

But such countries as El Salvador, Haiti, and most African nations received essentially none of that newly available investment capital. [38] (The trade story is similar—trade accounted for 37.4 percent of the economies of the rich countries in 1999 but only about 8 percent of the economies of the low-income countries that year. [39]) Similar stories apply in the cases of gross private capital flows and gross foreign direct investment—the rich countries account for the lion's share of economic integration. So to the degree that capital flows are desirable because they provide funds for productive investment, most countries have yet to benefit. [40]

Economic Development and Democracy

The third element of the postwar economic order, the World Bank, found its mission changing almost as soon as it was created. Born to rebuild Europe, it was quickly overshadowed by the Marshall Plan. But it soon found a new raison d'être—providing assistance to the huge numbers of countries seizing independence from their former European colonial masters. Most were poor, badly in need of foreign capital at a time when such capital was largely tied up inside the borders of rich countries. The World Bank stepped in to fill the gap.

The next several decades saw waves of development fashions come and go as the World Bank and others struggled to figure out how to turn poor countries into rich ones. But in the intervening decades, only a few, mostly Asian, countries have seen sustained economic growth. And when private capital markets grew to dwarf World Bank funds, the new fashion became one of figuring out what poor countries could do to attract some of those newly available moneys.

In the late 1980s, a broad consensus emerged, or at least received a label. The Washington Consensus (so tagged by economist John Williamson in

1989) purported to lay out a set of ten propositions for the steps poor countries and those "in transition" from Soviet-style central planning should follow to become richer. The rules called on countries to eliminate all sorts of barriers (to trade, financial flows, and competition) and to reform government practices regarding collection and expenditure of revenues.[41] As labels are wont to do, the term quickly took on a life of its own, standing as shorthand for getting the government out of the way of market forces and lowering barriers to exchange, both within a country and across its borders.

Some governments became true believers in pro-market reforms. Laggards were strongly pressured by the IMF and the World Bank, which made adoption of such reforms a condition of their new "structural adjustment" loans—loans to help countries in crisis get their internal economic houses in order. Because the IMF and the World Bank assumed they knew what proper internal economic structures should look like, the loans came with a wide range of conditions attached. Those conditions routinely required countries to cut public spending, which usually led to substantial decreases in education, health, and other social service budgets. The conditions also called for reduction or elimination of subsidies on everything from basic foods to gasoline. The IMF and the World Bank were often correct that such subsidies, intended to help the poor, more often benefited those better off, but their abrupt cutoff sparked widespread social unrest. The conditions also tended to demand liberalization—state-owned industries had to be sold to the private sector, interest rates raised to draw foreign investment, barriers to foreign ownership lowered, and currencies devalued to make exports more competitive. All were eminently sensible policies under some circumstances. Interest rates had often been kept artificially low, currencies were often overvalued, and protected domestic industries were often woefully inefficient. But the structural adjustment policies paid too little attention to the specific conditions prevailing in individual countries. In some cases, they demanded changes that were simply politically impossible to sustain, and in others they imposed unnecessary hardship.

Not surprisingly, the often simplistic application of pro-market reforms failed to achieve widespread, equitable, and sustainable growth. The relatively easy steps of lowering barriers to trade and financial flows took place in countries that were utterly incapable of regulating their banks, stock markets, or privatization programs. The national systems of regulation that allow confidence in national financial institutions and provide social safety nets for the losers in the economic game do not have enough in the way of international counterparts to regulate, stabilize, and legitimize what markets do, and poor countries almost by definition are short on the necessary institutional infrastructure to do the job themselves. Countries that have never had much in the way of stock markets are setting them up to provide a new means of corporate financing in which international investors can participate, for example. However, effective regulation of stock markets is a difficult task, one that countries such as the United States have spent decades attempting, and failing, to perfect. The result is often a highly concentrated stock market plagued by rampant insider trading and usurious commission fees.

Over the course of the 1990s, new preconditions for economic success kept being discovered and added to the original set—strengthening government institutions, increasing the domestic savings rate, fighting corruption, fostering transparency of both markets and governments, strengthening the rule of law. If poor (and middle-income) countries need to be efficient, well-run, incorrupt, transparent, and able to draw on significant domestic savings in order to make economic development happen, then their prospects would seem hopeless. Few of the world's rich countries fully measure up to these standards. The truth is, of course, that countries that are now rich have followed a wide range of paths to become so. Some, like the United States, engaged in massive environmental despoliation, savagely oppressed large parts of their population, cheerfully repudiated foreign debts, endured periods of massive corruption, and most emphatically maintained high trade barriers and restrictions on capital flows whenever they felt so inclined.

The mandarins who now so confidently prescribe various nostrums agree only on what fails—government control of the economy—not on what works. The debate over how poor countries should proceed remains very much alive.[42] Should all countries open up to unlimited financial and trade flows to benefit from access to capital, technology, and ideas, or should they reimpose controls to protect themselves from the devastating volatility that can wreak havoc on a society? When financial crisis does strike, as it did so often in the 1990s in so many countries, should governments raise interest rates to lure foreign capital back, even at the cost of throwing their economies into recession or depression? Should the responsibility for adapting to globalization lie with individual governments, or can the global financial system as a whole be made more stable?

In short, the growing degree of economic integration is no accident. It results from deliberate government decisions to lower the barriers that used to keep capital and products pretty well locked up within national borders. In response to the painful experience of the 1930s and 1940s, the major Western economies spent the last several decades of the twentieth century reducing barriers to trade. Recently, they have also dropped barriers to financial flows, allowing foreigners to buy and sell their currencies and invest in their stock markets. And as seen in chapter 5, production of goods and services also has globalized as countries that formerly mistrusted multinational corporations, seeing them as exploitative agents of neo-imperialism, have come to see them instead as, at least potentially, providers of needed capital, jobs, technology, and managerial know-how. In the last two decades of the century, the collapse of the Soviet communist model and the failures of closed economies in Latin America, in contrast with the striking economic successes of East Asia, have led most governments to conclude that open market systems will lead to greater prosperity than systems based on barriers to international exchange. Scores of countries decided to lower tariff barriers and deregulate their financial systems. Governments that showed signs of reluctance found themselves prodded along by the IMF and the United States.

Private capital flows between countries now far outweigh the foreign exchange reserves available to governments. Trade in goods and services is growing faster than the global economy as a whole, accounting for more than $4 trillion per year in a global economy of some $30 trillion.[43] Huge pools of capital are looking for somewhere to go, and those who control those pools prefer to go to countries that do not have controls on capital flows. A growing number of companies operate in several countries at once. All this, combined with still-present memories of the disastrous political and economic consequences of closure in the 1930s, will probably keep the pressures toward economic openness going for quite a while.

Making It Work Better

This increasingly integrated global economy, tied together by trade, financial flows, and production processes that cross borders, is improving the efficiency of investment and production in many places. That increases overall economic wealth. Globally, per capita gross national product (GNP) rose in the 1990s. But that blanket statement hides vast inequities and injustices and sheer human suffering. And creating a system that can do better is no easy task.

It is not clear that the same rules should apply to countries in wildly different stages of economic development. Some societies are more able and willing than others to pay for higher levels of environmental protection, unemployment benefits, and other societal goods that markets do not provide. Rules that make sense to Americans living on an annual income of $29,240 may make no sense to Indians living on $440 per year, not to mention Ethiopians living on $100 per year.[44] The idea of children working eight or ten hours each day to help feed their families may seem repugnant to the rich but simple necessity to the poor. As economic integration progresses, it becomes ever harder to determine what is a society's legitimate demand to set standards on social and environmental issues according to its own needs and preferences and what is merely a disguised barrier to trade.

The inequities in the system make it difficult to come up with solutions that are economically and politically sustainable. The rules are being made overwhelmingly by the biggest beneficiaries—the richer segments of the population of the United States, the members of the European Union, and Japan—and by the international financial institutions they dominate. They may be correct in their claim that the economic efficiency they are promoting could help everyone in the long run by increasing aggregate wealth. But so far the rules have not done much to protect the vulnerable from the costs of rapid change. This intense focus on economic efficiency ignores the reality that efficiency is not a goal. It is a means of enabling societies to use resources productively in the pursuit of goals. And some of those goals— long-term social justice and environmental sustainability—may conflict with short-term maximization of economic efficiency.

The unrepresentative process of global economic decision making threatens to trigger a backlash from those not represented. The trend toward greater integration is strong, but it is not irreversible. Although economic globalization results partly from technology—transportation and communications are now so cheap and easy that the economic rewards from trade and financial flows are higher than ever—integration takes place only to the degree that governments allow. Tariffs still exist. So do fixed exchange rates and controls on capital flows. Barriers may be harder to maintain, but if governments decide that the political or social costs of globalization outweigh the benefits, they could reinstitute controls. Malaysia did, as a temporary response to the Asian financial crisis of the 1990s. On trade, WTO member governments have agreed in principle on a new set of negotiations intended in part to overcome some of the existing trade inequities, but difficulties in those negotiations, along with recent protectionist moves on steel, agriculture, and timber by the United States, have raised doubts about whether much can be accomplished.

In a sense, we have been here before. Once the industrial revolution got under way in the mid-nineteenth century, trade and capital flows skyrocketed. In the period 1870–1914, those flows actually may have constituted a larger share of world economic activity than they do today.[45] But that historical experience does not give great cause for complacency about how well a nationally organized humanity can deal with a globally organized economy. The period 1870–1914 was followed not by a sustained period of global prosperity but by World War I, the creation of the Soviet empire, the Great Depression, and World War II.

Although some lessons have been learned from earlier mistakes, new pressures make management of economic integration even more difficult this time around. Trade and foreign direct investment cover a much broader range of the economy than was the case a hundred years ago, creating international competition where it did not previously exist.[46] Corporations operate transnationally to a degree not seen before, creating real trouble for governments trying to tax and regulate. Governments are now expected to protect their vulnerable citizens from the effects of economic volatility, and their failure to do so can create significant social unrest. Perhaps most important, the costs of getting it wrong are higher than ever. If economic breakdown could spark global depression and global warfare in the 1930s, what might it lead to in the far better armed and more crowded world of the early twenty-first century?

The mandarins say that is exactly why we need them to make the economic rules that can protect us all from catastrophe. But such a technocratic approach ignores the inherently political nature of the subject. There are real trade-offs to be made on everything from how much protection patents will receive to which environmental regulations will be struck down. And the rules governing those trade-offs will be effective only if they are both appropriately designed and seen as legitimate. Governments can enforce rules only if most people are willing to obey them, not if most people are looking to flout or overturn them. The rules will be neither well designed nor seen as legitimate if they are made behind closed doors by small cabals and then handed down from on high. As integration penetrates ever deeper behind national borders, a much broader, more open system of decision making is necessary. But how can that be brought about?

Opening Up

Bono has one answer. The renowned Irish rock star, lead singer of the band U2, has transformed himself into a policy wonk of no mean accomplishment. He dedicates much of his time to the campaign against poor-country debt. Scores of countries owe so much money to foreign creditors (both to private companies and to aid agencies and international institutions) that their required payments often exceed the sum total of new capital coming in. Often, the governments that incurred that debt were dictatorships—sometimes kleptocracies that spirited the funds out of the country—but even when the governments change, the debts remain. Bono thinks that much of that debt should be canceled. And he has a great deal of company in a transnational civil society network called Jubilee 2000. Bono's is the famous face, but it has taken the combined efforts of thousands of people in many countries, working through Jubilee 2000, to force the rich countries and the international financial institutions to pay serious attention to the world's highly indebted poor countries. The debts are obviously unpayable, but until Jubilee 2000 came along in the 1990s, few among the economic policy–making elite showed much interest in finding ways to relieve the burden.

Jubilee 2000 is just one of many civil society networks trying to force open the global economic decision-making process. In the late 1990s, a transnational coalition helped to kill international negotiations on the proposed Multilateral Agreement on Investment, an agreement that the coalition argued would protect the interests of investors over those of just about everyone else. The IMF is only beginning to attract a network of activists who do more than protest in the streets, but the World Bank has been surrounded by NGO coalitions demanding change since the early 1980s. Those coalitions have come at the World Bank from several directions. They include rich-country environmentalists outraged by the environmental destructiveness of many Bank-funded projects such as dams and roads, representatives of poor-country communities involuntarily resettled from lands made uninhabitable by those projects (and often dumped in new places that offered no prospect of livability), and proponents for indigenous peoples whose cultures and livelihoods were rapidly disappearing. Collectively, they have pushed the World Bank to adopt the disclosure policy described in chapter 4, to get serious about following its own environmental and human rights standards, and to establish a procedure to allow those affected by a Bank-funded project to complain directly to the World Bank.

As in the case of Jubilee 2000, many of the networks involve NGOs based in rich countries trying to collaborate with people in poor countries. Some of the American groups that led the Seattle protest worked for months in advance with counterparts in other countries, including Canada, India, France, Indonesia, Malaysia, Thailand, Japan, the United Kingdom, the Netherlands, Germany, Argentina, and Ecuador. What these networks represent is more than an inconvenience for business as usual. They are the first stirrings of a badly needed set of mechanisms for feedback and accountability.

But the networks by themselves can be only one part of the equation for imposing accountability and broadening the range of voices involved in economic decision making. The other factor will have to be a much greater degree of transparency. Citizens have a right to know about government economic plans and performance, and governments do not escape that obligation by delegating their authority to intergovernmental organizations. Consumers and investors have a right to know about the products they buy (including the processes by which those products are made) and about the companies they invest in. As economies cross borders, so do those rights. And everyone who is affected by the decisions of intergovernmental organizations such as the IMF, the World Bank, and the WTO has a right to know what decisions are being made, by whom, and with what consequences.

The reasonableness of expecting governments, corporations, and even intergovernmental organizations to let people know what they are up to seems widely accepted, even acclaimed. The World Trade Organization's Web site is full of references to the importance of transparency in the promotion of free trade, and its director-general, Mike Moore, said in May 2000: "We are trying to make the WTO's work even more accessible to the man and woman in the street. . . . We welcome public scrutiny. We have nothing to hide."[47]

Following the Asian financial crisis of the late 1990s, an array of global policy makers and pundits touted transparency as never before.[48] According to this new conventional wisdom, the trouble arose because secretive "crony capitalism," misleading government reports, and lack of adequate corporate financial disclosure left foreign investors unable to assess the true quality and risk of their investments. All sorts of new standards for corporate and government disclosures have popped up in recent years. The IMF has developed data dissemination standards specifying what economic performance and policy data governments should make publicly available and how often, how widely, and by what processes. Dozens of countries now provide such data on the IMF's Web site.

The trend may be toward greater transparency, but the rhetoric remains far stronger than the reality. That is because the incentives to hide economic information remain powerful. Citizens who know how the economy is actually doing and what government officials are doing about it might be tempted to demand changes in those policies—or in the officials. The World Bank and the IMF have become powerful promoters of the principle of transparency, but their own disclosure policies, as seen in chapter 4, leave much to be desired.[49]

Achieving the degree of transparency needed for informed widespread participation in the debate over economic globalization will be no easy task, but it is clearly possible. And it is essential. Secretive decision making by small groups of elites cannot and should not continue. Without broad and informed participation, policy decisions will fail to incorporate essential perspectives and will lack the legitimacy that only a public voice can bring. Good public policy, in economics as in other issue areas, has to be truly public.

8

Environment

If you want to think about what Mother Nature might have in store for us, consider the fate of Easter Island.[1] Easter Island is about as close as the world comes to a self-contained ecosystem. The nearest habitable island is 1,400 miles away, and South America lies more than 2,000 miles to the east. It should be an environmental Eden, given its subtropical location and fertile volcanic soil. And once, apparently, it was. Pollen from sediment samples reveals that for some 30,000 years, a thick forest covered the island, with shrubs, herbs, ferns, and grasses underneath. The lack of predators had made the island into a haven for seabirds of at least twenty-five nesting species, probably the richest breeding site in the Pacific Ocean.

When the first settlers canoed over from Polynesia perhaps 1,600 years ago, Easter Island must have seemed paradise indeed. The trees provided a source of rope, edible nuts, and sap that could be made into sugar or syrup. Big trees made it possible to build big canoes, go out to sea, and hunt the giant porpoises that were the only available large-animal source of meat, and the seabirds provided a readily available supplement. The soil would have supported a variety of crops.

So the settlers did what anyone would do. They prospered, multiplied, and created a complex civilization, with rival clans jockeying for status. That jockeying for status culminated in the giant stone statues that have made the island famous. These statues were as much as sixty-five feet tall, weighed as much as 270 tons, and were often transported several miles from where they were carved, despite the absence of either wheeled vehicles or beasts of burden.

Given the original abundance of natural resources, the creation of the statues is no great mystery, although it remains an impressive accomplishment. It would have required at most a few hundred people to load the statues onto wooden sleds and drag them from the quarries to their final sites, assuming abundant supplies of rope and wood were available. Archaeological sites suggest there was a population of 7,000 on the island, or possibly two or three times that number, ample for the task if readily available food supplies permitted sufficient spare time.

But sometime around A.D. 1500, the settlers stopped making statues. By the time the first European explorer dropped by, on Easter Sunday (hence the island's name) in 1722, the island was a wasteland, with no tall trees, few birds other than chickens, and almost none of the small trees from whose fibers rope could be made. With the forest gone, islanders could no longer go out to sea and hunt porpoises because there were no more big trees from which to carve seaworthy canoes. Deforestation led to soil erosion and degradation, so crop yields fell. As surplus food disappeared, so did the complex social structure and centralized government, replaced by a warrior class. The population had crashed to some 2,000 by the time Europeans found the island, and the survivors were living in caves for protection from one another. Rival groups began toppling one another's statues, and by 1864 none were left standing.

Is this our future? It could be. Biogeographer and Pulitzer Prize–winning author Jared Diamond, who wrote the article from which the above description was drawn, concludes his essay by pointing to disturbing parallels:

> Easter Island is Earth writ small. Today, again, a rising population confronts shrinking resources. We too have no emigration valve, because all human societies are linked by international transport, and we can no more escape into space than the Easter Islanders could flee into the ocean. If we continue to follow our present course, we shall have exhausted the world's major fisheries, tropical rain forests, fossil fuels, and much of our soil in the next few decades. If mere thousands of Easter Islanders with only stone tools and their own muscle power sufficed to destroy their society, how can billions of people with metal tools and machine power fail to do worse?

But, as Diamond points out, there is one crucial difference between us and the Easter Islanders. We know what happened to them. We can use that knowledge and all the advantages of a technologically sophisticated and literate civilization to head down a very different path. People have done so before, using technological and political innovations to fend off Malthusian predictions of imminent disaster. India and China no longer endure massive famines, thanks to higher-yielding crops combined with new agricultural techniques. And environmental degradation can sometimes be reversed, given sufficient time, money, and determination. The Cuyahoga River in Cleveland, Ohio, which caught fire in 1969, has since become the center of a thriving riverfront restaurant district and is used for boating.

Unfortunately, that the Easter Island outcome can be avoided does not mean that all will necessarily turn out well. No one really knows whether the guide to the future should be the continued failure of Malthusian fears to materialize or the horror of Easter Island. The scale and speed of environmental change are so much greater than anything seen before that history no longer serves as a reliable guide. What we *can* learn from Easter Island is a cautionary tale: what can happen to human populations that wear out their welcome with Mother Nature through ignorance or folly.

The threat is a systemic and far-reaching one. All that frenetic economic activity described in the previous chapter requires not only the infrastructure humanity builds but also the infrastructure and resources nature provides. Obviously, we do not make the air, water, and soil on which our lives depend. Less obviously, nature also provides essential—and irreplaceable—services. It cleans the air and water we pollute, recycles organic matter into usable form, and maintains the infrastructure of ecosystems that nurture all the species on which we depend for food and medicine, and all the natural resources that provide grist for the mills of our industrial civilization. Nature provides flood control, pollination, erosion control, and genetic resources.

Governments, and most citizens, pay much more attention to economic indicators than to environmental ones. That skewed focus not only brings about serious environmental degradation but also threatens long-term economic prospects because it encourages shortsighted exploitation of natural resources. People generally think it is good news if gross domestic product (GDP) goes up. GDP measures all the flows of money within an economy, and most people assume an increasing GDP is necessarily a sign of growing real wealth. As most economists would admit, it is not. If a country were to cut down all its forests and sell the lumber, GDP would go up—temporarily. GDP might even continue to show an upswing for a while after the forests were gone because the government would be pressed to spend money coping with the erosion, flooding, and other effects of ecosystem destruction.

Nature does not charge for its services. If it did, the bill could easily overwhelm the entire global GDP. One rough estimate cited a value of $33 trillion for nature's services in 1995, roughly equal to global GDP.[2] Perhaps if we did have to pay, we would take better care of those ecosystems. Because nature provides its goods and services at no monetary cost, there is no price mechanism to enforce their efficient allocation. As a result, no market incentive militates against damaging the ecosystems. And we are damaging those systems apace.

As the human population soars past the 6 billion mark, humanity has acquired the capacity to alter the environment on a planetary scale, changing the planet's physiology and potentially damaging its capacity to support life. Human action has already poked a hole in the stratospheric ozone layer that protects Earth from the sun's ultraviolet radiation. A strong scientific consensus now holds that the emissions of greenhouse gases such as carbon dioxide from fossil fuel use are trapping heat in the atmosphere, thus altering the climate. If unchecked, climate change could raise ocean levels enough to swamp the coastal areas and inundate the river deltas, where a large fraction of humanity lives. It may already be altering precipitation patterns, changes that eventually could turn grain belts into dust bowls, turn deserts into grain belts, and generally throw societies into turmoil as they attempt to cope with ever more variable weather patterns.[3] And as population growth, the global rise in living standards, and pollution interact to reduce the availability of renewable resources such as water, clean air, arable land, forests, and fisheries, the turmoil that can result from struggles for these increasingly scarce resources is unlikely to remain neatly contained within political boundaries in a highly interconnected world.[4]

The warnings are loud, clear, consistent, and numerous. One impressive scientific panel after another has come to sobering conclusions about how fast humanity is damaging the planet's environmental infrastructure. The United Nations' "Comprehensive Assessment of the Freshwater Resources of the World" reported in 1997 that "water resource constraints and water degradation are weakening one of the resource bases on which human society is built. Water shortages and pollution are causing widespread public health problems, limiting economic and agricultural development, and harming a wide range of ecosystems. They may put global food supplies in jeopardy and lead to economic stagnation in many areas of the world."[5] The World Commission on Forests and Sustainable Development warned in 1999 that "there has been a clear global trend toward a massive loss of forested areas. . . . The current trends are toward an acceleration of the loss of forested area, the loss of residual primary forests, and progressive reduction in the internal quality of residual stands."[6] The Consultative Group on International Agricultural Research recently reported that 40 percent of the land used for agriculture is already degraded by erosion, nutrient depletion, waterlogging, and other causes. Given that most arable land is already used for crops and that world cereal production must increase by 40 percent by 2020 to meet growing demands for food, that degradation bodes ill for the future.[7]

It has been evident for quite a while that all these pieces could add up to serious trouble for the planet as a whole. The Royal Society and the National Academy of Sciences, the top scientific institutions in the United Kingdom and the United States, respectively, and not noted for overreaction, warned in 1992 that "the future of our planet is in the balance. Sustainable development can be achieved, but only if irreversible degradation of the environment can be halted in time. The next thirty years may be crucial."[8]

Only recently has anyone tried to put the pieces together systematically to assess the overall condition of the planet's environmental health in the way the International Monetary Fund (IMF) and the World Bank routinely assess the global economy. The United Nations Development Programme, the United Nations Environment Programme, the World Bank, and the World Resources Institute (the latter a highly regarded private research institute in Washington, D.C.) recently undertook a pilot analysis of global ecosystems to provide a meaningful, reasonably objective overview of the state of the planet. Their report evaluates the health of the ecosystems on which economic activity—indeed, life itself—depends. Those ecosystems are of five kinds: agricultural land, coastal waters, forests, freshwater, and grasslands. From these, directly or indirectly, humanity and all other species derive the necessities of life, from water to fiber to food to less obvious but no less essential services such as carbon storage (to counter global climate change) and maintenance of biodiversity (essential to ecosystem resilience as well as provision of genetic resources for future foods and medicines).

Their findings are summed up in the subtitle of their report: *People and Ecosystems: The Fraying Web of Life.* They conclude that

> the capacity of ecosystems to continue to produce many of the goods and services we depend on is declining . . . human activities have begun to significantly alter the Earth's basic chemical cycles—the water, carbon, and nitrogen cycles—that all ecosystems depend on. Our emissions of CO_2 have brought the real threat of global climate change and, with it, potential changes in the distribution and productivity of ecosystems. Our emissions of nitrogen—in the form of fertilizer runoff and nitrogen oxides from fossil fuels and land clearing—have thrown off the balance of nutrients in many ecosystems. Our appropriation of more than half the planet's freshwater runoff has pushed aquatic ecosystems to the point of depletion. These stresses strike at the foundation of ecosystem functioning and add to the fundamental erosion of productive capacity that ecosystems face on a global scale.[9]

It is ironic how differently we treat natural and man-made infrastructures. If we were wearing out roads at the rate at which we seem to be wearing out our systems for purifying air and water, producing food, and generally keeping ourselves alive, action would be taken. Both roads and ecosystems are public goods, not likely to be adequately provided by market forces. Governments know they are responsible for roads, and it is easy to tell when roads are not being maintained, so governments tend to spend money on building and maintaining them. Who takes responsibility for maintaining wetlands, fisheries, forests, or topsoil in good enough condition that the planet as a whole does not end up like Easter Island? And who should?

The problem stems in part from the sheer number of people in the world. Global population has jumped from a mere 1 billion in 1800 to 3 billion in 1960 to a remarkable 6 billion sometime in 1999.[10] And it is growing at a rate of about 78 million people per year. That figure actually represents a slowing of the rate of increase; just a few years ago, births were outpacing deaths by 86 million per year. Part of the slowdown is due to a higher death rate in some places caused by such factors as the AIDS epidemic and the catastrophic collapse of the public health systems in the former Soviet Union, but most of it comes from families around the world deciding to have fewer children. Even so, we are still adding a new Philippines or Vietnam every year.

Total global population will continue climbing for quite a while, although how high it will get is anyone's guess. For the first three decades of the twenty-first century, we will be seeing the consequences of the high birthrates of the previous three decades as all those people grow up and have children of their own. This is what demographers call demographic momentum. Even if everyone in the world immediately decided to have only enough children to replace themselves, there are already so many young people in the world, with their childbearing years ahead of them, that by the year 2100 the world would have 7.3 billion people. A more likely number is a peak of at least 9 billion by the year 2050.

Can the environmental infrastructure support all these people? A large population does not necessarily have to pose environmental problems. There is a concept called the "ecological footprint": how much of Earth's productive capacity a given person appropriates for everything from food to transportation to commerce to waste absorption.[11] People who drive sport utility vehicles, eat lots of red meat, and draw power for home heating and air-conditioning from coal-fired power plants have vastly larger footprints than do people who rarely eat meat, do not have cars, and have never experienced air-conditioning. The average American has an ecological footprint ten times greater than that of the average person in a developing country.[12]

It is possible to imagine ways in which dense populations could live very lightly on the land—relying primarily on solar and wind power, recycling everything, devising production processes that produce few, if any, waste products.[13] Many types of pollution are decreasing in the rich countries, thanks partly to technological improvements and partly to powerful environmental advocacy movements that have helped to bring about strict environmental regulations.

But in general, the urban, industrialized or industrializing half of the world's population treads heavily on the planet. The problem runs deeper than can be solved by the clean-up-your-mess regulations that have partially detoxified the air over Los Angeles and London. The problem is the very nature of modern industrial production, predicated on burning fossil fuels and using up resources. Americans, Germans, and Japanese consume more than twenty tons of fuel, metals and minerals, food, and forest products per person every year.[14] Almost all this gets dumped back on Mother Nature as waste or pollution. And that is literally not even half the story of the ways in which rich people disturb the environment. Agriculture and forestry erode some 33,000 pounds of soil per American per year. Building roads, maintaining waterways, and getting at the coal that powers much of America's industrial activity requires moving some forty tons of rock and dirt each year for every person in the country. European figures are similar.[15]

The United States, Japan, and Europe together account for less than one-sixth of the world's 6 billion people but are responsible for a wildly disproportionate share of environmental problems. This small fraction of the world's population uses as much as ten to thirty times the energy of people in poorer countries such as China and India and contributes the lion's share of emissions of greenhouse gases from the burning of coal, oil, and natural gas.[16]

Those in the poorer half of humanity have a much smaller footprint per person, but they are much more directly hurt by environmental degradation. They often grow their own food, burn firewood for fuel, and get their water directly from local rivers. So when soils degrade, forests disappear, and rivers dry up or become contaminated, the half of humanity that still lives in rural areas suffers. And the pattern of population growth ensures that those problems are going to get worse. The overwhelming share of population growth will occur in what are presently the world's poorer countries, and among the poorer segments within those countries. Richer people tend to have far fewer children, partly because they are more likely to have access to adequate contraception, but mostly because they tend to *want* fewer children. The world's poorest people are those who make their living directly from the land, often by engaging in subsistence agriculture. For these people, children are an economic asset, an extra pair of hands to fetch the water or tend the cow. For the rich, who send their children to school, children are an economic liability. And although population growth rates are coming down even among the very poor, demographic momentum ensures that pressures on the soil, water, and forests will escalate in the first few decades of the century. There are also a couple of billion people in between these two extremes who have climbed out of poverty and are getting richer. As they get richer, they are adopting the consumption habits of the rich.

Some people think that stopping or reversing economic integration would solve environmental problems. They claim that developing countries cannot devote resources to environmental protection because they are forced to repay onerous foreign debts or to slash government spending in compliance with structural adjustment loan conditions of the IMF and World Bank. But the economic–environmental connection is not clear-cut. High debt levels do correlate with high levels of deforestation as countries sell off timber or convert forestland for cash crop production. But exports are not necessarily more environmentally harmful to produce than the domestic products they replace.[17] IMF-imposed austerity programs lead to reduced government spending, which is blamed for cuts in environmental protection programs. But the government spending that gets cut may also be the environmentally harmful kind, such as large road or dam projects, which often lack adequate environmental safeguards. IMF and World Bank structural adjustment requirements can help the environment quite directly if they force governments to cut energy or irrigation subsidies.[18]

The globalization of production has similarly mixed environmental effects. On the positive side, the more efficient technologies made available to poor countries should reduce some degree of waste. But the globalization of production also allows consumers in rich countries to benefit from environmentally harmful production processes without directly paying the environmental costs. The goods thus produced are cheaper because the environmental costs are pushed off on poor countries, which often lack the resources to regulate such production or to clean up its consequences.

Consumers in the rich countries may not intend to impose such costs, but they often have no way of knowing that they are doing so. As discussed in chapter 7, under the existing international trade agreements, governments are not allowed to ban or discriminate against imports of goods made by environmentally undesirable processes, even if they have banned such processes in their own territory. Even requiring labels to inform consumers about the way products are made may, under WTO rules, constitute a barrier to trade. The reasoning behind these rules seems to be that poor countries should be free to make their own decisions about how much environmental damage they are willing to inflict on themselves in the name of economic progress.

That reasoning is widespread in the economics profession. Former secretary of the U.S. Treasury Lawrence Summers once argued, when he was a World Bank official, that economic rationality called for encouraging the movement of dirty industries from rich countries to poor ones and for dumping toxic wastes in the lowest-wage countries. He reasoned that the costs in forgone wages from higher mortality and morbidity would be lowest where wages were lowest, and that the aesthetic objections to pollution matter more to the rich than to the poor.[19] When his memorandum expressing this view was leaked, igniting a firestorm of protest, Summers claimed he was merely trying to put some rigor into what was usually a muddled discussion of the relationship between environment and economics.[20] In fairness, the tone of the memo was clearly sarcastic and intended to provoke discussion. But the broader point that Summers and others repeatedly make—that economic reforms and economic growth are the best response to environmental degradation—has real flaws. The economist's answer to demands that environmental concerns be part of global economic decision making is often to counsel patience. The rich countries also had horrendous pollution when they first industrialized, a century or so ago. It is reasonable to expect that as societies grow richer, they will develop the same kind of stricter environmental standards.

But there are real differences between the situation a century ago and that of today that make such a let-the-market-solve-it approach seem more ostrich-like than sagacious. First, no rich country ever had to deal with the sheer scale of environmental pressures now facing the poor countries. Yes, when Europe was industrializing, it had dense populations living under environmental conditions every bit as appalling as those facing Mexico City or New Delhi today. But Europe did not have cities of tens of millions of people, and it had a vital safety valve—migration. Millions upon millions of Europeans simply left. Today's poor may be trying to do the same, but the rich are trying hard to keep them where they are.

Second, environmental degradation was not a global problem then. When it comes to such matters, especially climate change, rich countries have not solved them—instead, they are the main contributors to those problems. We in the rich countries never did solve the problem of biodiversity loss—we wiped out our share of species and are now making relatively feeble efforts to protect the remaining endangered ones. Issues that were local in a world of a billion people become global in a world six times as densely populated. Even if it were morally sound for the rich to push environmental costs onto the poor, the environmental consequences are unlikely to remain within the borders of developing countries. Toxins have a nasty habit of spreading throughout food chains, ending up on dinner plates far from their point of entry into an ecosystem. How the climatic disruptions induced by too much burning of fossil fuels will affect different regions is as yet unpredictable, but the atmosphere is unlikely to pay much attention to the political boundaries that separate rich and poor countries. To claim that production processes have only local environmental consequences is to reveal a profound misunderstanding of the way ecosystems work.

Third, there is no particular reason to believe that all regions will see significant economic growth in the first few decades of the century, even when measured in the traditional way—that is, not taking into account the degree to which economic "growth" may simply reflect overconsumption of natural resources such as forests and fisheries. Many countries have cloudy prospects. In much of Africa, the Middle East, and the former Soviet Union, it is quite possible that real per capita economic growth simply will not occur.

How to Solve the Problems

If it is unlikely that humanity will automatically grow its way out of environmental danger, are the prospects for governance—deliberate collective action—any brighter? Concerns about environmental issues, local and global, have spawned a vast array of meetings, agreements, treaties, laws, and other human efforts to clean up the mess. The first of the big United Nations conferences on global issues, the United Nations Conference on the Human Environment in 1972, brought together 113 countries, a wide array of intergovernmental organizations, and numerous nongovernmental organizations (NGOs), which declared the necessity of safeguarding the environment in the interests of present and future generations.[21] It also led to creation of the United Nations Environment Programme, which tries to catalyze and coordinate the environmental efforts of intergovernmental, nongovernmental, national, and regional bodies, essentially serving as the United Nation's environmental conscience.[22] Twenty years later, in 1992, the United Nations did it again with the United Nations Conference on Environment and Development (UNCED, popularly known as the Earth Summit or Rio conference) in Rio de Janeiro. The Rio conference came up with an ambitious strategy for future environmental problem solving known as Agenda 21. Ten years later, few of its goals had been achieved.

In addition to these overarching environmental discussions, diplomats and bureaucrats around the world are engaged in negotiations on and implementation of all sorts of environmental treaties. Every once in a while, these work. At the top of virtually every list of intergovernmental success stories is the series of agreements dealing with the abstruse, but potentially catastrophic, problem of stratospheric ozone depletion.

The problem was chlorine in the wrong place.[23] The place was the stratosphere, the upper reaches of the atmosphere, some six to thirty miles above Earth's surface. In the stratosphere, an unstable molecule of oxygen called ozone, with three atoms of oxygen instead of the usual two, absorbs certain wavelengths of ultraviolet radiation from the sun, keeping that radiation from reaching the ground below. Biological organisms cannot tolerate high levels of such radiation. If ozone fails to do its stratospheric duty, we here on the planet's surface fry. Stratospheric ozone occurs naturally in small but adequate quantities. But because ozone is inherently unstable, it can be easily broken apart. It turns out that chlorine is particularly good at breaking up ozone's ménage à trois. A single chlorine atom can cause a chain reaction that splits tens of thousands of ozone molecules.

In 1974, Mario Molina and Sherwood Rowland, two scientists at the University of California, Irvine, were investigating the properties of a widely used and apparently environmentally benign set of man-made chemicals called chlorofluorocarbons (CFCs). They found that these gases are, unlike ozone, highly stable. Unlike most gases, which break down in the lower atmosphere or are rained out of it, CFCs stick together for decades or even centuries and wend their leisurely way up to the stratosphere, where solar radiation finally splits them into their constituent atoms. That releases chlorine (the first *C* in *CFCs*) into the stratosphere.

When Rowland and Molina first figured this out, CFCs were widely used as everything from refrigeration coolants to spray can propellants to cleaning solvents, partly because they seemed so safe. They are not flammable or toxic or corrosive, and they are cheap to make. By 1974, nearly 900,000 tons of CFCs were being produced annually. Most of the millions of tons previously produced would not yet have reached the stratosphere, so the damage to come was not yet visible.

This is exactly the kind of problem governments are normally bad at handling. The science was extremely complex and still theoretical because massive ozone depletion had not yet occurred. The economics were troubling, with an international CFC-producing industry initially determined to deny any possible connection between their products and such a serious potential threat. The problem could not be solved without truly global cooperation, given that a relatively small number of free riders continuing to produce CFCs could devastate the ozone layer even if everyone else stopped.

At first, progress was indeed slow. Years of scientific and political wrangling followed. The chief American negotiator on ozone depletion, Richard Elliott Benedick, starts off the preface to his account of the negotiations as follows:

> In January 1985 I led a small U.S. delegation to a little noticed meeting in Geneva, where we failed to achieve an international agreement. The event attracted only perfunctory attention in the press, and its unremarkable results occasioned no diplomatic ripples in national capitals.[24]

Fortunately for the future of life on Earth, things changed, and fast. A few months after Benedick's dismal experience in Geneva, international negotiators managed to sign the Vienna Convention for the Protection of the Ozone Layer. The Vienna Convention did not actually do anything to protect the ozone layer. It merely provided for international cooperation on research and exchange of information and set up a procedure for starting negotiations on future protocols. But then British scientists published shocking findings showing that, starting in 1979, ozone levels over Antarctica during spring (September–November) had been plunging unnoticed to about 50 percent of the level measured in the 1960s. American and Japanese scientists soon confirmed this wholly unexpected finding. No one knew what was tearing the hole in the ozone layer over Antarctica, but it was widely suspected that CFCs might be the culprit, and this placed additional pressure on governments to take the threat of ozone depletion seriously. Less than two years after signing the Vienna Convention, some two dozen countries (notably including the United States, the world's largest producer of CFCs) signed a protocol, the Montreal Protocol on Substances That Deplete the Ozone Layer, that required them to drastically cut their use of CFCs and other ozone-depleting substances.

Over the next few years, prodded by research confirming that CFCs were in fact responsible for the Antarctic hole and other damage to the ozone layer, governments drastically speeded up the pace, adopting steadily more rigorous control measures, moving up the deadlines for the phaseout of CFCs, and adding other ozone-depleting chemicals to the list. They also created a fund to pay poor countries for the incremental costs of building their capacity to phase out the chemicals. Remarkably, many countries made progress even faster than the protocol and its amendments called for. By

1995, global production of the most significant ozone-depleting CFCs had declined by 76 percent from its peak in 1988.[25]

Thanks to all this, catastrophe has most likely been averted. We are still stuck with the very unpleasant consequences of the damage wrought by man-made chemicals currently in or en route to the stratosphere. Poor countries complain that the aid they were promised to support the transition away from ozone-depleting substances has turned out to be stingy, and a worrisomely large number of them have yet to sign on to the more rigorous control measures of the 1990s. Because of the time lag between production of CFCs and other chemicals and the arrival of those substances in the stratosphere, the peak damage will occur in the first years of the twenty-first century, with stratospheric ozone gradually recovering over the next fifty years. In other words, recovery will take three generations from the time of the original recognition of the problem. But this is by far the most successful international environmental treaty, and it is a pretty good effort.

What happened between the Vienna Convention in March 1985 and the Montreal Protocol in September 1987 was a combination of good science, good diplomacy, the development of enlightened self-interest on the part of businesses, effective lobbying and lawsuits by NGOs, and sheer good luck. The science and diplomacy took the form of a series of workshops prior to the Montreal negotiations at which negotiators heard the best available scientific evidence, evaluated the relative risks and options, and agreed that the rational solution would be to phase out production of CFCs.[26] Business enlightenment took the form of a decision by E. I. Du Pont de Nemours and Company and other American producers to proceed apace with the development of substitute, non-ozone-depleting substances. The Natural Resources Defense Council, an American NGO, sued the U.S. Environmental Protection Agency (EPA) and lobbied the United States Congress in pursuit of a decision to reopen the negotiations.[27] The luck came about because the first sign of serious damage to the ozone layer, in the form of the hole in the ozone layer over Antarctica, appeared just in time to spur action.

By the standards of global environmental issues, ozone depletion was in many ways an easy case. Industry readily found substitutes from which it could make a profit, and the industry consisted of a mere handful of producers. The danger was relatively easy to explain in direct and personal terms— stop using the chemicals or watch sunburn and cancer rates skyrocket. The

United States lived up to its responsibility as the biggest producer and played a leadership role.

If all intergovernmental environmental agreements had so much going for them, there would not be so much cause for concern about the global environment. There are hundreds of bilateral and multilateral environmental treaties, many of which have regular meetings of parties to promote implementation of and compliance with their various terms. Thousands of international meetings every year, governmental and nongovernmental, deal with everything from chemical management to desertification to wetlands.[28] The international environmental policy circuit is a busy one. But in general, the planet seems unimpressed by those efforts.

The scariest disjuncture between human governance and environmental degradation is found in the biggest problem of all—climate change. As in the ozone case, although the basic problem is simple, the science and politics are anything but. Despite the efforts of a few scientists (mostly funded by the coal and oil industries) to cast doubt on the reality of human-caused climate change, there is little question that humanity has already committed itself to living through a massive, planet-wide experiment.

This is the experiment: Take one planet. Note that the planet's atmosphere naturally contains significant quantities of certain gases, such as carbon dioxide, that trap heat as does the glass in a greenhouse. Because of those gases, some of the energy from the sun that can get in as light cannot bounce back out as heat—the reason why the planet is not a lifeless ball of ice. Now start changing the composition of that atmosphere, substantially increasing the relative proportion of carbon dioxide (mostly from burning of fossil fuels such as oil and coal) and other greenhouse gases. See what happens.

What happens, according to the most authoritative scientific source available, the Intergovernmental Panel on Climate Change (IPCC), is a "discernible human influence on global climate."[29] That discernible influence takes the form of a rising global temperature of about one degree Fahrenheit so far. Over the next century, depending on the ultimate outcome of an incredibly complicated set of interactions among cloud cover, ocean currents, and other phenomena, additional warming of as much as ten degrees Fahrenheit could occur.[30] The science is not precise enough to say exactly what the consequences will be for various parts of the world or even how much of the unusually hot weather we have experienced since the 1980s is our own fault. But the possibility of serious, possibly disastrous, consequences already exists and will grow stronger the longer we continue to pour greenhouse gases into the atmosphere.

It takes a shift of only a few degrees in average global temperature to make an enormous difference. The last ice age was only about nine degrees colder on average than today.[31] Even in the past 1,000 years, the planet's climate has varied significantly on the basis of shifts in average temperature no more than two degrees colder or warmer than today. From about A.D. 950 to 1250, Europe and North America were unusually warm, leading the Vikings to attempt to settle the misnamed Greenland. From approximately 1550 to 1850, Europe suffered a period of unusual cold termed the Little Ice Age, with London's Thames River freezing solid enough to allow a festival to be held atop it. These were minor fluctuations, natural variations that occur because of such causes as volcanic eruptions, shifts in the planet's orbit, and variations in solar output. Human-induced climate change could push us well beyond those minor fluctuations.

The warming itself could have nasty effects, such as migration of tropical diseases into areas formerly too cold to support the insects that carry them, or rising sea levels. Water expands as it warms, and the Antarctic ice pack is already beginning to break up. Since half the world's population lives near a coast, the potential for massive dislocation is clear. One particularly threatened group of countries has joined together in the Association of Small Island States, a group whose members may see their entire territories vanish beneath the waves.

An even bigger problem may be instability. Everything from ocean currents to wind patterns will be subject to rapid change, which can stress ecosystems and potentially freeze or heat up specific regions in ways that may average out to what seems a fairly small temperature increase but will not feel small to the places affected. All flora and fauna that are well adapted to their current local climates may have to migrate quickly to find the new locations of their environmental niches. And trees cannot run very fast.

There are those who point to all the uncertainties about the outcome of the planetary experiment as reason for doing nothing. Since it is possible that the outcome will not be awful, why pay the costs of cutting back on greenhouse gas emissions?

How much it would actually cost is a subject of heated dispute. Stabilizing the climate would require, among other things, cutting current annual carbon emissions by more than half. Since industrial activity and transportation both depend overwhelmingly on the burning of fossil fuels, which releases carbon, such big cuts would require very significant changes in the ways people move about and make things. Some oil and coal companies and a few governments, such as those of Saudi Arabia and Kuwait, claim that the costs of transformation are prohibitive. Others point out that relatively pain-less steps are available, such as cutting the billions of dollars of subsidies to the fossil fuel industry and encouraging the widespread adoption of already available energy-efficient technologies.

The do-nothing reasoning is flawed on at least two grounds. One is that the "costs" are ones it makes sense to bear in any case: a transition to sus-tainable energy sources such as solar and wind power has other benefits, such as reducing air pollution—which directly harms human health—and creating jobs, given the higher employment potential of the sustainable energy technologies. The other is that the uncertainties run in both direc-tions. The outcome of human-induced global climate change may be more benign than is currently projected by the consensus of scientific opinion. It may also be worse.

There is a distinct chance that we will stumble across tipping points as the planet warms. For example, a fairly limited degree of warming would suffice to start melting the permafrost that covers much of the northern reaches of Russia and Canada. Alaska is already seeing such melting, although it is not clear whether climate change is responsible. Such melting would lead to the release of methane currently trapped in the frozen ground. Methane is a potent greenhouse gas, far more effective at trapping solar radi-ation than is carbon dioxide. No one knows how much methane is in the permafrost, although it is believed to be a substantial quantity, or how quickly it would be released.

Given the scope of the problem, efforts at solutions are falling appallingly short. At the 1992 Earth Summit in Rio de Janeiro, governments signed the United Nations Framework Convention on Climate Change (FCCC, pop-ularly known as the Framework Convention), which proclaimed an "ulti-mate objective" of stabilizing greenhouse gas concentrations at levels that would not cause human-induced climate change, but the convention did not actually commit anyone to doing anything specific. The idea was that the Framework Convention would give rise to a series of operational protocols with real teeth, just as the Vienna Convention laid the basis for the subse-quent agreements cutting back on the use of ozone-depleting substances.

But cutting emissions of greenhouse gases is proving much harder. There is one protocol, agreed to in December 1997 in Kyoto, Japan. It commits industrial countries to reducing their overall emissions of six greenhouse gases by at least 5 percent below 1990 levels between 2008 and 2012. Since, in the absence of government action, emissions would be expected to rise sharply, this requirement actually constitutes a reduction (from what otherwise would have occurred) of about 30 percent.[32] But it is far, far less than what is needed for climate stabilization—probably an order of magnitude less.

It is not clear whether the Kyoto Protocol could accomplish even this much. In keeping with the current enthusiasm for finding market solutions to all problems, the climate change negotiators have set out to create an artificial market for emissions trading. Countries that find they can relatively cheaply cut emissions even more than they agreed will be allowed to sell an allowance to another country, which will then be entitled to emit more. The idea is to meet the collective goal of emissions cuts as cheaply, flexibly, and efficiently as possible.[33]

There is nothing inherently wrong with the idea of emissions trading. A similar approach helped to reduce acid rain in the United States. But it is tricky to get the rules for it right. Under the Kyoto rules, Russia and Ukraine ended up with emissions caps far higher than their emissions are actually likely to be, given the way their economies nose-dived in the 1990s. If they choose to sell their allowances to rich countries, few cuts might happen anywhere.

Another part of the Kyoto Protocol would allow rich countries to buy additional emissions credits by funding projects that reduce emissions, such as tree planting, in poor countries. The implementation of all this is even more complicated than it sounds. Deciding which projects deserve emissions credits will be difficult and fraught with potential for cheating.

The United States has never been wildly enthusiastic about the protocol, which is a problem given that the United States is the single largest emitter of greenhouse gases. During the presidency of Bill Clinton, whose administration negotiated the protocol, the U.S. Congress refused to accept the protocol because it requires rich countries, but not poor ones, to cut their emissions— a reasonable first step, since the rich countries currently account for most of the problem. The administration of President George W. Bush subsequently repudiated the agreement altogether, saying it would come up with something better, a something that has yet to emerge.

The climate change problem will not be solved by the usual government negotiators up to their usual tricks of trying to serve national over global interests. Greenhouse gases are not a minor by-product—they are inherent in the world's energy and land-use patterns. Effective action to quell climate change will happen only when the general public, national governments, and private industry form a greater consensus about the need and mechanisms for confronting the problem, and then work together creatively to remedy it.

This conclusion extends to most global environmental problems. Ozone depletion, unfortunately, was the exception. Like climate change, other global environmental threats, such as the spread of toxic substances, biodiversity decline, and ecosystem collapse, elicit much less agreement on the extent and shape of the problem and offer more incentives for specific groups to continue opposing changes in current practices. And at least we are talking seriously about climate change. Attention to the alarming deterioration of ecosystems the world over has barely reached the hand-wringing stage and is unlikely to get much further. Intergovernmental agreements would have to demand a draconian and politically unlikely surrender of national sovereignty in order to change existing practices sufficiently to solve these kinds of environmental problems.[34] The Convention on Biological Diversity, for example, claims more than 170 countries as parties, but species are being lost at perhaps a thousand times the natural rate of extinction, and one in every eight plant species is endangered.[35] Indeed, species are being lost more quickly than they can be discovered and catalogued as whole ecosystems are devastated in a kind of mass production approach to the destruction of flora and fauna. The convention is weak for a reason. To be made effective, it would have to become an international covenant laying out precise directives on how the countries of the world could manage their lands. But there is no agreed-upon set of indicators of ecosystem health that everyone could agree to try to maintain, no single concrete threat to human well-being on which government concern could focus, and not enough biologists in the world to effectively monitor compliance with detailed ecosystem-protecting treaties. The idea that the world's governments will calmly agree on a set of specifications about which wetlands could not be drained, which forests would have to be declared off-limits to logging, and which fields could be cultivated and which would have to be left fallow to revert to prairie is ludicrous on its face. Even if such a denigration of national sovereignty were politically feasible, it would be unworkable in practical terms. Ecosystem management requires *local* knowledge—exactly what a global-level agreement is ill-equipped to provide.

The Alternatives

Fortunately, there are alternative approaches to environmental governance. In the United States, for example, the Emergency Planning and Community Right-to-Know Act of 1986 requires companies to disclose what amounts of a few hundred specified toxic chemicals they release into the air or water or on land (above certain threshold levels). The companies must send the information to the EPA, which uses it to compile a Toxics Release Inventory (TRI) that is then made public. The act itself puts no limits on emissions of these toxic chemicals. It merely requires companies to own up publicly to what they are emitting. But that has proved sufficient to help bring about an enormous change in behavior. Emissions of the indexed chemicals at facilities covered by the law fell by 44 percent between 1988 and 1994, even though production of those chemicals rose by 18 percent. Some of the decline probably stemmed from other regulatory changes, but no environmentalist would have dared dream of getting a 44 percent reduction mandated solely by the usual types of environmental regulations.

The success of this new approach has drawn the most sincere form of flattery—imitation. In 1991, the United Kingdom introduced its Chemical Release Inventory (CRI) and the Netherlands began allowing public access to information that companies had been providing to the government under legislation dating back to 1974. As a follow-up to UNCED in 1992, the Organization for Economic Cooperation and Development (OECD) began to develop manuals and host meetings to promote the development of what came to be called Pollutant Release and Transfer Registers (PRTRs).[36]

Indonesia recently adopted a simpler transparency-based approach to managing environmental problems. It publicly grades facilities by color according to how well they meet existing regulations. According to the World Bank, the program is significantly increasing compliance with environmental regulations.[37] Its success, due to the pressure of both local public opinion and the business community's desire to market to environmentally sensitive foreign consumers, has spurred further imitation. In 1997, the Philippines announced the introduction of a public information program called Ecowatch. Mexico's environmental agency recently announced that it will begin to publish information about the environmental performance of 3,000 industries to provide incentives for them to clean up their act.[38]

Governments are not the only bodies attempting to use information to improve the state of the environment. In 1998, a major U.S. environmental group, Environmental Defense, launched a World Wide Web site called "Scorecard" (http://www.scorecard.org) that makes TRI and other data accessible to anyone with an Internet connection. The site is very user-friendly. For instance, if an American types in his or her postal code, up pops information about local TRI releases as well as local air pollution, nearby toxic dump sites, and more. By navigating through various layers, users can get data on the relative toxicity of specific compounds and rankings showing which facilities pose the biggest health threats. The site has been covered by national television news and national news magazines. And it is heavily used, with more than 11 million visitors in its first year of operation.

An Indian NGO, the Centre for Science and Environment (CSE), is also pursuing the transparency approach to environmental regulation, publishing ratings that compare companies within a given industry on their environmental performance.[39] Since the Indian government does not require companies to provide public information about environmental records, the CSE decided to ask the companies directly. To induce companies to provide information, the CSE adopted a carrot-and-stick policy. The stick was that any company that failed to provide information would automatically be ranked at the bottom. The carrot was that if companies could prove they were trying to improve their environmental performance, their efforts would be reflected in the rankings.

With funding from the United Nations Development Programme (funneled through the Indian government), the CSE set out to rank companies in the pulp and paper industry, a renowned polluter. Much to the surprise of the CSE, by the time the ratings were released, every company in the industry had provided the requested information, apparently convinced that the harm to their reputations of refusing to comply—and thus being ranked last—outweighed any possible harm from complying with the survey.

The transparency approach to environmental problem solving is spreading beyond the issue of toxic chemicals. The World Resources Institute has set up an international data and mapping network called Global Forest Watch (http://www.globalforestwatch.org) that provides an up-to-date picture of where forests are threatened by corruption, mismanagement, and illegal logging. This is a rearguard action—some 80 percent of the planet's original forest cover is already gone or degraded—but Global Forest Watch aims to protect the blocks of relatively intact forest that remain. No one had previously tried to provide such an overview. Its findings are posted on the Internet, enabling anyone interested to demand better protection for the forests. The project currently works with scores of partners in seven countries and plans to triple that number by 2005.

European governments seem to be trying to give networks and transparency approaches a systematic helping hand. In 1998, thirty-five European countries and the European Union met in Aarhus, Denmark, to sign the United Nations Economic Commission for Europe Convention on Access to Information, Public Participation in Decision-Making, and Access to Justice in Environmental Matters (better known, fortunately, as the Aarhus Convention). The Aarhus Convention takes broad pro-transparency language that was included in the final document of the 1992 Rio conference and turns it into a binding international agreement. It lays out what kind of environmental information should be made public and by what processes, and it stipulates that governments should create registries like the U.S. Toxics Release Inventory. It allows individuals and NGOs to seek redress in court when governments or corporations fail to meet these obligations to provide information. And the transparency requirements do not discriminate on the basis of citizenship or geography. An NGO or individual in one country can demand information from a government or corporation in another.[40]

Saving the Planet for Fun and Profit

Because so many environmental problems result from activities carried out by businesses, and because governments do not seem to be adequately regulating those businesses, civil society groups are putting intense pressure directly on businesses to clean up the mess. The private sector has responded in two ways. One group, the membership of the World Business Council for Sustainable Development (WBCSD), has essentially agreed that it needs to be less dirty and more efficient in its use of resources so that less waste is dumped into the environment.[41]

And some businesses are doing just that. British Petroleum (BP Amoco) and Shell are not waiting for government regulators to tell them to curb greenhouse gas emissions. They have publicly announced that they believe in adopting a precautionary approach and have pledged to cut their greenhouse gas emissions by 10 percent of 1990 levels by 2010—a bigger cut than the Kyoto Protocol requires of any government.[42] This is in sharp contrast with the stance of other fossil fuel companies. In advance of the Kyoto negotiations, a group of such firms, along with labor unions, created an organization called the Global Climate Information Project, which barraged U.S. television viewers with advertisements warning of dire threats to the U.S. economy should the Kyoto accord come into force.[43] Many of these firms, along with others, are members of the vociferous Global Climate Coalition, a group dedicated to the proposition that all evidence showing that climate change is real and growing can safely be ignored.

The Global Climate Coalition is breaking up almost as fast as the Antarctic ice shelf. BP Amoco and Shell used to be members but have withdrawn. An alternative organization now exists for businesses prepared to take climate change seriously—the Business Environmental Leadership Council, organized through the Pew Center on Global Climate Change.

But with climate stabilization requiring cuts in greenhouse gas emissions of more than 50 percent below those prevailing in 1990, the commitments of a few corporations to cut emissions by 10 percent fall far short of the need. The Business Environmental Leadership Council and the Global Climate Coalition can fight all they want over what constitutes corporate responsibility, but environmental protection may be even more demanding than the WBCSD is prepared to recognize. It may require changes not only in how closely businesses adhere to environmental codes or how ardently they pursue greater efficiencies to reduce waste but even in what products they choose to make. If the problem is inherent in the way products are made, from natural resources to product to waste, then reducing waste just buys us a little time until the growing size and affluence of the global population buries us all in waste. Maybe we have to rethink the ways in which things get made.

Enter the Hypercar. The Hypercar is one of those ideas cynics would assume could not possibly work because it has no downside and enormous potential benefit. It is a car conceived by energy analyst Amory Lovins, a visionary with a remarkable record of being right about the ease with which societies can grow economically without necessarily increasing their energy consumption. The car combines the best of all the technologies now available.

It has superstrong alloys that greatly reduce its weight and, thus, its fuel demands. Its fuel cells could actually add clean energy to the electricity grid when the car is plugged in but emit nothing harmful. It even has ways of capturing and using the heat energy otherwise lost in braking. The perfect Hypercar is not yet available, but the Japanese automotive industry is already selling models that incorporate some of Lovins' suggestions. With the current world inventory of more than half a billion vehicles projected to double in the first few decades of the century, widespread adoption of the Hypercar could go a long way toward meeting the goals of climate stabilization—not to mention cleaning up the nearly unbreathable air of poor-country megalopolises such as Mexico City and New Delhi.

The Hypercar is just one example of the kinds of products companies could choose to produce and promote if they got serious about making environmentally clean products. Another striking example is that of a carpet tile manufacturing company called Interface. Its chief executive officer, Ray Anderson, simply decided one day that his company's business was environmentally unsustainable, and that had to change. The company began investing heavily in radical energy efficiency, using renewable energy sources, and attempting to produce zero waste. In its most challenging effort, the company now proposes to lease rather than sell its carpet tiles. When the tiles wear out, the company will take them back and recycle them—quite a change from usual business practices.[44] And it is still making money.

Yet another example comes from American architect William McDonough and German chemist Michael Braungart. They teamed up to design an upholstery fabric that does no environmental damage at all. As they put it, their aim was "to design a fabric so safe that one could literally eat it."[45] After eliminating almost all of the 8,000 finishes, dyes, and other processing chemicals used in the textile industry as too hazardous to go back into the soil safely, they created a fabric of ramie and wool that requires the use of only 38 chemicals, now produced in a factory in Switzerland. It is so environmentally safe that Swiss regulators who came by to test the mill's effluent thought their instruments were broken until they came to a surprising realization. The water coming out of the plant was as clean as the water going in.

There is ample reason to believe that such products can turn a tidy profit. Assumptions that it is cheaper to pollute wastefully than to produce cleanly have been proved wrong time and time again. What is in the interest of society—a widespread transformation of production processes and products to make them much less polluting or pollution-free—is also in the interest of a huge swath of the business community. Big profits await those firms nimble enough to seize the opportunity, especially if governments can be persuaded to stop subsidizing many of their dirtier competitors.

Is It Enough?

Will the combination of old and new approaches suffice to fend off climate change, replenish fisheries, restore degraded soils, halt the rapid extinction of species, keep toxic substances out of ecosystems and human bodies, and generally restore Mother Nature to good health? So far, the evidence from planet Earth is that our efforts lag behind the environmental damage we are inflicting. Action remains woefully disproportionate to the scale of the problems.

Global-level environmental problems, such as climate change and ozone depletion, clearly require global collective action. They threaten everyone and require that all countries participate in the solutions. It does little good for some countries to control their emissions of greenhouse gases and ozone-depleting substances if others continue merrily pumping the stuff out. But it is essential to start thinking about other kinds of environmental pressures in the same way—as global issues needing global collective action. Scarcity of basic environmental resources such as clean water and arable land can spill over borders in wars, refugee flows, political tensions, and humanitarian crises, especially in parts of the world where government institutions and civil societies are too weak to solve the problems directly or mediate the resulting conflicts.[46]

Too often, governments have proved unwilling or unable to undertake significant environmental steps except under intense public pressure. Governments could do considerably better through such obvious steps as taxing fossil fuel use. But pious exhortations to governments to stop doing environmentally stupid things and start doing smart ones are making slow headway.

Bringing about the changes necessary to protect the planet will require governance that goes beyond governments. Corporations will need to change their production processes. And the public will need to change its consumption patterns, buying only goods that are made through environmentally sustainable processes and that are not inherently excessively damaging. Enabling the public to do that will require a massive shift toward greater transparency about the environmental consequences of production and consumption of all kinds of goods and services, as with the nutritional labels on foods that Americans have come to take for granted.

What is truly needed is something from everyone—governments, corporations, and networks of civil society groups all prodding one another along the route to environmental sustainability, using the global spotlight as a major source of encouragement. How well they play their respective roles will determine whether we end up closer to the rosy scenario or the gloomy one.

⟨9⟩

The Fourth Revolution

John Man starts off his fascinating account of Johannes Gutenberg's life and times by noting that "on a graph of human contact over the last 5,000 years, the line from rock-art to e-mail is not a regular curve. It has four turning-points, each recording moments at which written communication flicked to a new level of speed and outreach." First came writing itself, which made possible large-scale societies; then came the alphabet, which made writing broadly accessible; and then there was Gutenberg's printing press, which led to the modern world. The fourth, he says, is the coming of the Internet, "which seems to be turning us into cells in a planet-sized brain."[1]

What kind of world will we make out of this latest turning point? The need to do something constructive is clear. The world remains plagued by problems ranging from severe to horrific. Ethnic conflict may not be as pervasive and destructive as media portrayals would suggest, but it does dominate the lives of far too many people. Some rich countries are seeing improvements in their environmental conditions, but for the most part the state of the environment is deteriorating, not improving. The global economy is unstable and highly inequitable, with nearly half the world's population barely surviving on a couple of dollars per day. Terrorism remains an unpredictable but ever-present threat.

It is disturbingly easy to imagine ways in which things could get worse in the next several years. Russia could disintegrate into the world's first nuclear-armed state run by organized crime rings. Climate change could reach a tipping point that simultaneously sends northern Europe into a new ice age and overheats the great North American breadbaskets. Japan's long-standing economic misery could end in a banking system collapse that pulls the global financial system down with it. Can we hope to create a system of global governance that is effective enough to ward off most such catastrophes and resilient enough to cope with the stresses and shocks that do occur?

Contrary to the views of the many prophets of doom and gloom who simply assume a bleak future, plentiful meaningful opportunities exist to make the world a better place and to overcome the collective problems we face. Nascent but discernible is the development of a cosmopolitan mentality among people who have a growing power to effect change, thanks in part to the new capacity to form effective networks. Transparency is providing new opportunities both to enforce rules and standards and to hold accountable those who purport to act in the public interest. And information technology is facilitating the creation of networks among governments, the private sector, and, especially, civil society that engage a wide range of voices in determining the global future.

Imagining success in such an endeavor is harder than envisioning failure. It calls for a fairly messy approach to governance rather than one grandly designed New World Order. But given how the efforts of ideologues to create rationally ordered societies in the twentieth century have fared, the unlikelihood of a grand design should be cause for a large collective sigh of relief.[2]

Because imagining a better future is the essential first step toward creating one, what follows is one such flight of fancy that draws on all the themes covered in the previous eight chapters. Imagine it is the year 2020—a favorite date for builders of futurist scenarios who like to indulge in puns about "2020 vision." This world is still far from perfect, but it is in much better shape than ours is today. How will that have come about?

A 2020 Vision

At the beginning of the twenty-first century, the world faced a seemingly insurmountable gulf between the needs for global action and the woefully underdeveloped mechanisms for meeting those needs. Poverty afflicted half of humanity. New and resurgent diseases, from AIDS to tuberculosis to the West Nile virus, threatened millions. Environmental degradation on a massive scale, from the unpredictable consequences of global warming to the spread of toxic chemicals, endangered everyone. Sharply contending views about what should be done about it all increasingly led to violence on the part of protestors, overwhelmed or repressive governments, and ideologically inspired terrorists. Political leaders gathered for frequent gabfests but seemed unable or unwilling to commit themselves to serious action on any subject other than promoting ever deeper economic integration. The systems for making and enforcing global rules were generally feeble, and where strong, they were widely seen as unfair.

Now, in 2020, the widespread violence, terrorist assaults, and sense of despair of this century's first several years are a rapidly fading memory. Although serious problems persist, an extraordinary range of mechanisms has developed that offer real hope that humanity may at last have found ways to live mostly in peace and growing prosperity on a planet no longer so sharply divided.

To see how far we have come in just two decades, look back at how the world was organized at the opening of the century. If one merely looked at numbers of efforts, global governance seemed to be thriving. In thousands of bilateral and multilateral treaties and statements, governments offered repeated declarations of their determination to address the problems that came with a global economic system, porous borders, and the ever greater scope of human effects on Earth's biosphere. A vast array of international organizations regularly held meetings and generated an extraordinary number of documents. But a closer look made clear that, with a few notable exceptions, all the sound and fury were not accomplishing much.

A handful of rich and powerful countries dominated international negotiations and organizations. Their say in running the world was wildly disproportionate to their share of the world's population. And the richest and most powerful of all, the United States, was increasingly refusing even to make a good-faith effort to participate in global negotiations. When governments did manage to reach agreements, implementation often fell far short. Some crucial environmental treaties, such as the Convention on Biological Diversity, had essentially no effect on the problems they were meant to address. Often, governments signed on to agreements they had little capacity to implement.

Even in those areas where treaties had teeth and international organizations were playing a serious, substantive role, success sometimes seemed to engender as many problems as it solved. This was particularly notable in the international arrangements governing trade. Having created a trade regime that largely served their own economic interests, the world's rich countries seemed perplexed by the vehement objections to that regime that emerged both from other governments and from an increasingly vociferous network of civil society organizations. Developing countries argued that the rich countries were failing to live up to promises made years ago, and civil society groups raised complaints that the rules and procedures favored private over public interests. Countries flocked to join the World Trade Organization (WTO) not necessarily because they believed the new trade regime was fair and effective but because the alternative was to remain excluded from the only trade system available.

The need for major reform of the systems of global governance was clear. Proposals abounded, but few offered much real hope of redressing what ailed humanity. Some people drew their lessons from familiar patterns of national laws and law enforcement, proposing, for example, that environmental and labor standards be included in trade agreements, enforced by trade sanctions. Such suggestions foundered over questions of how to make such processes both effective and broadly legitimate. At the other extreme were occasional calls for the reversal of globalization, with a retreat to national borders. But despite the frequent mislabeling of the public backlash as anti-globalization, in fact relatively few people were demanding a retreat to impermeable national borders. Most critics objected to specific rules and institutional behaviors, not to the idea of integration.

Despite the apparent impasse, there were glimmerings of better ideas for running the world. Growing public scrutiny of intergovernmental organizations was making it increasingly difficult for the governments of rich countries to treat these organizations as mere instruments for achieving purely national ends, as they had long been wont to do. Corporations were increasingly adopting an ethos of corporate social responsibility that had the potential to reduce the need for direct government supervision. Proliferating civil society networks gave voice to people from all parts of the world who shared grievances about the rules governing global integration.

At the turn of the century, *transparency* ran second only to *globalization* as a prominent buzzword, touted as the solution to everything from financial volatility to environmental degradation to corruption. It seemed as though everyone was calling for everyone else to be transparent. Civil society groups demanded transparency from intergovernmental organizations, corporations, and governments, which in turn began demanding it of civil society groups. Transparency's popularity varied in inverse proportion to its distance: those who demanded disclosures from others often resisted providing detailed information about themselves. But all those demands did lead to real changes in behavior that in turn provided the foundation for a major shift in patterns of governance.

Three changes proved crucial. First, citizens demanded, and got, new laws entitling them to access to information about their governments. The new laws enabled civil society groups working on all kinds of issues to hold their governments accountable for the ways in which tax funds were spent and decisions were made. The new transparency did not work perfectly, of course. All too often, the black hole of secrecy gave way to a cacophony of white noise as information spewed in all directions. And moneyed interests found ways to promote their ends through proxy organizations that ostensibly worked in the public interest. But overall, as norms of government accountability and citizens' right to know spread and became entrenched, national governments changed for the better. The incidence of corruption decreased substantially, and open political debates upgraded the quality of government policies.

Second, such organizations as the International Monetary Fund (IMF), the World Bank, and the WTO began disclosing information they (and their member governments) had previously kept secret. Nongovernmental organizations (NGOs) swarmed all over that information, ensuring that citizens and the media were kept well informed. Such scrutiny quickly improved the performance of those organizations. As they found themselves forced to defend their policies to an ever larger and more attentive public, bureaucratic rigidities and power politics alike withered under the glare.

Third, new agreements began to entrench the emerging transparency norms at the global level. The model was Europe's Aarhus Convention.[3] Unlike the multitude of largely ineffective agreements that had focused on specific environmental problems, the Aarhus Convention set out to change the *process* by which environmental decisions were made. To do so, it required governments to disclose relevant information to the public. "Relevant information" included data on the state of the environment, planned or operational policies and measures, international conventions and other documentation, institutional mandates, and information about institutional performance. The convention also required its adherents to establish Pollutant Release and Transfer Registers, under which corporations that released toxic emissions would have to report publicly on the extent of those emissions. Similar registries in other countries had already dramatically reduced the level of toxic emissions, proving that corporations could be shamed by public pressure into improving their environmental performance.

The Aarhus Convention also laid out ground rules for civil society participation in decision making. All sorts of activities that had particularly significant environmental consequences, from the energy sector to the chemical industry to waste management, became subject to public review and consultation. Government policies and programs related to the environment, such as national environmental action programs and waste management policies, also had to undergo public consultation. If governments or corporations failed to provide the required information and opportunities for public voice, the convention gave civil society groups the right to seek judicial remedies for noncompliance. And all these rights and rules applied across borders, enabling citizens from one country to demand Aarhus-related information from public authorities and private entities in another.

The Aarhus Convention proved so successful that it became a model even in other issue areas, particularly economics. Most national governments are parties to the Economic Information Convention, negotiated in 2010. Originally promoted primarily by the IMF and the United States, the Economic Information Convention builds on IMF data dissemination standards but also includes a broader range of information of interest to citizens as well as investors. The information flows fostered by that convention have gone far to reduce the suspicion and ignorance in which earlier debates over global economic governance were conducted.

At the same time that Aarhus-type standards began to spread across regions and into more and more issue areas, major corporations continued to find themselves subjected to relentless demands that they become more transparent and adopt new standards of corporate social responsibility. Initially, most simply paid lip service to one of a bewildering variety of codes of conduct, refusing to allow any independent verification of their behavior. But a few enlightened corporate leaders seized the opportunity to please customers and investors by undertaking more dramatic action. Some adopted meaningful codes of responsible corporate conduct regarding the environment and human rights, with their performance verified by independent external bodies. Others established new practices that preceded or exceeded government requirements, or both, such as the internal emissions trading mechanisms adopted by BP Amoco and Shell. Over time, these corporations found their good deeds amply rewarded both by customers, who flocked to buy products and services provided by reliably certified companies, and by investors in the rapidly growing movement of socially responsible investing. Their success led other major companies to emulate their example, setting off a virtuous cycle of rising corporate standards of behavior.

Although large corporations in particular still speak with a loud voice in international negotiations, that voice is now better balanced by the presence of citizens' groups speaking on behalf of a wider range of interests. National-level debates also enjoy a better balance thanks to the improvements in national governance described earlier that have created much more transparent and participatory systems. The once popular (in some circles) notion that a corporation's only social responsibility was to maximize shareholder return within the limits of legality, often by stretching those limits as far as possible, is now rarely heard. The bewildering array of corporate codes of conduct was eventually winnowed down to a handful of relatively well designed and widely adopted ones, making it easier for customers, communities, employees, and other stakeholders to monitor corporate behavior.

But perhaps the most important shift has come not in how well corporate behavior is circumscribed but in what a growing number of businesses are setting out to do. One key change is a revolution in the attitude of big corporations regarding the poor. Rather than seeing them as merely occasional targets for corporate charity, businesses began to recognize that even quite poor people could constitute a profitable market if products and production methods were geared toward what they could afford. With nearly half the world living on two dollars per day or less, sheer size made that potential market too large to ignore.

Another major development came in the form of a few key intergovernmental agreements, such as the Kyoto Protocol to the United Nations Framework Convention on Climate Change. Such clear signals from governments, along with pressure from transnational networks of environmental groups and consumer demand, spurred extraordinary innovation on the part of certain enlightened sectors of the business community aimed at creating

new technologies and production processes. Those technological innovations are coming together in a trend called industrial ecology, wherein
industrial production systems are designed so that they generate no environmental problems at all. These will take time to diffuse completely, but
already they have made it much easier for governments to agree on steadily
improving global environmental standards.

All this was the result of a profound change in the relationship between
governments and the governed, a new global social contract of sorts, in
which civil society forged a new role for itself, often in the form of NGOs.
Early in the twenty-first century, the first response of befuddled functionar-
ies to the massive protests that were the most visible element of civil society's global flowering had been to throw up walls around their conference
sites, as they did in Davos, Quebec City, and Genoa in 2001, or to move
the conferences to isolated locations such as Doha, the capital of Qatar.
Such moves did little to alter widespread perceptions that global governance
had become the province of aloof, remote elites. But over time, policy makers came to understand that unless they wanted to relocate their meetings
to Antarctica, they needed to provide meaningful channels for a public
voice in global decision making. They found useful models dating back
years or even decades. The original plan for the International Trade Organization back in the 1940s, for example, envisaged that NGOs would
receive documents, propose agenda items, and even speak at conferences.
Many environmental agreements already contained language allowing nongovernmental groups that were "technically qualified" in areas related to the
agreement to be admitted as observers, to assist the secretariat of the organization charged with overseeing implementation of the treaty, or both. To
permit broad participation while keeping out the lunatic fringe, nongovernmental groups were allowed in unless a supermajority of member states
voted to exclude them.

Bit by bit, such groups began to work more closely with, rather than
against, governments and corporations. They helped to negotiate and draft
the Aarhus Convention, for example. Others deserved credit for spearhead-
ing the public pressure that led intergovernmental organizations such as the
IMF, the WTO, and the World Bank to adopt increasingly forthcoming
disclosure policies. National civil society networks took the lead in lobbying
for national freedom of information policies, and over time those national
networks began to link up across borders to share resources and lessons. A

wide variety of civil society networks constituted the force behind the corporate social responsibility trend, as their "naming and shaming" strategies
sparked significant changes in corporate behavior. And transnational civil
society networks increasingly came to redefine the international agenda by
means of campaigns on issues ranging from debt relief to trade reform to
human rights.

Although there are still frequent complaints about the lack of formal
accountability mechanisms for this sector, the problem has proved somewhat
self-correcting. Transparency has become so widespread and the perspectives
represented in transnational civil society so diverse that the various groups
now monitor one another as avidly as they monitor everyone else. When the
resulting cacophony began to get out of hand, many groups adopted codes
of appropriate conduct for nongovernmental organizations, complete with
their own certification procedures, leading to the emergence of monitors for
the monitors.

The various intergovernmental organizations, such as the United
Nations, the World Bank, the IMF, and the WTO, still matter. They provide
important forums within which all the many actors on the global scene—
governments, corporations, civil society groups, and international civil ser-
vants—try to persuade one another about what rules should be made and
how they should be implemented. The series of "Financing for Development" conferences that the United Nations began in 2002, for example,
mattered despite the lack of success in increasing the transfer of capital from
rich countries to poor ones. Those conferences brought together staff and
government officials from the United Nations, the IMF, and the World Bank
in a public setting that required them to defend their views about what economic policies should be adopted and why. One unexpected benefit was that
some governments found themselves embarrassed by the inability of their
national representatives to engage effectively in such public debates, and this
sparked a growing tendency to search out leading thinkers to serve on the
executive boards and governing councils of the institutions. That improved
oversight in turn changed the atmosphere within the organizations as staff
and management were required to make rigorous and persuasive arguments
in defense of their plans and policies.

For the most part, these organizations still do not act independently of
governments in setting the rules and are not evolving into supranational
authorities telling governments what to do. In one sense, their "enforcement"

capacities have actually declined. The two-decade experiment with ever more intrusive conditionality attached to loans from the international financial institutions has been widely acknowledged a failure because the conditions generated great bitterness and did little good. The World Bank now makes few loans, giving most of its help in the form of grants and technical assistance. The IMF still serves as lender of last resort for the international system, but its conditions are now broad outcome requirements (e.g., holding international reserves above a certain level) that do not prescribe *how* countries should achieve those outcomes. The WTO's dispute resolution mechanism has evolved substantially to incorporate a much wider range of perspectives on whether a given measure is truly a protectionist trade barrier or is a legitimate measure serving a non-trade-related end. The push to do away with all national regulations that might impede trade or foreign investment has given way to a more balanced assessment that allows equal standing to other goals.

Thanks to such measures as the Economic Information Convention and the Environmental Information Convention (a geographically expanded version of the Aarhus Convention, adopted in 2012), intergovernmental organizations are also playing a more extensive version of their long-standing role as monitors of the state of the world. In this role, they provide a vital early warning function, combining data flows with crucial analysis of emerging problems. They also frequently monitor compliance with international agreements (often in association with NGOs, although sometimes in competition with them). To a limited extent they serve as the mechanisms for resource transfers, although (with the exception of the Initiative for Global Health, described later in this chapter) much of this function has been taken over by private sector and civil society actors.

The institutions of environmental governance have taken on greater relative weight in the international system than they had two decades ago, even though years of sporadic discussions about the creation of a World Environment Organization led nowhere. One major development came with negotiation of the Environmental Information Convention mentioned earlier, which built on Principle 10 of the agreement that emerged from the 1992 United Nations Conference on Environment and Development. Most countries are now parties to that convention. The convention, like many other advances in transparency, came about after a sustained transnational civil society campaign that was conducted in alliance with a number of like-minded governments. That campaign began as the Access Initiative, an alliance of four leading environmental NGOs from around the world, and quickly blossomed into a network of thousands.[4] As a result, most governments are now committed to releasing vast quantities of information about their environmental negotiations, plans, policies, and activities. The convention also called for additional funds to support efforts to monitor the state of the global environment. Although, as always, the response to requests for funding to address a global public good is less than ideal, both governments and private actors contributed enough that monitoring has improved significantly. The United Nations Environment Programme, in association with a number of NGOs such as the World Resources Institute, is the primary keeper of the world's environmental database, although the secretariats of a number of environmental conventions also play that role in their specific areas.

One of the few new formal organizations is the Initiative for Global Health, an outgrowth of the Global Fund to Fight AIDS, Tuberculosis, and Malaria, first proposed by the United Nations' secretary-general, Kofi Annan, in 2001. At the time, despite repeated government proclamations of the goal of universal basic health, the previous century's progress in extending life spans and improving the health of the world's citizens was severely threatened. The collapse of many public health systems and the spread of AIDS were dramatically reducing life expectancies in many regions. Much of the previous century's improvement in life expectancy could be traced to the widespread use of antibiotics, but massive misuse of those antibiotics in both health care and agriculture had created the chilling phenomenon of microbes resistant to most, or all, known treatments. Vast numbers of people still lacked such basic prerequisites to good health as safe drinking water. And global expenditures on health care were extremely skewed, with most health research funds dedicated to diseases that affected only 10 percent of the world's population. The consequences were already becoming grave, particularly in sub-Saharan Africa, where the human and social capital of an entire generation was disappearing.

The Initiative for Global Health became the catalyst for the most significant official transfer of resources from rich countries to poor ones in this century. Governments of rich countries initially responded poorly to Annan's call for significant funding to address the AIDS crisis and other health catastrophes afflicting the developing countries. But activists came to the rescue, mobilizing public opinion in scores of countries to push governments and corporations to do something about an increasingly visible crisis. Within a few years, the fund was receiving the $7–$10 billion per year Annan had said was necessary to begin creating an infrastructure that could deliver health services effectively.

But the money was not simply transferred to governments to spend as they would. Instead, much of it was channeled through a wide array of NGOs, international organizations, and private companies. Although some of the funding was inevitably lost to mistakes and corruption, by and large the fund operated transparently and with a high degree of accountability. In time, it evolved into a formal organization that helped developing countries create effective and efficient health services.

The money also enabled the Initiative for Global Health and the World Health Organization together to take on a leading policy role in key global governance debates. They successfully challenged the international financial institutions' claims about the virtues of privatizing health care provisions and charging access fees for health care. And they spearheaded the fight against the common but absurd agricultural practices of feeding massive quantities of antibiotics to livestock to compensate for the disease-promoting conditions in which the livestock were kept. Although the countries hardest hit by AIDS and other health catastrophes may still take decades to recover fully, and although antibiotic resistance, among other infectious disease problems, continues to plague the world, the Initiative for Global Health clearly constitutes an enormous advance over the situation of two decades ago.

It took longer for substantial funding to start flowing into developing countries to help them address global environmental issues such as climate change. Not until a series of killer hurricanes devastated the state of Texas and swarms of disease-laden mosquitoes made their lethal way up America's East Coast did the United States adopt serious policies related to climate change, such as tax incentives to support less damaging goods and technologies. Thanks to both American and European support, the Global Environment Facility has been expanded beyond recognition and can now offer assistance to nearly every worthwhile project proposed to it regarding both climate change and biodiversity. The World Bank and other development funders have become far more careful about assessing the environmental implications of projects they support, and environmental impact statements are routinely conducted independently and made public.

Unfortunately, all this comes too late to stave off a significant warming of the planet or to rescue the nearly one million species driven to extinction in the twentieth century alone.

Twenty years into the twenty-first century, the major development in global governance comes less in the form of institutional changes than in the answer to the question, Governance for what purpose? Early in the century, conventional thinking saw the purpose of global governance as "to facilitate free trade, freedom of capital movements, and unrestricted access by multinational firms to markets around the globe."[5] Such thinking confused means with ends. It forgot that those steps are merely instruments toward what should be the purposes of governance: solving dilemmas of collective action in just and legitimate ways. The ultimate end, as Nobel laureate Amartya Sen argued, is to advance the ability of those being governed to develop fully their capacities to achieve.[6]

Earlier in the century, we saw years of controversy about whether global economic governance, as it was being practiced, would in fact lead from those steps to the broader ends. As the debate grew more heated, the growing strength of the doubters forced substantial changes in the processes by which intergovernmental organizations and other instruments of global governance operate. The institutions of global governance superficially resemble those of the beginning of the century. We still have a World Trade Organization, a World Bank, an International Monetary Fund, the various "G-groups," and only a handful of new or substantially expanded international organizations. Governments still negotiate international treaties that are crucial to establishing the rules by which the world runs.

Governments remain the ultimate sources of legitimate authority in global rule making. But the processes by which those rules are made have become far more transparent, and a much wider variety of actors regularly participate. The broad acceptance of the idea of transparency, though still imperfect, reflects a general recognition that transparency is crucial to providing a reasonable semblance of democracy at the global level of decision making.

Over the past two decades, it became clear that global decision making required the combined efforts of governments, intergovernmental organizations, business, and civil society. The private sector and civil society have shown themselves capable of helping to devise and implement global rules that serve the broad public interest. Corporations and civil society organizations now routinely join with governments in setting the international agenda, negotiating and implementing agreements (formal or informal), and monitoring and enforcing compliance with the standards of behavior set by those agreements. In addition to transparency, all this has required broad acceptance of the right of the various actors to participate in making the rules that govern us all.

The new reliance on transparency and participation as fundamental principles of global governance does not work perfectly. A transparency-based system of governance is vulnerable to misinformation and deliberate deception. The voices of the rich still too often speak more loudly than the voices of the poor. And as technology, the physical realities of living on a single planet, and deliberate policy choices continue to tie people more closely together into a community of shared fate, we may in time find it necessary to devise more systematic methods of running the world.

But in the meantime, global governance in 2020 is far more legitimate and far more effective than was the case a mere two decades ago. We have found that, as the clichés have it, sunlight really is the best disinfectant and honesty really is the best policy. In the process of trying to figure out which cross-border problems really matter and how to deal with them, even with the best of intentions everyone involved is bound to make many mistakes. Certainly, the world would be blessed if we could find a few brilliant and compassionate philosopher-kings able to make all the necessary decisions and painful trade-offs on behalf of the public interest. We could put them in charge of the national governments or the international organizations and wait for the rules to be handed down. But absent such wisdom from on high, the messy muddle of transnational governance, quite different from traditional patterns of national government, is probably the best we can do. It is hard to see what alternatives, at this point in human history, would better reconcile the sometimes competing demands for effectiveness, efficiency, fairness, and legitimacy in global governance.

Back to the Present

One final word from the world of today: there is a serious danger that, in the words of William Yeats' famous poem, the center will not hold. All we have to array against the forces of intolerance, greed, and sheer human pettiness are a few ideas about the necessity of holding power accountable and providing voice to the powerless. The fourth revolution that we are now undergoing may make possible a highly democratic, albeit nonelectoral, system of transnational governance. It will not be perfect. It is inherently messy, difficult to institutionalize, subject to co-optation by the rich and powerful, and hard to explain. As Winston Churchill famously said of national democracy, it may even be the worst form of governance—except for all the alternatives.

That messy new system will contain many features that Churchill would have recognized as democracy, including regular elections for national representatives empowered to make binding laws and to delegate some powers to inter-governmental organizations. But such formal governmental structures of decision making won't be enough. Indeed, governments alone can only be part of the solution.

Such alternative or supplementary approaches as corporate codes of conduct or civil society campaigns can help to provide accountability and feedback at the global level, where direct electoral systems would be unwieldy. There will still be plenty of questions about the effectiveness of the resulting system, and indeed about the extent to which it is truly or fully democratic. But that is true today about governance at the national level. The challenge is not to design a theoretically perfect system for running the world. The challenge is to take account of the scale of global problems and the diversity of the world's cultures while taking advantage of the new possibilities opened up by information technology in ways that will maximize the rule of the people. That, after all, is the literal meaning of democracy.

NOTES

Chapter 1: A Time of Transformation?

1. John Man, *Gutenberg: How One Man Remade the World with Words* (New York: Wiley, 2002).
2. For an exploration of some of the consequences of the print revolution, see Elizabeth L. Eisenstein, *The Printing Revolution in Early Modern Europe* (Cambridge, England: Cambridge University Press, 1983).
3. Man, *Gutenberg,* 270–273.
4. Eisenstein, *Printing Revolution,* 81–82.
5. Ibid., 77.
6. Ibid., 170.
7. Man, *Gutenberg,* 105.
8. Peter Schwartz, Peter Leyden, and Joel Hyatt, *The Long Boom: A Vision for the Coming Age of Prosperity* (Reading, Mass.: Perseus Books, 1999).
9. Robert Kaplan, *The Ends of the Earth: A Journey at the Dawn of the 21st Century* (New York: Random House, 1996).
10. See, e.g., George Friedman and Meredith LeBard, *The Coming War with Japan* (New York: St. Martin's Press, 1997), and Richard Bernstein and Ross H. Munro, *The Coming Conflict with China* (New York: Knopf, 1997).
11. Samuel Huntington, *The Clash of Civilizations and the Remaking of World Order* (New York: Simon and Schuster, 1996).
12. For more information on future military security issues, see Zalmay Khalilzad and Ian O. Lesser, eds., *Sources of Conflict in the 21st Century: Regional Futures and U.S. Strategy* (Santa Monica, Calif.: RAND, 1998); Lawrence Freedman, *The Revolution in Strategic Affairs* (New York: Oxford University Press for the International Institute of Strategic Studies, 1998); and John Arquilla and David Ronfeldt, *In Athena's Camp: Preparing for Conflict in the Information Age* (Santa Monica, Calif.: RAND, 1997). On trade

in dual-use technology, see Wolfgang H. Reinicke, *Global Public Policy: Governing without Government?* (Washington, D.C.: Brookings Institution Press, 1998).

13. Christopher J. L. Murray and Alan D. Lopez, eds., *The Global Burden of Disease: A Comprehensive Assessment of Mortality and Disability from Diseases, Injuries, and Risk Factors in 1990 and Projected to 2020,* vol. 1, Global Burden of Disease and Injury Series (Cambridge, Mass.: Harvard School of Public Health, Center for Population and Development Studies, Burden of Disease Unit, on behalf of the World Health Organization and the World Bank, 1996), Executive Summary, http://www.hsph.harvard.edu/organizations/bdu/summary.html; "Infectious Diseases and Global Change: Threats to Human Health and Security," *Aviso,* no. 8 (June 2001). About 90 percent of those deaths result from just six diseases: pneumonia; tuberculosis; diarrheal illnesses such as dysentery and cholera; malaria; measles; and AIDS.

14. Stuart B. Levy, "The Challenge of Antibiotic Resistance," *Scientific American* 278, no. 3 (March 1998): 46.

15. Christopher P. Howson, Harvey V. Fineberg, and Barry R. Bloom, "The Pursuit of Global Health: The Relevance of Engagement for Developed Countries," *Lancet* 351, no. 9102 (February 21, 1998): 586–590.

16. "AIDS and Violent Conflict in Africa," *Peace Watch* 7, no. 4 (June 2001).

17. Joint United Nations Programme on HIV/AIDS (UNAIDS), "Global Estimates of HIV/AIDS Epidemic as of End 2001," Fourteenth International Conference on AIDS, Barcelona, July 7–12, 2002, http://www.unaids.org/barcelona/presskit/barcelona%20report/Global_estimate.pdf.

18. The projection is according to UNICEF. Erica Barks-Ruggles, *Meeting the Global Challenge of HIV/AIDS,* Policy Brief no. 75 (Washington, D.C.: Brookings Institution, April 2001), http://www.brook.edu/comm/policy-briefs/pb075/pb75.htm.

19. Barbara Crossette, "Worldwide Tourist Industry Takes Off," *International Herald Tribune,* April 13, 1998.

20. World Health Organization, "Tuberculosis," Fact Sheet no. 104, revised August 2002, http://www.who.int/mediacentre/factsheets/who104/en/index.html.

21. Kathryn S. Fuller, "Balancing Trade and Sea Turtles," *International Herald Tribune,* May 16, 1998.

22. A few farsighted thinkers have tried to take what Nobel laureate Murray Gell-Mann calls "a crude look at the whole." In the early 1990s, for example, the Brookings Institution, the Santa Fe Institute, and the World Resources Institute undertook a multiyear effort called the 2050 Project aimed at considering the interactions among the many trends affecting the world. But such efforts are rare.

23. A standard approach to collective action problems is to try to turn them into individuals' problems by assigning "property rights" that give ownership to individuals rather than groups. But privatization is not an option for solving many global problems, such as the need for climate protection or financial stability. Even where it *is* possible, privatization just moves the collective action problem to a different place. Assigning property rights is itself a collective action problem. If external authorities do it, they face enormous problems in gathering information about how to divide the resource, particularly if they try to combine considerations of efficiency and fairness. Then someone has to enforce those rights. If the group acts internally to assign and enforce property rights, it still faces a collective action problem. See Elinor Ostrom, *Governing the Commons: The Evolution of Institutions for Collective Action* (Cambridge, England: Cambridge University Press, 1990).

24. There is an enormous literature in the social sciences on collective action theory. One classic book is Mancur Olson's *The Logic of Collective Action: Public Goods and the Theory of Groups* (Cambridge, Mass.: Harvard University Press, 1965). See also Russell Hardin, *Collective Action* (Baltimore, Md.: Johns Hopkins University Press for Resources for the Future, 1982), and Todd Sandler, *Collective Action: Theory and Applications* (Ann Arbor: University of Michigan Press, 1992). This brief overview of collective action theory lumps together some distinct subjects. Collective goods are not created equal. All share the characteristic of nonexcludability—that is, once they exist, everyone can use them. Pure public goods have a second characteristic known as nonrivalry in consumption. My "consumption" of a stable climate or a strong national defense does not detract from yours. But my consumption of a fishery or of irrigation water does prevent others from using that share of the good. This latter type of collective good is called a common pool resource. Free riding, in such cases, is not merely a failure to contribute to the collective good but a direct taking from what other members of the group can do or have.

25. Olson, *Logic of Collective Action*, 64.

26. Janna Thompson, "Community Identity and World Citizenship," in *Reimagining Political Community: Studies in Cosmopolitan Democracy*, ed. Daniele Archibugi, David Held, and Martin Köhler (Stanford, Calif.: Stanford University Press, 1998).

27. Robert Keohane, "International Institutions: Can Interdependence Work?" *Foreign Policy* 110 (spring 1998): 82–97.

28. For some types of problems, such as the need to develop treatments or vaccines for resurgent diseases, the benevolent hegemon remains humanity's best hope. It makes far more sense for the U.S. Centers for Disease Control and Prevention to spend a fair amount of money on an AIDS vaccine than

for twice the expenditure to be evenly divided among the health research centers of, say, fifty of the world's poorest countries. See Todd Sandler, *Global Challenges: An Approach to Environmental, Political, and Economic Problems* (Cambridge, England: Cambridge University Press, 1997), 20.

29. For an impassioned plea in favor of promoting transparency and accountability for all, rather than restricting information flows in the name of privacy, see David Brin, *The Transparent Society: Will Technology Force Us to Choose between Privacy and Freedom?* (Reading, Mass.: Addison-Wesley, 1998).

Chapter 2: The Global Spotlight

1. So far, high-resolution imagery is expensive to buy—as much as $4,000 per image—and difficult and costly to interpret. Space Imaging and the other commercial satellite operators are betting that local governments and a wide range of companies, not to mention national governments that lack their own satellites, will find the combination of comprehensive vistas and impressive detail irresistible. If a market large enough to drive prices down does develop, satellite imagery could play a significant role in diffusing knowledge away from governments and thus in shifting power to nongovernmental actors.

2. Pike has since left the Federation of American Scientists. He has continued his work at GlobalSecurity.org; see http://www.globalsecurity.org/eye/index.html.

3. Yahya A. Dehqanzada and Ann M. Florini, *Secrets for Sale: How Commercial Satellite Imagery Will Change the World* (Washington, D.C.: Carnegie Endowment for International Peace, 2000).

4. Vipin Gupta and Adam Bernstein, "Keeping an Eye on the Islands: Cooperative Remote Monitoring in the South China Sea," in *Commercial Observation Satellites: At the Leading Edge of Global Transparency,* ed. John C. Baker, Kevin M. O'Connell, and Ray A. Williamson (Santa Monica, Calif.: RAND, 2001), 327–360.

5. David Albright and Corey Gay Hinderstein, "Nongovernmental Use of Commercial Satellite Imagery for Achieving Nuclear Nonproliferation Goals: Perspectives and Case Studies," in Baker, O'Connell, and Williamson, *Commercial Observation Satellites,* 381–402.

6. Jeremy Bentham, *Panopticon* (London: R. Baldwin, 1812).

7. Michel Foucault, *Discipline and Punish: The Birth of the Prison* (New York: Vintage Books, 1979).

8. William J. Mitchell, *City of Bits: Space, Place, and the Infobahn* (Cambridge, Mass.: MIT Press, 1995).

9. David Brin, *The Transparent Society: Will Technology Force Us to Choose*

between Privacy and Freedom? (Reading, Mass.: Addison-Wesley, 1998), chap. 1.

10. Ibid., 4.

11. Communities for a Better Environment–California, *Oil Rag: Newsletter of the National Oil Refinery Action Network (NORAN),* no. 1 (October 1995), http://www.cbecal.org/oldcbe/cbesf/rag1.html.

12. David Patterson, "Microprocessors in 2020," *Scientific American* 273, no. 3 (September 1995): 48–51.

13. William Wresch, *Disconnected: Haves and Have-Nots in the Information Age* (New Brunswick, N.J.: Rutgers University Press, 1996).

14. Katie Hafner, "Common Ground Elusive as Technology Have-Nots Meet Haves," *New York Times,* July 8, 1999; World Bank, *World Development Indicators, 2000* (Washington, D.C.: World Bank, 2000), 10.

15. Hafner, "Common Ground Elusive."

16. See the Web site of the Global Information Infrastructure Commission, http://www.giic.org.

17. Jay Ulfelder, "Into the Breach: Tackling the Digital Divide," *Worldlink: The Magazine of the World Economic Forum* (January–February 2002): 63–66.

18. Jon B. Alterman, "How World-Wide Is the Web?" *Information Impacts Magazine,* December 1999, http://www.cisp.org/imp/december_99/12_99alterman-insight.htm.

19. Andy Pasztor, "Hughes Electronics Agrees to Provide Satellite-Based Web Service in India," *Wall Street Journal,* March 24, 2000, B-4.

20. World Bank, *World Development Indicators, 1998* (Washington, D.C.: World Bank, 1998), 290.

21. Miriam Jordan, "It Takes a Cell Phone," *Wall Street Journal,* June 25, 1999; Kenneth J. Cooper, "One Moment, Please, Ganganagar Calling the World," *Washington Post,* March 1, 2000, A15.

22. G. Russell Pipe, Carol Charles, and Symon Visser, eds., *Assessing Data Privacy in the 1990s and Beyond* (Washington, D.C.: Global Information Infrastructure Commission, 1996).

23. For more information on such vulnerabilities, see Kenneth B. Malpass et al., *Workshop on Protecting and Assuring Critical National Infrastructure* (Stanford, Calif.: Stanford University, Center for International Security and Cooperation, 1997); Stuart J. D. Schwartzstein, ed., *The Information Revolution and National Security: Dimensions and Directions* (Washington, D.C.: Center for Strategic and International Studies, 1996); John Arquilla and David Ronfeldt, *The Advent of Netwar* (Santa Monica, Calif.: RAND, 1996); Roger C. Molander, Andrew S. Riddie, and Peter A. Wilson, *Strategic Information Warfare: A New Face of War* (Santa Monica, Calif.: RAND, 1996).

24. Stephen M. Kobrin, "Electronic Cash and the End of National Markets," *Foreign Policy*, no. 107 (summer 1997): 65–77.

25. David E. Sanger and Jeri Clausing, "U.S. Removes More Limits on Encryption Technology," *New York Times*, January 13, 2000.

26. This language is taken from the standard license issued by the National Oceanic and Atmospheric Administration (NOAA), U.S. Department of Commerce, to companies wishing to operate private satellites under the terms of Title II of the Land Remote Sensing Policy Act of 1992 (P.L. 102-555). A copy of the license form was faxed to the author by NOAA on March 17, 1999.

27. Reporters sans frontières (Reporters without Borders), "The Twenty Enemies of the Internet," press release, August 9, 1999, http://www.fiu.edu/~fcf/twnetyenemies.html.

28. Garry Rodan, "The Internet and Political Control in Singapore," *Political Science Quarterly* 113, no. 1 (spring 1998): 63–89.

29. Elizabeth Rosenthal, "China Issues Rules to Limit E-Mail and Web Content," *New York Times*, January 27, 2000.

30. Shanthi Kalathil and Taylor C. Boas, *The Internet and State Control in Authoritarian Regimes: China, Cuba, and the Counterrevolution*, Working Paper no. 21 (Washington, D.C.: Carnegie Endowment for International Peace, July 2001).

31. Leonard R. Sussman, "Censor Dot Gov: The Internet and Press Freedom 2000," Freedom House Press Freedom Survey, 2000, http://www.freedomhouse.org/pfs2000/sussman.html.

32. François Fortier, "Power@Grassroots.org" (paper presented at conference of the United Nations Research Institute for Social Development, Geneva, June 22–23, 1998).

33. Rodan, "Internet and Political Control in Singapore."

34. Nina Hachigian, "China's Cyber Strategy," *Foreign Affairs* 80, no. 2 (March 2001): 118–134.

35. Sheila McNulty and Peter Montagnon, "Getting Ready to Take a More Relaxed Approach: Singapore Is Poised for Further Economic Liberalization," *Financial Times*, March 13, 2000, 21.

36. Rafal Rohozinski, *Mapping Russian Cyberspace: Perspectives on Democracy and the Net*, Discussion Paper no. 115 (Geneva: United Nations Research Institute for Social Development, October 1999).

37. Laurent Belsie, "Technology Thwarted Coup Leaders' Success," *Christian Science Monitor*, August 26, 1991, 2.

38. Bob Travica and Matthew Hogan, "Computer Networking in the xUSSR: Technology, Uses, and Social Effects," listserv message, July 15, 1992,

http://www.funet.fi/pub/culture/russian/politics/coup/papers/Travica-Hogan92.

39. Chris Hedges, "Serbs' Answer to Tyranny? Get on the Web," *New York Times,* December 8, 1996, 1.

40. "Internet Played Role in Suharto Overthrow," *Boston Globe,* May 1998.

41. Ibid.

42. See, e.g., Fortier, "Power@Grassroots.org"; Gerald Sussman, *Communication, Technology, and Politics in the Information Age* (Thousand Oaks, Calif.: Sage Publications, 1997); George Spencer, "Microcybernetics as the Meta-Technology of Pure Control," in *Cyberfutures: Culture and Politics on the Information Superhighway,* ed. Ziauddin Sardar and Jerome R. Ravetz (London: Pluto Press, 1996), 61–89.

43. This discussion of transparency is adapted from Ann Florini, "The End of Secrecy," *Foreign Policy,* no. 111 (summer 1998): 50–63.

44. Henry L. Stimson Center, "Other CWC Implementation Facts" (Washington, D.C.: Henry L. Stimson Center, Chemical and Biological Weapons Nonproliferation Project, updated February 5, 2002), http://www.stimson.org/cbw/?sn=cb20011220108.

45. Ibid.

46. Ann M. Florini, "The Politics of Transparency" (paper presented at the annual meeting of the International Studies Association, Los Angeles, March 15–19, 2000).

47. I am indebted to Jordan Tama for this point.

48. Brin, *Transparent Society,* 301.

49. Lou Dolinar, "Access Denied: Government Agencies Criticized for 'Scrubbing,'" *Newsday,* October 24, 2001, http://www.newsday.com.

50. Robin Toner, "A Nation Challenged," *New York Times,* October 27, 2001.

51. The Risk Management Plan information was collected under Section 112(r) of the Clean Air Act. See OMB Watch, "Access to Government Information Post September 11th," February 1, 2002, http://www.ombwatch.org/article/articleview/213/1/1/.

52. Ibid.

53. David Colker, "Despite Government Efforts, the Web Never Forgets," *Los Angeles Times,* November 27, 2001.

54. Amartya Sen, *Resources, Values, and Development* (Cambridge, Mass.: Harvard University Press, 1984).

55. David F. Ronfeldt, *Tribes, Institutions, Markets, Networks: A Framework about Societal Evolution,* RAND Report no. P-7967 (Santa Monica, Calif.: RAND, 1996).

56. Sidney Tarrow, "Fishnets, Internets, and Catnets: Globalization and Transnational Collective Action," in *Challenging Authority: The Historical*

Study of Contentious Politics, ed. Michael P. Hanagan, Leslie Page Moch, and Wayne te Brake (Minneapolis: University of Minnesota Press, 1998), 145.

Chapter 3: The Global We

1. Abraham H. Maslow, *Motivation and Personality* (New York: Harper and Row, 1987).
2. See Benedict Anderson, *Imagined Communities: Reflections on the Origin and Spread of Nationalism* (London, New York: Verso, 1991).
3. For excellent overviews, see Robert Wright, *The Moral Animal* (New York: Pantheon Books, 1994); Steven Pinker, *How the Mind Works* (New York: Norton, 1997); and Henry Plotkin, *Evolution in Mind: An Introduction to Evolutionary Psychology* (Cambridge, Mass.: Harvard University Press, 1998).
4. Richard Dawkins, *The Selfish Gene* (Oxford, England: Oxford University Press, 1989); Edward O. Wilson, *Sociobiology: The New Synthesis* (Cambridge, Mass.: Harvard University Press, 1975).
5. Pinker, *How the Mind Works;* Wright, *Moral Animal.*
6. These ideas about reciprocal altruism draw from game theory. See, e.g., Robert Axelrod, *The Evolution of Cooperation* (New York: Basic Books, 1984).
7. Plotkin, *Evolution in Mind,* chap. 3, provides a strong argument about the pitfalls of trying to claim too much explanatory power for evolutionary psychology.
8. Dawkins, *Selfish Gene.*
9. For a fascinating exploration of these ideas, see Robert Wright, *Non-Zero: The Logic of Human Destiny* (New York: Pantheon Books, 2000).
10. Robert D. Putnam, "Bowling Alone: America's Declining Social Capital," *Journal of Democracy* 6, no. 1 (1995): 65–78; quote on p. 67.
11. See Edward O. Wilson, "The Biological Basis of Morality," *Atlantic Monthly,* April 1998, 53–70, especially p. 59.
12. Samuel Huntington, *The Clash of Civilizations and the Remaking of World Order* (New York: Simon and Schuster, 1996), 20.
13. Clare Ansberry, "Diverted on Sept. 11, Stranded Fliers Make Enduring Connections," *Wall Street Journal,* November 7, 2001, A-1.
14. Richard Rorty, "Human Rights, Rationality, and Sentimentality," *Yale Review* 81, no. 4 (October 1993): 1–20; quote on p. 2.
15. Verena Stolcke, "Talking Culture: New Boundaries, New Rhetorics of Exclusion in Europe," *Current Anthropology* 36 (February 1995): 1–24.
16. Ernest Gellner, *Nations and Nationalism* (Ithaca, N.Y.: Cornell University Press, 1983).

17. The formal study of nationalism dates back less than a century; see Carlton Hayes, *The Historical Evolution of Modern Nationalism* (New York: R. R. Smith, 1931), and Hans Kohn, *The Idea of Nationalism: A Study in Its Origin and Background* (New York: Macmillan, 1944).

18. Eugen Weber, *Peasants into Frenchmen* (Stanford, Calif.: Stanford University Press, 1976).

19. Eric Hobsbawm and Terence Ranger, eds., *The Invention of Tradition* (Cambridge, Mass.: Cambridge University Press, 1983).

20. David Laitin, *Ethnic Cleansing, Liberal Style,* MacArthur Foundation Program in Transnational Security Working Paper Series (Cambridge: Massachusetts Institute of Technology, Center for International Studies, 1995), 5.

21. Ted Gurr, "Minorities, Nationalists, and Ethnopolitical Conflict," in *Managing Global Chaos: Sources of and Response to International Conflict,* ed. Chester A. Crocker, Fen Osler Hampson, and Pamela Aall (Washington, D.C.: United States Institute of Peace Press, 1996).

22. Scholars have made quite a cottage industry of generating competing explanations for what drove this relatively recent triumph of nationalism as the reigning form of group identity. Although most agree that nationalism arose as a political tool, used by political elites to mobilize populations by appealing to a largely mythical and invented national consciousness, no one agrees about why, when, or where they did so. Charles Tilly contends that the demands of war sparked the invention of nationalism as political elites used appeals to a deliberately created national identity to mobilize large numbers of people to fight in and pay for war—as he put it, "war made the state, and the state made war." Charles Tilly, ed., *The Formation of National States in Western Europe* (Princeton, N.J.: Princeton University Press, 1975). Elsewhere, however, Tilly has said that nationalism is not merely a political phenomenon—it is also a set of principles of national self-determination, principles whose power and implications need explanation. See Charles Tilly, "National Self-Determination as a Problem for All of Us," *Daedalus* 122 (spring 1993): 29–36. Ernest Gellner argues that nationalism arose in the industrial age when the leaders of industrial societies needed to mobilize large groups for labor in the new industries. Gellner, *Nations and Nationalism.* Liah Greenfeld claims it was invented by upwardly mobile commoners in early-sixteenth-century England to make room for themselves in the rigidly stratified society of the time, which had no place for them. Liah Greenfeld, *Nationalism: Five Roads to Modernity* (Cambridge, Mass.: Harvard University Press, 1992).

23. Anderson, *Imagined Communities,* 87.

24. Manuel Castells, *The Power of Identity* (Malden, Mass.: Blackwell, 1997). Anthony Smith points out that elites do not work from a tabula rasa: "Cer-

tainly the state and political action play important roles in crystallizing ethnic sentiments and national identities, notably through protracted warfare
and territorialization. But ethnic ties and national sentiments are created by
a variety of factors—ecological, social, and especially cultural and symbolic,
such as religion, language and the arts." Anthony Smith, "Culture, Community, and Territory: The Politics of Ethnicity and Nationalism," *International Affairs* 72, no. 3 (1996): 448.

25. Walker Connor, *Ethnonationalism: The Quest for Understanding* (Princeton,
    N.J.: Princeton University Press, 1994), 197.
26. Yael Tamir, "The Enigma of Nationalism," *World Politics* 47 (April 1995):
    426.
27. Ibid., 425. Liah Greenfeld similarly focuses on the psychological gratifica-
    tion offered by national identity to explain its power.
28. Eric Hobsbawm, *Nations and Nationalism since 1780: Programme, Myth,
    Reality* (Cambridge, England: Cambridge University Press, 1990).
29. Ibid., 109.
30. Hobsbawm, *Nations and Nationalism since 1780.*
31. Ibid., 134.
32. Rupert Emerson, *From Empire to Nation: The Rise to Self-Assertion of Asian
    and African Peoples* (Cambridge, Mass.: Harvard University Press, 1960),
    158; Hans Kohn, *Nationalism: Its Meaning and History* (Princeton, N.J.:
    Van Nostrand, 1955), 89, cited in Mark Juergensmeyer, *The New Cold War?
    Religious Nationalism Confronts the Secular State* (Berkeley: University of
    California Press, 1993).
33. Juergensmeyer, *New Cold War?* 14.
34. Monroe Price, "The Market for Loyalties: Electronic Media and the Global
    Competition for Allegiances," *Yale Law Journal* 104, no. 3 (December
    1994): 667–705.
35. Ibid., 673.
36. Ibid., 677 n. 48.
37. Eric Hobsbawm, "The Perils of the New Nationalism," *Nation* 253, no.
    151 (1991): 556.
38. Ted Gurr and James Scarritt, "Minorities at Risk: A Global Survey," *Human
    Rights Quarterly* 11 (1989): 375.
39. The quote is from Samuel Huntington, "If Not Civilizations, What? Para-
    digms of the Post–Cold War World," *Foreign Affairs* 72, no. 5 (Novem-
    ber–December 1993): 194.
40. This would be the argument in Francis Fukuyama, *The End of History and
    the Last Man* (New York: Maxwell Macmillan International, 1992), and
    Gellner, *Nations and Nationalism,* among other sources.
41. Huntington, "If Not Civilizations, What?"; Huntington, *Clash of Civiliza-*

tions; Connor, *Ethnonationalism;* Liah Greenfeld, "Transcending the Nation's Worth," *Daedalus* 122, no. 3 (1993): 47–62.

42. Greenfeld, "Transcending the Nation's Worth."

43. V. P. Gagnon, "Ethnic Nationalism and International Conflict: The Case of Serbia," *International Security* 19, no. 3 (1995): 130–166.

44. Hobsbawm, *Nations and Nationalism since 1780.*

45. Ibid., 177. E. H. Carr argued in 1945 in *Nationalism and After* (London: Macmillan, 1945) that nationalism would have to be replaced by a kind of functional internationalism because national self-determination necessarily creates units that can neither protect themselves nor survive economically.

46. Yahya Sadowski, "Ethnic Conflict," *Foreign Policy* (summer 1998): 12.

47. David Lake and Donald Rothchild, "Ethnic Fears and Global Engagement: The International Spread and Management of Ethnic Conflict," *Ethnic Fears,* January 8, 1996, 41.

48. Dale Eckelman, "Trans-state Islam and Security," in *Transnational Religion and Fading States,* ed. S. H. Rudolph and James Piscatori (Boulder, Colo.: Westview Press, 1997), 31.

49. Daniel Levine and David Stoll, "Bridging the Gap between Empowerment and Power in Latin America," in Rudolph and Piscatori, *Transnational Religion and Fading States,* 3.

50. Rudolph and Piscatori, *Transnational Religion and Fading States.*

51. Peter L. Berger, "Four Faces of Global Culture," *National Interest* 49 (fall 1997): 27–28.

52. Levine and Stoll, "Bridging the Gap."

53. Robert Boynton, "The Two Tonys," *New Yorker,* October 6, 1997, 74.

54. Pippa Norris, "Global Governance and Cosmopolitan Citizens," in *Governance in a Globalizing World,* ed. Joseph S. Nye Jr. and John D. Donahue (Washington, D.C.: Brookings Institution Press, 2000), 155–177.

Chapter 4: Why Governments Won't Solve Everything

1. Daniel Yergin and Joseph Stanislaw, *The Commanding Heights: The Battle between Government and the Marketplace That Is Remaking the Modern World* (New York: Simon and Schuster, 1998).

2. See, e.g., Stephen Krasner, "Approaches to the State: Alternative Conceptions and Historical Dynamics," *Comparative Politics* 16, no. 2 (January 1984): 223–246, and Peter B. Evans, Dietrich Rueschemeyer, and Theda Skocpol, eds., *Bringing the State Back In* (New York: Cambridge University Press, 1985).

3. Hendrik Spruyt, *The Sovereign State and Its Competitors* (Princeton, N.J.: Princeton University Press, 1994).

4. Charles Tilly, "War Making and State Making as Organized Crime," in Evans, Rueschemeyer, and Skocpol, *Bringing the State Back In,* 183.

5. Norman Davies, *Europe: A History* (New York: Oxford University Press, 1996).

6. Charles Tilly, ed., *The Formation of National States in Western Europe* (Princeton, N.J.: Princeton University Press, 1975), 71.

7. Tilly, "War Making and State Making," 185–186.

8. Michael Mann, "Nation-States in Europe and Other Continents: Diversifying, Developing, Not Dying," *Daedalus* 122, no. 3 (summer 1993): 116–117.

9. Ibid., 117.

10. See Mohammed Ayoob, *The Third World Security Predicament: State Making, Regional Conflict, and the International System* (Boulder, Colo.: Lynne Rienner, 1995), 50 n. 15.

11. Mann, "Nation-States in Europe," 137.

12. World Bank, *World Development Report 1997: The State in a Changing World* (New York: Oxford University Press, 1997), 2. The figure is for all government expenditures, central and local, including social security expenditures.

13. World Bank, *World Development Report 1996: From Plan to Market* (New York: Oxford University Press, 1996).

14. See Sven Steinmo, *Taxation and Democracy: Swedish, British, and American Approaches to Financing the Modern State* (New Haven, Conn.: Yale University Press, 1993), and Alberto Giovannini, "National Tax Systems versus the European Capital Market," *Economic Policy* 9 (October 1989): 345–386.

15. Reint Gropp and Kristina Kostial, "FDI and Corporate Tax Revenue," *Finance and Development* 38, no. 2 (June 2001): 10–13.

16. AccountancyMagazine.com, "OECD and European Corporate Taxes Fall for Fifth Year," February 8, 2001, http://www.smartpros.com/x29281.xml.

17. Martha Finnemore, "Norms, Culture, and World Politics: Insights from Sociology's Institutionalism," *International Organization* 50, no. 2 (1996): 332.

18. Ayoob, *Third World Security Predicament.*

19. Ibid., 41.

20. John Stremlau, "Antidote to Anarchy," *Washington Quarterly* 18, no. 1 (winter 1995): 29–44.

21. Susan Strange, *The Retreat of the State: The Diffusion of Power in the World Economy* (Cambridge, England: Cambridge University Press, 1996), 14.

22. See, e.g., Michael Specter, "Low Birth Rates Cause Alarm: There Are Too Few Newborns in Europe to Renew Populations," *International Herald Tribune,* July 11–12, 1998, 1.

23. Thomas Homer-Dixon, "The Rise of Complex Terrorism," *Foreign Policy* (January–February 2002): 52–62.

24. The literature on regimes is enormous. The classic work is Stephen Krasner, ed., *International Regimes* (Ithaca, N.Y.: Cornell University Press, 1983). Other important volumes include Volker Rittberger and Peter Mayer, eds., *Regime Theory and International Relations* (Oxford, England: Clarendon Press, 1983), and Robert Keohane, *International Institutions and State Power: Essays in International Relations Theory* (Boulder, Colo.: Westview Press, 1989).

25. World Trade Organization, *The Multilateral Trading System: Fifty Years of Achievement* (Geneva: World Trade Organization, May 1998); Joan E. Spero and Jeffrey A. Hart, *The Politics of International Economic Relations,* 5th ed. (New York: St. Martin's Press, 1997), 49–95, 215–248; Bernard M. Hoekman and Michel M. Kostecki, *The Political Economy of the World Trading System: From GATT to WTO* (New York: Oxford University Press, 1995); John Croome, *Reshaping the World Trading System: A History of the Uruguay Round,* 2nd ed. (The Hague: World Trade Organization; Boston: Kluwer Law International, 1999); World Trade Organization Secretariat, *Guide to the Uruguay Round Agreements* (The Hague: World Trade Organization; Boston: Kluwer Law International, 1999).

26. Marvin S. Soroos, *The Endangered Atmosphere: Preserving a Global Commons* (Columbia: University of South Carolina Press, 1997), 147–175; Richard Elliot Benedick, "Ozone Diplomacy," and Ian H. Rowlands, "Ozone Layer Depletion and Global Warming: New Sources for Environmental Disputes," in *Green Planet Blues: Environmental Politics from Stockholm to Rio,* ed. Ken Conca, Michael Alberty, and Geoffrey D. Dabelko (Boulder, Colo.: Westview Press, 1995); Edward A. Parson, "Protecting the Ozone Layer," in *Institutions for the Earth: Sources of Effective International Environmental Protection,* ed. Peter M. Haas, Robert O. Keohane, and Marc A. Levy (Cambridge, Mass.: MIT Press, 1993).

27. Rodney W. Jones and Mark G. McDonough, with Toby F. Dalton and Gregory D. Koblentz, *Tracking Nuclear Proliferation: A Guide in Maps and Charts, 1998* (Washington, D.C.: Carnegie Endowment for International Peace, 1998).

28. Most of the goals were reiterated in the declaration of the Millennium Summit of the United Nations, signed by nearly all national governments in September 2000. The text of the United Nations Millennium Declaration is available at http://www.un.org/millennium/declaration/ares552e.pdf.

29. "Shots for All Children," *International Herald Tribune,* January 23, 2002, 8.

30. Michael Cranna, ed., *The True Cost of Conflict* (London: Earthscan with Saferworld, 1994).

31. In 1999, the United States spent approximately $260 billion. The next

eight were are follows: Japan, $51 billion; France, $47 billion; Germany, $40 billion; the United Kingdom, $32 billion; Italy, $23 billion; Russia, $22 billion; China, $18 billion (although this figure is almost certainly an underestimate, given that China excludes many items normally included in military budgets); and South Korea, $15 billion. Stockholm International Peace Research Institute, *SIPRI Yearbook 2000: Armaments, Disarmament, and International Security* (Oxford, England: Oxford University Press, 2000), 270–274.

32. See chapter 7 for the distinction between exchange rate measurement and purchasing power parity.

33. Joseph S. Nye, *Bound to Lead: The Changing Nature of American Power* (New York: Basic Books, 1990).

34. Stewart Patrick, "America's Retreat from Multilateral Engagement," *Current History* (December 2000): 430–439.

35. Ibid., 433.

36. Associated Press, "Bush Approves Payment on Back Dues to United Nations, Hopes for Help Fighting Terrorism," October 5, 2001; Juliet Eilperin, "House Approves UN Payment," *Washington Post*, September 25, 2001.

37. Eilperin, "House Approves UN Payment."

38. Steven Kull, *Americans on the War on Terrorism: A Study of U.S. Public Attitudes* (Washington, D.C.: Program on International Policy Attitudes, November 13, 2001), 5.

39. Ibid., 4, 8.

40. Max Boot, "The Case for American Empire," *Weekly Standard* 7, no. 5 (October 15, 2001): 27.

41. Joseph Nye, "The New Rome Meets the New Barbarians," *Economist*, March 23, 2002, 23–25.

42. Anne-Marie Slaughter, "The Real New World Order," *Foreign Affairs* 76, no. 5 (September–October 1997): 183–197.

43. Ibid., 190.

44. See the International Hydrographic Organization's World Wide Web site at http://www.iho.shom.fr/iho.html.

45. For an overview of perspectives about intergovernmental organizations, see Michael N. Barnett and Martha Finnemore, "The Politics, Power, and Pathologies of International Organizations," *International Organization* 53, no. 4 (autumn 1999): 699–732. See also Robert O. Keohane, *After Hegemony: Cooperation and Discord in the World Political Economy* (Princeton, N.J.: Princeton University Press, 1984).

46. See the annual Human Development Reports published by Oxford University Press for the United Nations Development Programme.

47. Lloyd Gruber, *Ruling the World: Power Politics and the Rise of Supranational Institutions* (Princeton, N.J.: Princeton University Press, 2000), xiii–xiv.
48. Peter Evans and Martha Finnemore, "Organizational Reform and the Expansion of the South's Voice at the Fund" (report prepared for the G-24 Technical Group meeting, Washington, D.C., April 12–18, 2001), 12–13.
49. John Audley and Ann M. Florini, *Overhauling the WTO: Opportunity at Doha and Beyond,* Policy Brief no. 6 (Washington, D.C.: Carnegie Endowment for International Peace, October 2001).
50. Naomi Koppel, "Poor Nation Dilemma: How to Shape the World without Being There," Associated Press, June 25, 2000.
51. Robert O. Keohane, "International Institutions: Can Interdependence Work?" *Foreign Policy* (spring 1998): 93.
52. Thomas S. Blanton, "The International Movement for Freedom of Information" (paper presented at annual meeting of the International Studies Association, New Orleans, March 27, 2002, based on interview with Shekhar Singh, Washington, D.C., May 23, 2001).

Chapter 5: Business

1. The description of the corporate role in the battle over intellectual property rights is based on the extensive work of scholar Susan Sell. See, e.g., Susan Sell, "Multinational Corporations as Agents of Change: The Globalization of Intellectual Property Rights," in *Private Authority and International Affairs,* ed. A. Claire Cutler, Virginia Haufler, and Tony Porter (Albany: State University of New York Press, 1999), 169–197.
2. The IPC included the CEOs of the Bristol-Myers Squibb Company, CBS, E. I. Du Pont de Nemours and Company, General Electric Company, General Motors Corporation, Hewlett-Packard Company, IBM, Johnson & Johnson, Merck & Co., Monsanto Company, and Pfizer. Ibid., 169.
3. Agreement on Trade-Related Aspects of Intellectual Property Rights, Article 33. Legal text of the TRIPS Agreement (Annex 1C of the Marrakesh Agreement Establishing the World Trade Organization) is available on-line at http://www.wto.org/english/tratop_e/trips_e/t_agm0_e.htm.
4. Ibid., Article 34.
5. Ibid., Article 66.
6. Arlene Buleta, "Drug Firms Take South Africa's Government to Court," *Lancet* 357 (March 10, 2001): 775.
7. David Wilson et al., "Global Trade and Access to Medicines: AIDS Treatments in Thailand," *Lancet* 354 (November 27, 1999): 1893–1895, http://www.transnationale.org/anglais/sources/sante/influence_profits__la ncet_thailand.htm.

8. Michael Hirsh, "Has the White House Really Changed Its Tune on AIDS Drugs?" Newsweek.com Web exclusive, http://discuss.washingtonpost.com/nw-srv/printed/us/na/a10740-2000feb1.htm.

9. Shawn Crispin, "New World Disorder," *Far Eastern Economic Review,* February 17, 2000; Sarah Boseley, "Struggle for Cheap Medicines: Anti-Drugs War between the Big Firms and the Poor Countries," *Guardian,* November 27, 1999, 15; Thomas Fuller, "Asia Battles AIDS with Cheaper Medicines," *International Herald Tribune,* October 27, 1999, 1.

10. Gumisai Mutume, "AIDS Drug Firms Practice New Global Racism," African Eye News Service, http://www.afrol.com/News2001/sa013_medicine_racism.htm.

11. Rachel L. Swarns, "Drug Makers Drop South Africa Suit over AIDS Medicine," *New York Times,* April 20, 2001, A-1.

12. Dagi Kimani, "Price Cuts for AIDS Drugs Welcomed," *Africa News,* May 25, 2000.

13. "GlaxoSmithKline Gives AIDS Drug Rights to Generic Maker," *New York Times,* October 9, 2001, C-4.

14. "Caribbean Nations Get Deal on HIV-Fighting Drugs from U.S. Drug Company," Associated Press, August 28, 2001.

15. Francesco Neves, "The Right Prescription," *Ethnic News Watch (Brazil)* 13, no. 182 (April 30, 2001): 11.

16. Robert Evans, "Leaders Say Eased Patent Accord Could Hurt AIDS Research," *Boston Globe,* September 20, 2001, A3.

17. Ibid.

18. World Trade Organization, "Declaration on the TRIPS Agreement and Public Health," WT/MIN(01)/DEC/2, adopted November 14, 2001, Doha, Qatar, http://www.wto.org/english/thewto_e/minist_e/min01_e/mindecl_trips_e.htm.

19. Cutler, Haufler, and Porter, *Private Authority.*

20. David C. Korten, *When Corporations Rule the World,* 2nd ed. (Bloomfield, Conn.: Kumarian Press, 2001).

21. John Braithwaite and Peter Drahos, *Global Business Regulation* (Cambridge, England: Cambridge University Press, 2000), 145.

22. Ibid.

23. Jack Beatty, ed., *Colossus: How the Corporation Changed America* (New York: Broadway Books, 2001), 45.

24. Ibid., 168–186.

25. Ibid., 141.

26. Marina von Neumann Whitman, "The Corporation and Society," in *New World, New Rules: The Changing Role of the American Corporation* (Boston:

Harvard Business School Press, 1999), reprinted in Beatty, *Colossus,* 468–484.

27. Rhys Jenkins, *Corporate Codes of Conduct: Self-Regulation in a Global Economy,* Programme Paper no. 2 (Geneva: United Nations Research Institute for Social Development; Technology, Business and Society Programme, April 2001), 1–2.

28. U.S. Senate, Select Committee to Study Governmental Operations with Respect to Intelligence Activities, *Covert Action in Chile, 1963–1973,* 94th Cong., 1st sess., Committee Print (Washington, D.C.: U.S. Government Printing Office, 1975).

29. Virginia Haufler, *A Public Role for the Private Sector: Industry Self-Regulation in a Global Economy* (Washington, D.C.: Carnegie Endowment for International Peace, 2001), 16.

30. Jenkins, *Corporate Codes of Conduct,* 2.

31. Peter Martin, "Multinationals Come into Their Own," *Financial Times Millennium Survey,* December 6, 1999, 16.

32. Daniel Yergin and Joseph Stanislaw, *The Commanding Heights: The Battle between Government and the Marketplace That Is Remaking the Modern World* (New York: Simon and Schuster, 1998).

33. Susan Strange, *The Retreat of the State: The Diffusion of Power in the World Economy* (Cambridge, England: Cambridge University Press, 1996), 9.

34. Frederic F. Clairmont, "Power of the World's True Masters: When the Giants Play with Fire," *Le Monde Diplomatique,* December 1999, http://www.globalpolicy.org/socecon/tncs/wrldpwr.htm.

35. Michael Renner, "Worldwide Mergers and Acquisitions, 1980–1999," http://www.globalpolicy.org/socecon/tncs/mergdata.htm.

36. United Nations Conference on Trade and Development, *World Investment Report 1992: Transnational Corporations as Engines of Growth* (New York: United Nations, 1992), 5.

37. United Nations Conference on Trade and Development, *World Investment Report 1999* (New York: United Nations, 1999), overview, 1.

38. World Bank, *World Development Report 1998/99: Knowledge for Development* (New York: Oxford University Press, 1999), table 21, 230, http://www.worldbank.org/wdr/wdr98/contents.htm; World Bank, *World Development Report 1999/2000: Entering the 21st Century* (New York: Oxford University Press, 2000), table 21, 270, http://www.worldbank.org/ wdr/2000/fullreport.html.

39. United Nations Conference on Trade and Development, *World Investment Report 1999,* overview, 9.

40. Jeffrey Garten, "Mega-Mergers, Mega-Influence," *New York Times,* October 26, 1999, http://www.globalpolicy.org/socecon/global/merger.htm.

41. "$37 Million Fine Levied for Clean Air Violation," *New York Times,* May 28, 1998, A-22.
42. Ibid.
43. Russell Mokhiber, "Top 100 Corporate Criminals of the Decade," http://www.corporatepredators.org/top100.html.
44. Thelma Mejia, "Company Charged in Death of Union Leader," Inter Press Service, May 19, 1998.
45. Larry Rohter, "Where Banana Is King, a Revolt over Farmlands," *New York Times,* July 22, 1996, A-4.
46. Paul Lewis, "Blood and Oil," *New York Times,* February 13, 1996, A-1.
47. Oliver F. Williams, "A Lesson from the Sullivan Principles," in *Global Codes of Conduct: An Idea Whose Time Has Come,* ed. Oliver F. Williams (Notre Dame, Ind.: University of Notre Dame Press, 2000), 57–82.
48. Jenkins, *Corporate Codes of Conduct,* 4–5.
49. E. J. Dionne, "Swoosh! Public Shaming Nets Results," *International Herald Tribune,* May 15, 1998.
50. Debora L. Spar, "The Spotlight and the Bottom Line: How Multinationals Export Human Rights," *Foreign Affairs* 77, no. 2 (March–April 1998), 8.
51. Stephan Schmidheiny, Rodney Chase, and Livio DeSimone, *Signals of Change: Business Progress towards Sustainable Development* (Geneva: World Business Council for Sustainable Development, n.d.).
52. Spar, "Spotlight and the Bottom Line."
53. Kofi Annan, "A Compact for the New Century" (speech given to the World Economic Forum, Davos, Switzerland, January 31, 1999), http://www.un.org/partners/business/davos.htm.
54. Caux Roundtable, "The Caux Principles: Business Behavior for a Better World," reprinted in Williams, *Global Codes of Conduct,* 384–388.
55. Gerald F. Cavanaugh, "Executives' Code of Business Conduct: Prospects for the Caux Principles," in Williams, *Global Codes of Conduct,* 172.
56. Ibid., 176.
57. Amy Zuckerman, "Global Standards Can Be a Drag on the Bottom Line," *Journal of Commerce,* July 7, 1998.
58. Louise Lee and Aaron Bernstein, "Who Says Student Protests Don't Matter?" *Business Week,* June 12, 2000, 94–96.
59. Dara O'Rourke, "Monitoring the Monitors: A Critique of PriceWaterhouse Coopers (PwC) Labor Monitoring," unpublished manuscript, September 28, 2000.
60. John Gerald Ruggie, "The Global Compact as Learning Network," *Global Governance* 7, no. 4 (October–December 2001): 371–378.
61. Maria Livanos Cattaui, "Business Takes Up Kofi Annan's Challenge," March 15, 1999, http://www.un.org/partners/business/iccwbo.htm.

62. Dionne, "Swoosh!"

63. See the Global Reporting Initiative's Internet site at http://globalreporting. org.

64. Josephine Shaw Lowell, founder of the New York City Consumers League, cited in Linda F. Golodner, "The Apparel Industry Code of Conduct: A Consumer Perspective on Social Responsibility," in Williams, *Global Codes of Conduct*, 241.

65. Social Investment Forum, "2001 Report on Socially Responsible Investing Trends in the United States," November 28, 2001, http://www.socialinvest.org/ areas/research/trends/2001-Trends.htm. The discussion of socially responsible investing that follows is drawn from this document, except where otherwise noted.

66. The revised version of the principles was released in June 1998 by three groups: in the United States, the Interfaith Center on Corporate Responsibility, a coalition of 275 Protestant, Roman Catholic, and Jewish institutional investors; in the United Kingdom, the Ecumenical Council for Corporate Responsibility; and in Canada, the Taskforce on the Churches and Corporate Responsibility.

67. "Pensions and Investment 2001 Databook," *Pensions and Investments,* December 24, 2001, 11.

68. Hunter Lovins and Walter Link, "Insurmountable Opportunities? Steps and Barriers to Implementing Sustainable Development" (speech given to the United Nations Regional Roundtable for Europe and North America, Vail, Colorado, June 2001).

69. "Very Well Then, I Contradict Myself," *Business Ethics* 15, no. 5 (September–October 2001), 21.

Chapter 6: Civil Society

1. For an assessment of Western efforts to channel funding in support of democracy, see Thomas Carothers, *Aiding Democracy Abroad* (Washington, D.C.: Carnegie Endowment for International Peace, 1999). For an assessment of assistance to civil society, see Marina Ottaway and Thomas Carothers, eds., *Funding Virtue: Civil Society Aid and Democracy Promotion* (Washington, D.C.: Carnegie Endowment for International Peace, 2000).

2. For an evocative scenario along these lines, see Allen Hammond, *Which World? Scenarios for the 21st Century* (Washington, D.C.: Island Press, 1998).

3. Adam Seligman, *The Idea of Civil Society* (New York: Macmillan, 1992).

4. Ibid., 33.

5. Ibid., 57.

6. Seligman, *Idea of Civil Society.*

7. Sidney Tarrow, *Power in Movement: Social Movements, Collective Action, and Politics* (Cambridge, England: Cambridge University Press, 1994), 66.

8. Susanne Hoeber Rudolph, "Introduction: Religion, States, and Transnational Civil Society," in *Transnational Religion and Fading States,* ed. S. H. Rudolph and J. Piscatori (Boulder, Colo.: Westview Press, 1997), 1.

9. Carl Kaysen, "The Abolition of Slavery in the West" (paper presented at Conference on Norms and International Governance, University of California, Los Angeles, July 17–20, 1997).

10. Betty Fladeland, *Men and Brothers: Anglo-American Antislavery Cooperation* (Urbana: University of Illinois Press, 1972), 258; Steve Charnovitz, "Two Centuries of Participation: NGOs and International Governance," *Michigan Journal of International Law* 18, no. 2 (1997): 183–286.

11. Charnovitz, "Two Centuries of Participation," 191–208.

12. Martha Finnemore, *National Interests in International Society* (Ithaca, N.Y.: Cornell University Press, 1997), chap. 3.

13. Ibid. See also the World Wide Web site of the ICRC, at http://www.icrc.org/eng.

14. Except where otherwise noted, this section draws from Motoko Mekata, "Building Partnerships toward a Common Goal: Experiences of the International Campaign to Ban Landmines," in *The Third Force: The Rise of Transnational Civil Society,* ed. Ann M. Florini (Tokyo: Japan Center for International Exchange; Washington, D.C.: Carnegie Endowment for International Peace, 2000), 145–178.

15. Protocol on Prohibitions or Restrictions on the Use of Mines, Booby-Traps and Other Devices, United Nations Convention on Prohibitions or Restrictions on the Use of Certain Conventional Weapons Which May Be Deemed to Be Excessively Injurious or to Have Indiscriminate Effects, adopted October 10, 1980, entered into force December 2, 1983.

16. I witnessed this technique used by Susannah Sirkin of Physicians for Human Rights at a conference titled "Reaching Beyond States: The Role of International NGOs," held at Star Island, Portsmouth, New Hampshire, July 24–31, 1999.

17. "Anti-mine NGO's Resolve Strengthened," *Daily Yomiuri,* October 12, 1997.

18. Center for Negotiation and Dispute Resolution, *A Working Chronology of the International Movement to Ban Anti-Personnel Mines* (Ottawa, Canada: Carleton University, 1997).

19. Jessica Mathews, "The New, Private Order," *Washington Post,* January 21, 1997.

20. Asahi Shimbun, "NGOs, Governments Work Together to Achieve Peace," Asahi News Service, October 20, 1997.

21. Steven Lee Myers, "A 'Maybe' on Land-Mine Ban," *International Herald Tribune*, May 23, 1998.

22. Norma Greenway, "Delegates Vow to Keep Up Momentum: With 'Agenda for Action' in Place, Focus Shifts to 'Non-sexy' Subjects," *Ottawa Citizen*, December 5, 1997.

23. Randy Boswell, "Mines Treaty Boosts Spirits at 'Lost Causes,'" *Ottawa Citizen*, December 5, 1997.

24. Jon Fransen, "International Campaign to Ban Land Mines Receives Nobel Peace Prize," Gannett News Service, December 9, 1997.

25. Juliet O'Neill, "Ottawa Process a One-Time Affair, Canadian Officials Insist," *Ottawa Citizen*, December 6, 1997.

26. Tom Farer, "The UN and Human Rights: More Than a Whimper, Less Than a Roar," in *United Nations, Divided World*, ed. Adam Roberts and Benedict Kingsbury (Oxford, England: Oxford University Press, 1988), 98.

27. Except where otherwise noted, the remaining discussion of human rights is drawn from Thomas Risse, "The Power of Norms versus the Norms of Power: Transnational Civil Society and Human Rights," in Florini, *Third Force*, 179–211.

28. Margaret E. Keck and Kathryn Sikkink, *Activists beyond Borders* (Ithaca, N.Y.: Cornell University Press, 1998); Jackie Smith, Charles Chatfield, and Ron Pagnucco, eds., *Transnational Social Movements and Global Politics: Solidarity beyond the State* (Syracuse, N.Y.: Syracuse University Press, 1997).

29. See Sanjeev Khagram, "Toward Democratic Governance for Sustainable Development: Transnational Civil Society Organizing around Big Dams," in Florini, *Third Force*, 83–114.

30. This section is drawn from Rebecca Johnson, "Advocates and Activists: Conflicting Approaches on Nonproliferation and the Test Ban Treaty," in Florini, *Third Force*, 49–81.

31. If you have been following these notes, you will know that in fact I have done exactly that in an edited volume called *The Third Force: The Rise of Transnational Civil Society*. The authors of those case studies in turn often drew on books they had written on single case studies. Several other books describe additional case studies, such as Keck and Sikkink, *Activists beyond Borders*, and Sanjeev Khagram, James V. Riker, and Kathryn Sikkink, eds., *Restructuring World Politics: Transnational Social Movements, Networks, and Norms* (Minneapolis: University of Minnesota Press, 2002).

32. Tarrow, *Power in Movement*, 143.

33. Charnovitz, "Two Centuries of Participation," 261–262; United Nations, *The World Conferences: Developing Priorities for the 21st Century*, UN Brief-

ing Papers series (New York: United Nations, Department of Public Information, 1997), http://www.un.org/geninfo/bp/worconf.html. The conferences were the World Population Conference (Bucharest, 1974); the World Food Conference (Rome, 1974); the Conference of the International Women's Year (Mexico City, 1975); the United Nations Conference on Human Settlements (Habitat I; Vancouver, 1976); the United Nations International Conference on Population (Mexico City, 1984); the World Conference on Women (Nairobi, 1985); the World Summit for Children (New York, 1990); the United Nations Conference on Environment and Development (Rio de Janeiro, 1992); the World Conference on Human Rights (Vienna, 1993); the International Conference on Population and Development (Cairo, 1994); the World Summit for Social Development (Copenhagen, 1995); the Fourth World Conference on Women (Beijing, 1996); the second United Nations Conference on Human Settlements (Habitat II; Istanbul, 1996); and the World Food Summit (Rome, 1996).

34. See, e.g., Tadashi Yamamoto, ed., *Emerging Civil Society in the Asia Pacific Community: Nongovernmental Underpinnings of the Emerging Asia Pacific Regional Community,* rev. ed. (Singapore: Institute of Southeast Asian Studies; Tokyo: Japan Center for International Exchange in cooperation with the Asia Pacific Philanthropy Consortium, 1996).

35. Tarrow, *Power in Movement,* 147.

36. In the United States and most of Europe, private giving accounts for less than 20 percent of nonprofit income, with more than 80 percent coming from a combination of government support and fees. Lester Salamon et al., *The Emerging Sector: A Statistical Supplement* (Baltimore, Md.: Johns Hopkins University Institute for Policy Studies, 1996).

37. Steven Commins, "World Vision International and Donors: Too Close for Comfort?" in *NGOs, States, and Donors: Too Close for Comfort?* ed. David Hulme and Michael Edwards (New York: St. Martin's Press in association with Save the Children, 1997), 141; Anthony Bebbington and Roger Riddell, "Heavy Hands, Hidden Hands, Holding Hands? Donors, Intermediary NGOs, and Civil Society Organizations," in Hulme and Edwards, *NGOs, States, and Donors,* 111.

38. Hulme and Edwards, *NGOs, States, and Donors,* 11.

39. For a country-by-country analysis of the status of civil society and the extent of government control, see Civicus, *The New Civic Atlas: Profiles of Civil Society in 60 Countries* (Washington, D.C.: Civicus, 1997).

40. Tadashi Yamamoto, ed., *Emerging Civil Society in the Asia Pacific Community: Nongovernmental Underpinnings of the Emerging Asia Pacific Regional Community: A Twenty-Fifth Anniversary Project of the Japan Center for International Exchange* (Singapore: Institute of Southeast Asian Studies and

Japan Center for International Exchange in cooperation with the Asia Pacific Philanthropy Consortium, 1995), 26–27.

41. Matt Forney, "Voice of the People," *Far Eastern Economic Review,* May 7, 1998, 11.

42. Japan Center for International Exchange, "New NPO Law Fosters Enabling Environment," *Civil Society Monitor,* no. 4 (April 1998): 1.

43. Keck and Sikkink, *Activists beyond Borders;* Smith, Chatfield, and Pagnucco, *Transnational Social Movements.*

44. John Boli and George Thomas, "World Culture in the World Polity: A Century of International Non-Governmental Organization," *American Sociological Review* 62 (1997): 171–190.

Chapter 7: Economic Integration

1. The Raging Grannies of Seattle are one of several dozen such groups that have sprung up in recent years in North America, starting in British Columbia in a protest against the presence of U.S. nuclear submarines in Canadian waters. This account is based on telephone interviews. The quotation is from the Seattle Raging Grannies' Web site, http://www.raginggrannies.com/home.html.

2. "The World Trade Organization / Supersedes the laws of all the nations / Trade is the answer, profit is the king / To heck with human rights, they don't mean a thing. . . ." Lyrics by Kay Thode of the Seattle Raging Grannies.

3. Knight Kiplinger, *World Boom Ahead,* cited in Reginald Dale, "So Far, Prophesy of Boom Has the Edge," *International Herald Tribune,* February 19, 1999, 11.

4. "Customs Reports Year 2000 Status of Cross-Border Inspection Program," U.S. Customs Service press release, October 15, 1999, cited in Stephen E. Flynn, "Drugs, Thugs, and Trade: Border Control in an Era of Hemispheric Economic Integration" (report prepared for meeting of the Council on Foreign Relations' Study Group on Globalization and the Future of Border Control, Houston, Texas, February 7, 2000).

5. Timothy Gorringe, *Fair Shares: Ethics and the Global Economy,* cited in Tom Plate, "Lend an Ear to Complaints from the Emerging Countries about Globalization," *International Herald Tribune,* February 22, 1999, 6.

6. Nancy Birdsall, "Life Is Unfair: Inequality in the World," *Foreign Policy,* no. 111 (summer 1998): 76–93. The 60 to 1 ratio reflects what goods and services people in different countries are actually able to buy. Thus, even though Ethiopians live on the dollar equivalent of $110 per year, compared with rich-country averages of close to $30,000 per year, the appropriate income

ratio of rich to poor is not 300 to 1. That Ethiopian income is adjusted to reflect purchasing power parity (PPP), or the number of units of Ethiopian currency required to buy the same quantity of comparable goods and services as one U.S. dollar would buy in an average country. With PPP figures rather than exchange rate equivalents, Ethiopia's per capita income shoots up to more than $500 per year, leading to the 60 to 1 ratio.

7. If calculated as a percentage of total world GDP, the U.S. economy weighs in at a whopping 28 percent. By PPP calculations (see note 6), the United States is still at a respectable 21 percent. The G-7 countries are Britain, Canada, France, Germany, Italy, Japan, and the United States. They began meeting as a group in 1975. Their combined GDP in 1998 was $18.68 trillion, 65 percent of the total world GDP of $28.73 trillion, or, by PPP calculations, about 45 percent. World Bank, *World Development Indicators, 2000* (Washington, D.C.: World Bank, 2000), table 4.2, 186.

8. This was recognized as a problem in the recent debate on IMF conditionality. See, e.g., Mohsin S. Khan and Sunil Sharma, *IMF Conditionality and Country Ownership of Programs,* IMF Working Paper WP/01/142 (Washington, D.C.: International Monetary Fund, 2001), http://www.imf.org/external/pubs/cat/longres.cfm?sk=15374.0.

9. The reality was, of course, more complicated. British pounds were generally held to be as good as gold and could be exchanged in place of gold, so Britain was free to fiddle with its money supply, and trade was not so strictly bound to the supply of gold.

10. Gretchen Ritter, "Silver Slippers and a Golden Cap: L. Frank Baum's *The Wonderful Wizard of Oz* and Historical Memory in American Politics," *Journal of American Studies* 31, no. 2 (1997): 171–202; Hugh Rockoff, "The 'Wizard of Oz' as Monetary Allegory," *Journal of Political Economy* 98, no. 4 (1990): 739–760.

11. Rockoff, "'Wizard of Oz' as Monetary Allegory," 744.

12. Joan E. Spero and Jeffrey A. Hart, *The Politics of International Economic Relations,* 5th ed. (New York: St. Martin's Press, 1997).

13. Ibid., 54.

14. Brian McDonald, *The World Trading System: The Uruguay Round and Beyond* (New York: St. Martin's Press, 1998), 32.

15. "The World Economy: Survey," *Economist,* September 26, 1987, 33.

16. Spero and Hart, *Politics of International Economic Relations,* 82–87.

17. Paul Krugman and Maurice Obstfeld, *International Economics,* 5th ed. (Reading, Mass.: Addison-Wesley, 2000).

18. John Burgess, "Green Room's Closed Doors Couldn't Hide Disagreements," *Washington Post,* December 5, 1999.

19. Nancy Dunne, "The Next Round," *International Economy* 13, no. 33

(May–June 1999): 20.

20. Kathryn S. Fuller, "Balancing Trade and Sea Turtles," *International Herald Tribune,* May 16–17, 1998.

21. Stephen L. Kass and Jean M. McCarroll, "Fidel, Saddam, and the World Trade Organization," *Linkages Journal* 4, no. 1 (February 1999): 13–16.

22. Ibid.

23. Kathleen Newland, "Workers of the World, Now What?" *Foreign Policy,* no. 114 (spring 1999): 52–65.

24. Capital can come from three sources, other than the funds firms retain from profits: bank loans (the major source of corporate financing in most of the world), bond or debt issuance by corporations, or sales of shares of direct ownership in a stock market. Despite all the attention given to Wall Street, stocks account for less than 10 percent of investment even in countries, such as the United States, with well-developed stock markets. But the global trend is toward a growing importance for bonds and stocks.

25. Barry Eichengreen, "The Only Game in Town," *World Today* 54, no. 12 (December 1998): 317.

26. Some governments still set the exchange rate for their currency in a fixed ratio to the dollar, and some Latin American countries are considering using the dollar as their own currency. Most European governments irrevocably fixed their exchange rates vis-à-vis one another's currencies in preparation for the launch of the single common currency, the euro, in stages from 1999 to 2002. But beyond this, exchange rates float freely, and the market, not governments or the International Monetary Fund, decides how much one currency is worth in relation to another.

27. Stanley Fischer, "Exchange Rate Regimes: Is the Bipolar View Correct?" *Journal of Economic Perspectives* 115, no. 2 (spring 2001): 3–24.

28. Eichengreen, "Only Game in Town," 318.

29. Spero and Hart, *Politics of International Economic Relations,* 27.

30. Joseph E. Stiglitz, "What Happened to the Debate on the New Financial Architecture?" (speech given at Plenary Session of the Global Development Network, Bonn, December 5, 1999).

31. Robert M. Solow, "The Amateur," *New Republic* February 8, 1999, 30.

32. "Korea's Widening Social Safety Net Could Threaten Sustained Economic Growth—ADB," News Release no. 53/99, June 18, 1999, http://www.adb.org/Documents/News/1999/nr1999053.asp. For an IMF perspective on the Asian crisis, see Jack Boorman et al., "Managing Financial Crises: The Experience in East Asia," *Carnegie-Rochester Conference Series on Public Policy* 53 (December 2000): 1–79.

33. "Future Indonesian Development Affected by Asia's Economic Woes, Says

ADB Report," News Release no. 52/99, June 18, 1999, http://www.adb. org/Documents/News/1999/nr1999052.asp.

34. "Asia Continues to Be World's Fastest Growing Region," News Release no. 39/00, April 26, 2000, http://www.adb.org/Documents/News/2000/ nr2000039.asp.

35. "Asia Faces a Formidable Challenge in Dealing with Poverty in the New Millennium," News Release no. 41/00, April 26, 2000, http://www.adb. org/Documents/News/2000/nr2000041.asp.

36. *Global Poverty Report,* prepared for the G-8 Okinawa Summit, July 2000, executive summary, 1, http://www.worldbank.org/poverty/library/G8_2000.htm.

37. World Bank, *World Development Indicators, 2000.*

38. World Bank, *World Development Indicators, 2001* (Washington, D.C.: World Bank, 2001), 322.

39. Ibid.

40. Wolfgang H. Reinicke, *Global Public Policy: Governing without Government?* (Washington, D.C.: Brookings Institution Press, 1998), 43. In 1996, the vast majority of developing countries—140 of 166—received only 5 percent of private capital flows to all developing countries.

41. John Williamson, ed., "What Washington Means by Policy Reform," in *Latin American Adjustment: How Much Has Happened?* ed. John Williamson (Washington, D.C.: Institute for International Economics, 1990), 7–20.

42. Moises Naim, "Washington Consensus or Washington Confusion?" *Foreign Policy,* no. 118 (spring 2000): 86–103.

43. The story of economic integration in the twentieth century is obviously far more complex than can be conveyed in a few pages. A good introduction is Spero and Hart, *Politics of International Economic Relations.* For more information about the problems of and prospects for economic integration, see Paul Hirst and Grahame Thompson, *Globalization in Question: The International Economy and the Possibilities of Governance* (Cambridge, England: Polity Press; Oxford, England: Blackwell, 1996); Reinicke, *Global Public Policy,* 29–39, 102, 134; Richard J. Herring and Robert E. Litan, *Financial Regulation in a Global Economy* (Washington, D.C.: Brookings Institution Press, 1995); Organization for Economic Cooperation and Development, *The New Financial Landscape: Forces Shaping the Revolution in Banking, Risk Management, and Capital Markets* (Paris: Organization for Economic Cooperation and Development, 1995), 38–39; and David Folkerts-Landau and Takatoshi Ito, *International Capital Markets: Developments, Prospects, and Policy Issues* (Washington, D.C.: International Monetary Fund, August 1995).

44. World Bank, *World Development Indicators, 2000,* table 1.1, 10.

45. Hirst and Thompson, *Globalization in Question.*

46. Michael D. Bordo, Barry Eichengreen, and Douglas A. Irwin, *Is Globalization Today Really Different than Globalization a Hundred Years Ago?* Working Paper 7195 (Cambridge, Mass.: National Bureau of Economic Research, June 1999).

47. Mike Moore, director-general of the World Trade Organization, "The Post-Seattle Trade Agenda" (speech given at the 33rd World Congress of the International Chamber of Commerce, Budapest, Hungary, May 5, 2000), http://www.wto.org/english/news_e/spmm_e/spmm30_e.htm.

48. International Monetary Fund, "G7 Leaders' Statement on the World Economy," October 30, 1998, http://www.imf.org/external/np/g7/103098ld.htm; International Monetary Fund, "Declaration of G7 Finance Ministers and Central Bank Governors," October 30, 1998, http://www.imf.org/external/np/g7/103098dc.htm; International Monetary Fund, "Report of the Working Group on Transparency and Accountability," October 15, 1998, http://www.imf.org/external/np/g22/taarep.pdf.

49. For assessment of these policies, see *IMF Study Group Report: Transparency and Evaluation* (Washington, D.C.: Center of Concern, 1998), and Lori Udall, "The World Bank and Public Accountability: Has Anything Changed?" in *The Struggle for Accountability: The World Bank, NGOs, and Grassroots Movements,* ed. Jonathan A. Fox and L. David Brown (Cambridge, Mass.: MIT Press, 1998), 391–436.

Chapter 8: Environment

1. Jared Diamond, "Easter's End," *Discover* (August 1995): 62–69.

2. A literature is emerging on the services ecosystems provide and what monetary value those services would have if we had to pay for them. See Stuart L. Pimm, "The Value of Everything," *Nature* 387 (May 5, 1997): 231–232; Robert Costanza et al., "The Value of the World's Ecosystem Services and Natural Capital," *Nature* 387 (May 5, 1997): 253; Gretchen C. Daily, ed., *Nature's Services: Societal Dependence on Natural Ecosystems* (Washington, D.C.: Island Press, 1997); and Yvonne Baskin, *The Work of Nature: How the Diversity of Life Sustains Us* (Washington, D.C.: Island Press, 1997).

3. Jessica Mathews, "Redefining Security," *Foreign Affairs* 68, no. 2 (1989): 162–177.

4. For more information, see Thomas F. Homer-Dixon, *Environment, Scarcity, and Violence* (Princeton, N.J.: Princeton University Press, 1996); Worldwatch Institute, *State of the World, 1998* (New York: Norton, 1998); and World Resources Institute, United Nations Environment Programme, United Nations Development Programme, and World Bank, *World*

Resources 1996–97: A Guide to the Global Environment (New York: Oxford University Press, 1996).

5. "United Nations Comprehensive Assessment of the Freshwater Resources of the World: Report of the Secretary-General," executive summary, paragraphs 1 and 3, http://www.un.org/esa/sustdev/freshwat.htm.

6. World Commission on Forests and Sustainable Development, *Our Forests, Our Future: Report of the World Commission on Forests and Sustainable Development* (Cambridge, England: Cambridge University Press, 1999), 3.

7. Anita Manning, "Report Finds Much of World's Soil Is 'Seriously Degraded,' Food Production Could Be at Risk across the Globe," *USA Today,* May 22, 2000, 5A. That 40 percent increase assumes that a significant number of people continue to consume a meat-intensive diet.

8. Michael Atiyah and Frank Press, "Population Growth, Resource Consumption, and a Sustainable World," joint statement issued by the Royal Society and the National Academy of Sciences, February 1992, http://www.sustdev.org/industry.news/042000/0060.shtml.

9. World Resources Institute, *A Guide to World Resources, 2000–2001: People and Ecosystems: The Fraying Web of Life* (Washington, D.C.: World Resources Institute, 2000), 9.

10. Donella Meadows, "Six Billion of Us: Boo? Hooray?" *(Lebanon, N.H.) Valley News,* October 7, 1999. Also available at http://iisd1.iisd.ca/pcdf/meadows/six_billion.html.

11. Edward O. Wilson, "The Age of the Environment," *Foreign Policy,* no. 119 (summer 2000): 34.

12. Ibid., 34–35.

13. Paul Hawken, Amory Lovins, and L. Hunter Lovins, *Natural Capitalism* (Boston: Little, Brown, 1999).

14. Allen Hammond, *Which World? Scenarios for the 21st Century* (Washington, D.C.: Island Press, 1998), 91.

15. Ibid., 92.

16. Hammond, *Which World?*

17. David Pearce et al., "Debt and the Environment," *Scientific American* 272, no. 6 (June 1995): 53.

18. Ibid., 53–54.

19. "Let Them Eat Pollution," *Economist* 322, no. 7745 (February 8, 1992): 66.

20. Mike McNamee, "The In-Your-Face Economist at the World Bank," *Business Week,* no. 3265 (May 11, 1992): 76.

21. "Declaration of the United Nations Conference on the Human Environ-

ment," June 16, 1972, http://www.unep.org/Documents/Default.asp?DocumentID=97&ArticleID=1503.

22. See the United Nations Environment Programme's World Wide Web site at http://www.unep.org.

23. The following discussion draws from Richard Elliott Benedick, *Ozone Diplomacy: New Directions in Safeguarding the Planet* (Cambridge, Mass.: Harvard University Press, 1991).

24. Ibid., xi.

25. Hilary French, "Learning from the Ozone Experience," in Worldwatch Institute, *State of the World, 1997* (New York: Norton, 1997), 151.

26. Richard Elliott Benedick, speech given at Workshop on Global Resources and Environment, University of California, Berkeley, March 15–17, 1990.

27. Sharon L. Roan, *Ozone Crisis: The Fifteen-Year Evolution of a Sudden Global Emergency* (New York: Wiley, 1989).

28. For a sampling of these meetings between 1996 and 2002, see archived issues of the International Institute for Sustainable Development's *Linkages Journal* at http://www.iisd.ca/journal/previous.htm.

29. J. T. Houghton et al., *Climate Change 1995—The Science of Climate Change: Contribution of Working Group I to the Second Assessment Report of the Intergovernmental Panel on Climate Change* (Cambridge, England: Cambridge University Press, 1996).

30. Daniel L. Albritton et al., "Summary for Policymakers: A Report of Working Group I of the Intergovernmental Panel on Climate Change," http://www.ipcc.ch/pub/spm22-01.pdf, 13.

31. Environmental Defense, "Fact Sheet: Global Warming and Climate Change," June 1, 2001, http://www.environmentaldefense.org/documents/380_global%20warming%20fact%20sheet%2Ehtm.

32. Gail V. Karlsson, "Environment and Sustainable Development," in *A Global Agenda: Issues before the Fifty-Third General Assembly of the United Nations,* ed. John Tessitore and Susan Woolfson (Lanham, Md.: Rowman & Littlefield, 1998), 123–124.

33. Michael Grubb, "Protecting the Planet," *World Today* 56, no. 5 (May 2000): 9.

34. I am indebted to Allen Hammond for this point.

35. Karlsson, "Environment and Sustainable Development," 126, citing an April 1998 report of the World Conservation Union (IUCN) titled "Red List of Threatened Plants," as reported in *Earth Times,* April 16–30, 1998, 5.

36. Organization for Economic Cooperation and Development, "Pollutant Release and Transfer Registers," http://www.oecd.org/EN/home/0,,EN-home-540-14-no-no-no-0,00.html.

37. David Wheeler et al., *Greening Industry: New Roles for Communities, Mar-*

kets, and Governments (Oxford, England: Oxford University Press for the World Bank, 1999).

38. Mexico's environmental enforcement agency, Procuraduría Federal de Protección al Ambiente (PROFEPA), plans to put the rankings on its Web site, at http://www.profepa.gob.mx.

39. "Green Rating Project," *Down to Earth* 8, no. 5 (July 31, 1999), http://www.cseindia.org/html/eyou/grp/grp_index.htm.

40. Elena Petkova and Peter Veit, *Environmental Accountability beyond the Nation-State: The Implications of the Aarhus Convention,* Environmental Governance Note (Washington, D.C.: World Resources Institute, April 2000).

41. Cited in Adil Najam, "World Business Council for Sustainable Development: The Greening of Business or a Greenwash?" in Fridtjof Nansen Institute, *Yearbook of International Co-operation on Environment and Development, 1999–2000* (Lysaker, Norway: Fridtjof Nansen Institute, 2000), 65–75.

42. Intriguingly, BP Amoco uses a system of group-wide emissions trading to make the cuts as cost-effective as possible.

43. Hilary French, *Vanishing Borders: Protecting the Planet in the Age of Globalization* (New York: Norton, 2000), 98.

44. Donella Meadows, "A CEO Responds to a Spear through the Heart," *(Lebanon, N.H.) Valley News,* November 28, 1996.

45. William McDonough and Michael Braungart, "The NEXT Industrial Revolution," *Atlantic Monthly* (October 1998), http://www.theatlantic.com/issues/98oct/industry.htm.

46. Thomas F. Homer-Dixon, "On the Threshold: Environmental Changes as Causes of Acute Conflict," *International Security* 16, no. 2 (1991); Thomas F. Homer-Dixon, "The Ingenuity Gap: Can Poor Countries Adapt to Resource Scarcity?" *Population and Development Review* 21, no. 3 (1995): 587–612. The connections between environmental breakdown and social breakdown are complex and remain hotly debated. For an overview of the debate on the connection between environment and security, see Ann M. Florini and P. J. Simmons, "North America," in *The New Security Agenda: A Global Survey,* ed. Paul B. Stares (Tokyo: Japan Center for International Exchange, 1998), 23–74.

Chapter 9: The Fourth Revolution

1. John Man, *Gutenberg: How One Man Remade the World with Words* (New York: Wiley, 2002), 1.

2. In a recent book, James C. Scott argues that the inherently misguided desire

to shape society according to some rational, "scientific" scheme led to some of the greatest tragedies of the twentieth century, particularly when civil society was too weak to temper such schemes with practical knowledge. See James C. Scott, *Seeing Like a State: How Certain Schemes to Improve the Human Condition Have Failed* (New Haven, Conn.: Yale University Press, 1998).

3. As mentioned in chapter 8, the formal name of the Aarhus Convention is the United Nations Economic Commission for Europe Convention on Access to Information, Public Participation in Decision-Making, and Access to Justice in Environmental Matters. See Elena Petkova and Peter Veit, *Environmental Accountability Beyond the Nation-State: The Implications of the Aarhus Convention,* Environmental Governance Note (Washington, D.C.: World Resources Institute, April 2000).

4. The four founding members of the Access Initiative were the World Resources Institute (Washington, D.C.), the Environmental Management and Law Association (Budapest), the Corporacíon PARTICIPA (Santiago), and the Thailand Environment Institute (Bangkok). Information is available at http://www.wri.org/wri/governance/access_summary.htm.

5. Robert Gilpin, *Global Political Economy: Understanding the International Economic Order* (Princeton, N.J.: Princeton University Press, 2001), 401.

6. Amartya Sen, *Development as Freedom* (New York: Knopf, 1999).

ABOUT THE AUTHOR

Ann Florini is Senior Fellow in the Governance Studies Program at the Brookings Institution. From 1997 to 2002, she was Senior Associate at the Carnegie Endowment for International Peace. She received her Ph.D. degree in political science from the University of California, Los Angeles, and her master's degree in public affairs from Princeton University. She has previously been associated with the University of California, Los Angeles; the Rockefeller Brothers Fund; and the United Nations Association of the United States of America. Her edited volume, *The Third Force: The Rise of Transnational Civil Society*, was published in October 2000 by the Japan Center for International Exchange and the Carnegie Endowment. She is coauthor of the monograph *Secrets for Sale: How Commercial Satellite Imagery Will Change the World*. Her articles have appeared in such journals as *Foreign Policy*, *International Studies Quarterly*, *World Link*, and *International Security*.

INDEX